ROUTEM

DISPERSAL

Keith A. Jenkinson

An Autobus Review Publication

Published by Autobus Review Publications Ltd.,
42 Coniston Avenue, Queensbury, Bradford BD13 2JD.

Printed by Impressions Ltd., Leeds.

ISBN 0 907834 34 5

Above : Awaiting their fate in 1987 in the yard of PVS, Carlton, the last resting place of vast quantities of former London buses are a pair of recently-arrived Routemasters. (K.A.Jenkinson)

Front cover upper : This rare sight of RMs 1, 2, 3, 4 & 5 was captured by the photographer at the Routemaster's 40th anniversary celebrations in 1994. (J.A.Godwin)

Front cover lower : RM133 is seen here in its final hour being dismantled at the yard of Rollinson, Carlton in July1985. (M.Lockyer)

Back cover upper : Looking immaculate in the livery of its current owner. Antenna Television of Athens, Greece is ALD991B which left its native London in December 1990. (Antenna TV)

Back cover lower : Passing through the centre of Glasgow, Kelvin Central Buses 1926 (ex.RM799) has gained the front grille from a sister vehicle whose registration plate has been removed. 1926's number (EDS312A) is being temporarily displayed on a paper sticker in its windscreen. (K.A.Jenkinson)

The last bus to be wholly designed by London Transport for use in the capital, the Routemaster despite its advancing years has in recent times become a cult vehicle, attracting interest from operators all around the world as well as in several parts of the United Kingdom.

Despite the first examples being withdrawn from service almost twenty years ago and numerous examples finding their way to the scrap yards, a large number of buses of this type are still to be seen in everyday service both in London and elsewhere and seem likely to survive well into the twenty-first century.

Within the pages of this book is a complete record of the disposal of all 2875 Routemasters built, the first of which made its debut in 1954, the last being completed in 1968. In addition, the original and final depots from which each operated in London is shown as is the date it entered service, was withdrawn and sold and the final body it carried. As will be seen, whilst some were sold for scrap, many others have had a succession of owners since their departure from London whilst others are still hard at work in the area for which they were originally designed.

Without the assistance of others, such a comprehensive record would not have been possible and in particular I would thank the PSV Circle whose monthly newsheets have been an invaluable source of reference; Brian and Geoff Laverack of PVS, Carlton for their generous help and for allowing me access to their records; Ted Brakell of Brakell Bus Sales for information relating to vehicles sold through his company and to several of the operators whose fleets currently contain one or more Routemasters.

Stevenson of Spath's former Northern General RCN699 stands alongside Hewitts Farm's ex.London Transport RM58 at the Showbus rally at Woburn in September 1983. (T.G.Walker)

THE ROUTEMASTER

from the cradle to the grave

First appearing on the streets of London in February 1956 after being exhibited at the Commercial Motor Show two years earlier, the Routemaster proved to be the last bus to be wholly designed by London Transport for operation within its own fleet and was initially intended as a replacement for the capital's trolleybuses. In the event, however, it was the Routemaster's predecessor, the RT and RTL which was used during the first stages of the electric traction conversion programme and it was not until November 1959 that the RM took up its originally intended role. Apart from the first four prototypes, the Routemaster was built solely by Park Royal who used chassis sub-frames produced by AEC and during the period 1959 to 1968 constructed a total of 2871 such buses of which 2756 were for operation by London Transport. Although the RM had been offered for sale to provincial operators, only the Northern General Transport Co. of Gateshead availed itself of this new model by taking a total of 50, the remaining 65 being purchased by British European Airways for use on its service to Heathrow Airport which was operated on its behalf by London Transport. Although initially the vast majority of Routemasters were powered by AEC engines, from 1962 a number were fitted from new with Leyland engines whilst a year earlier a 30ft. long variant had been introduced, classified the RML by London Transport.

Although at first confined to London's red-liveried central area fleet (except for RM2 and Green Line Leyland-engined prototype RCL4), a special version of the Routemaster fitted with rear platform doors made its debut in August 1962 for operation on London Transport's long distance Green Line services. Classified the RMC, these 68 vehicles were joined three years later by a batch of 43 RCLs (30ft. long variants) and the first of a number of RMLs for conventional country area services. Following the debut of an experimental forward entrance Routemaster (RMF1254) in 1962, this layout was selected by BEA for its 65 Routemasters delivered in 1966/7 and by Northern General for its 30ft. long variants in 1964/5.

Despite the Routemaster still being built, during the mid 'sixties the need for buses suitable for one-person-operation led London Transport to give consideration to a double decker with its entrance alongside the driver and initially, rather than buy 'off the peg' vehicles, it was decided to design a new version of the Routemaster to meet this requirement. This resulted in the construction of FRM1 whose engine was relocated at the rear, its body owing much of its parentage to the standard Routemaster, and although it was duly unveiled to the public in 1966, it was destined to remain unique due to its high production cost. As is well known, rather than put this new model into production, London Transport instead purchased a large quantity of Daimler Fleetlines with standard bodywork modified to incorporate its operators own features.

Thus, Routemaster production ceased during the early part of 1968 and, despite several of its RT-type predecessors having given thirty or so years service in the capital, it was at that time envisaged that the Routemaster would have a somewhat shorter life and would have disappeared completely from the streets of London by the mid 'nineties. This prediction appeared to be 'on target' when, in 1982, the first mass withdrawals commenced - but how wrong this proved to be as will be clearly seen in the following chapters.

As with most types of London Transport's buses, upon overhaul at Aldenham works the Routemaster fleet was subjected to a series of body exchanges, the sub frames and running units from one bus being overhauled and fitted to a different body, and thus it was for many years unusual for a bus to re-emerge in the same guise as that in which it entered the works. As a result, many of the earlier bodies with fixed front upper deck glazing subsequently appeared with higher stock numbers and with the constant interchange of chassis sub frames, few, if any, Routemasters can now be considered to be original in the true sense of the word. This method of overhaul was continued until 1984 after which such separation was discontinued and work was undertaken in complete vehicle form.

Apart from a tiny handful of Routemasters which were withdrawn as a result of accident or fire damage, the sale of experimental forward entrance RMF1254 to Northern General in 1966, the removal from passenger service of three of the four prototypes and the transfer on 1 January 1970 of the Green Line and country area vehicles to the newly formed NBC subsidiary London Country Bus Services, it was not until 1975 that the first 'proper' Routemaster withdrawals commenced when, following the removal of check-in facilities from Gloucester Road Air Terminal in London, British Airways found itself with a surplus of its forward entrance examples. Numbering 13, these were sold in August of that year to London Transport who were suffering an acute vehicle shortage at that time and two months later were placed in service by their new owner from North Street, Romford garage on route 175. Initially entering service in their existing British Airways orange & white livery and lacking a front destination box, a repainting programme was quickly put in hand and although this did not include the fitting of destination equipment, a canopy route number box was added. Given fleet numbers RMA1-13, these buses were, however, never popular with staff and were taken out of service in September 1976 when sufficient RTs became available for their replacement. Three of the RMAs were then converted to driver training buses, and for these duties had their staircase removed to allow an instructor's seat to be placed behind the driver, whilst the remainder were placed in store or used to transport staff from various points to Aldenham overhaul works.

Further reductions in the Heathrow Airport service rendered 14 more of British Airways' forward entrance Routemasters surplus to requirements during 1976 and these too were purchased by London Transport who put all but two of them to use as Aldenham staff buses between January and August 1978. A year later, in June 1979 BA withdrew all its remaining Routemasters following the cessation of the airport service, selling them to London Transport where they joined their sisters. Although a few were immediately placed in service on Aldenham staff bus duties, others were stored for eventual use as driver trainers whilst some were never used at all by their new owner and were ultimately sold.

Meanwhile, NBC subsidiary London Country had begun the progressive withdrawal of its Routemasters, the first examples of which were taken out of service as early as 1973 as had Northern General who started in 1977 and had eliminated the type by the beginning of 1981. Being of conventional rear entrance layout, the London Country examples, all of which had begun their lives with London Transport, attracted the interest of the latter who saw them as a means of enhancing its own large fleet of this type and thus when they were offered for sale, it came as no surprise when towards the end of 1977 a number were purchased to rejoin the fleet from which they had been separated several years earlier. Although the intention was to repurchase all 208 buses (68 RMC, 43 RCL & 97 RML - RMC4 being retained by London Country), after more than half had been returned to their original owner a disagreement between London Transport and London Country resulted in 14 being sold instead to Wombwell Diesels, a Yorkshire breaker. Immediately London Transport made contact with Wombwell in an attempt to secure these buses, and although successful in gaining 12, the scrapping procedure had already commenced leaving 2 of the RMLs beyond resuscitation. Their differences resolved, London Transport then acquired all London & Country's remaining Routemasters between June 1979 and March 1980. At first, a handful of the RMLs together with several RCLs and around half of the RMCs were put to use on driver training duties whilst most of the other RMLs were progressively overhauled and repainted red for inclusion in the normal passenger-carrying fleet. Those RCLs and RMCs not used for driver training were placed in store for possible future use and although many of these eventually saw active duties in the capital, a few which were in poor condition along with 17 RMLs were sold to Wombwell Diesels for scrap early in 1978.

Similarly, Northern General began selling its Routemasters to various dealers and breakers in December 1977, the last examples being disposed of in February 1982 after spending varying periods in store since their withdrawal from service. Surprisingly, 14 of these ultimately found their way to London Transport between December 1979 and August 1980 either direct from Northern or via various dealers (including two which never left Wombwell Diesels who stripped them on LTE's behalf and delivered their parts to London) although they were never overhauled and placed in service had been originally intended and were instead soon resold. Prior to the commencement of the withdrawal of London's production Routemasters, except for those whose days ended prematurely as a consequence of accident or fire damage, only RML2691 was taken out of stock

Two of the Routemasters sold to W.Norths of Sherburn-in-Elmet in October 1982, RM1298 and RM1402 await dismantling during the spring of 1983. (K.A.Jenkinson)

for sale, this being acquired in September 1972 by Gala Cosmetics who converted it into a mobile beauty salon to publicise Mary Quant products. In its new role it was to travel abroad extensively and although all of its movements are not known, it has been seen as far afield as Scandinavia, Western Europe, Canada and the USA and is believed to be still extant.

Following the abortive Fares Fare policy which was politically inflicted on London Transport in May 1981 when fares were cut by an average 32% and the subsequent failure of the scheme which resulted in fares rocketing to 33% above those charged prior to May 1981, the number of passengers carried almost immediately fell by 20%, thus causing numerous service cuts to be made and, as a consequence, rendering a large number of buses surplus to requirements. In the September 1981 service revisions alone, 220 RMs, 19 RMLs and 5 RCLs were no longer needed and with the prospects of an upturn in its fortunes seeming bleak, London Transport took the decision to implement a fleet reduction programme which involved the demise of around 200 Routemasters. Rather than sell these buses for use elsewhere, it was instead decided that all would be dismantled and that their reusable parts would be retained in stock at Aldenham to provide a bank of low-cost spares. Being unable to cope with this process itself, London Transport invited tenders for this work and in August 1982 despatched a 'pilot' Routemaster to each of several breakers to enable them to undertake a costing excersise. After examining the tenders received during the following month, Berry of Leicester and W.Norths of Sherburn-in-Elmet were each given contracts for the first 150 Routemasters to fall under this scheme. Berry was already well established as a scrap merchant, having cut up numerous British Railways steam and diesel locomotives whilst surprisingly W.Norths, who in the 1950s had purchased over 2000 former London buses for resale, was primarily a dealer rather than a breaker. Rather than take its 100 Routemasters to Leicester for dismantling, Berry instead reached an agreement with London Transport to carry out this task at Aldenham overhaul works and this commenced in November 1982 progressing to May 1983 by which time 98 had been dealt with. The remaining 2 were, instead of being dismantled, reinstated to the passenger-carrying fleet and thus survived to fight another day! The 50 contracted to W.Norths, however, were driven the 200 miles to Sherburn in Elmet in October 1982 where they were dismantled during the next twelve months, their reusable parts being returned to London as and when required. The only other RMs to leave the fleet during 1982 were 4 which in October were sold to a Japanese buyer for export to that country where they were to be exhibited in various classic car museums.

1983 witnessed the withdrawal of further Routemasters and whilst a number were sold to Wombwell Diesels and Booth of Rotherham for scrapping, others were more fortunate and found new owners who were able to offer them a more secure future. Amongst these was a small number sold to overseas buyers and an even smaller quantity which remained in Britain, albeit not in revenue-earning passenger-carrying roles. Similarly, as more RMs were taken out of service in 1984, so these too left the fleet with some being sold for scrap, others to overseas customers and the first to preservationist owners in England. Indeed, 1984 proved to be a momentous year as far as the Routemaster was concerned, for during the summer agreement was reached with PVS of Carlton, near Barnsley in South Yorkshire for that concern to purchase all London's redundant Routemasters destined for scrap in the future. This has led to more than 1000 buses of this type ending their days in the Carlton yards between 1984 and 1995 in addition to several which were initially sold by London Transport to other users and operators. Had plans materialised for the sale of up to 1300 Routemasters to China following the despatch of two demonstrators in 1988, the number gained by PVS would have been minimal, of course, but in the event the anticipated deal was never concluded ...... On occasions, so great was the number of RMs arriving at Carlton that PVS was unable to cope with their scrapping and whenever this situation arose, several buses were 'sold-on' to other breakers in the vicinity who completed their demise.

At first, the Routemasters selected for withdrawal were those fitted with - in London terms - non standard units such as Leyland engines and Simms electrical equipment but later this was changed to those buses which during 1985 would be coming up to their fifth body overhaul. As a

Following fire damage, RM1368 was converted into a single decker in June 1975 but was never used in revenue-earning service in its new form. (T.G.Walker)

Seen enroute to the Derby at Epsom Downs in June 1984 whilst employed as a courtesy bus is ex.Northern General front entrance FPT603C. (T.G.Walker)

result of this shift of emphasis, numerous Leyland engined examples were given a reprieve, and indeed some were to soldier on well into the next decade. Meanwhile, although initially no British operator had expressed an interest in purchasing Routemasters for addition to their fleets, no doubt believing them to be a specialist London vehicle which would be difficult to maintain, in May 1985 Stagecoach, then a small independent operator in Perth, Scotland, ventured forth and purchased 5 for use on rural and schools services on Tayside. Obviously satisfied with these buses and finding them both reliable and cost effective, they later added several more to their rapidly expanding fleet. Seeing the success of these buses and looking towards deregulation which was then looming on the horizon, Scottish Bus Group subsidiary Clydeside Scottish decided to test a Routemaster in service and in July 1985 borrowed RM652 from London Transport for evaluation. Proving favourable with passengers and crews alike, this led to an order being placed for a large quantity of buses of this type which began to migrate northwards in October and continued well into 1986. Initially, all were prepared for their new owner by BEL at Aldenham works prior to delivery and after entering service in their new home they immediately attracted attention from two other SBG subsidiaries - Kelvin Scottish and Strathtay Scottish - both of whom borrowed Clydeside examples for in-service trials. Their success was born out by orders from each company, and as with the Clydeside buses, preparation work and repainting was carried out at Aldenham before they were despatched north of the border. The Clydeside examples, attractively wearing a yellow & red livery, were at first used in service in and around Paisley, although it was not long before they became a familiar sight in central Glasgow when they were introduced to several cross-city services. Similarly, the Kelvin Scottish Routemasters in their distinctive two-tone blue and yellow colour scheme were also used on services running into Glasgow where, from October 1986, numerous Stagecoach examples could also be found operating for the company's new subsidiary Magicbus. Across in eastern Scotland, Strathtay Scottish's Routemasters were confined to local services in both Perth and Dundee initially wearing an orange, blue & white livery which was later modified in its application eliminating the white. Following an attack on its Perth services by Stagecoach in 1989, Strathtay repainted six of its Routemasters into the erstwhile Perth City Transport livery of red & cream for use in that city and during the previous year loaned examples from its standard-liveried fleet to Highland Omnibuses and surprisingly (for a couple of weeks) to Northern General who was at that time considering reintroducing the Routemaster to its fleet after withdrawing the last of its own forward entrance buses of this type in 1981. In addition to the large fleets of Routemasters operated by Clydeside, Kelvin and Strathtay, these companies also purchased a number of RMs solely for cannibalisation, athough Clydeside upon finding itself with an increased requirement of buses of this type, particularly during the Glasgow Garden Festival, placed some of these in service, thus bolstering its Routemaster fleet considerably. Meanwhile, in London itself, Blue Triangle of Rainham began to use Routemasters on sightseeing tours of the capital with a forward entrance ex.British Airways example and a 30ft. long former Green Line RCL.

Thus what had previously appeared to many to be a specialised, and somewhat elderly model suddenly had become a vehicle which was able to offer operators a cheap and effective means of dealing with new competition which it was anticipated would appear in large quantities once deregulation began. This led several companies including Brighton & Hove, Provincial of Hoeford and Southend Transport to each borrow a Routemaster for evaluation during 1987 and although the two first mentioned did not persue matters further, Southend in September 1988 placed 12 buses of this type in service and later added several further examples to its fleet. Meanwhile, in 1986 Blackpool Transport after evaluating a Routemaster in service during the early spring purchased 6 for use on its promenade service and two years later added a further 6 to use in competition with Fylde's Blue Buses who had begun services into its neighbour's territory. Perhaps more surprising, however, was the acquisition of 2 RMs by small Nottinghamshire independent, Gash of Newark who employed them on local town services initially still in London red livery. A year earlier, Leicestershire independent Confidence of Oadby had purchased a solitary example, using this on schools contracts and a local service and so popular did this prove, that a second Routemaster was acquired in June 1986. Gash added a third RM to its fleet at the start of 1987 whilst closer to Nottingham, Gagg of Bunny purchased RM1314 in May 1987, regarding this as

Former Green Line coach RMC1518 was, after its return to London Transport from London Country, used as a driver training skid bus and is seen in this role at Aldenham Works in July 1983. (T.G.Walker)

being semi-preserved as well as using it on normal passenger carrying duties upon which it was joined six months later by a second example.

More companies joined the ranks of Routemaster operators during May 1987 when Pulfrey of Great Gonnerby near Newark purchased a solitary example, Southampton Citybus introduced several to the city and more unusually Verwood Transport of Poole, Dorset placed a forward entrance former British Airways variant in service. Later, in October, Cumberland Motor Services became the first privatised NBC subsidiary to add Routemasters to its fleet when a total of 8 made their debut on Carlisle city services. Six of these had previously operated in the fleet of Kelvin Scottish, being made redundant along with many others when severe service cuts were implemented by that company in July.

During 1988 the number of operators who decided that the Routemaster would be of benefit was further increased and added Burnley & Pendle, East Yorkshire Motor Services, United Counties Omnibus Co. and Greater Manchester Buses into the cult. Burnley & Pendle bought 7 (although one was never operated and was instead used for spares) and after placing them in service still in their capital red livery on a service between Burnley and Colne began to paint them in a new red & cream scheme with EastEnders route branding and names of characters from the BBC television soap of that title. Surprisingly Greater Manchester Buses whose standard colour scheme was orange & white repainted its Routemasters in full London Transport livery and even designed a new fleet name logo for them based on the London bullseye. The service upon which they were used (Manchester Piccadilly to West Didsbury) was one on which a great deal of competition was being experienced and in order to further attract public interest, the RMs were given route branding under the title of 'Piccadilly Line'. The other two operators who introduced Routemasters to their fleets - East Yorkshire and United Counties - both unusually reverted to old style liveries for the buses concerned, the former whose current colours were red & white painting its 7 RMs in the old dark blue & primrose used in pre NBC days, the latter using post NBC green & orange instead of Stagecoach corporate white with orange, red & blue stripes. Additionally the United Counties 16, which were used at Bedford and Corby, were all given 'Routemaster' fleet names.

Additionally, several other operators borrowed Routemasters for in service evaluation including Eastern Scottish who tried a couple of Clydeside Scottish examples and Blue Bus of Eccles who hired one from London Coaches (and later exchanged it for another from the same source) for use on its service from Culcheth to Manchester. The first - and only - Routemaster operation in Wales came in 1989 when South Wales Transport hired a Strathtay Scottish example for trials in Swansea. Presumably not found to meet the needs of this operator, its visit failed to produce an order, although a London Buses RML was briefly used by this same operator more recently when in the area on a private hire duty from the capital. One of the most significant sales during this period, however, was that of 40 Routemasters to the Crown Agents for despatch to Sri Lanka Transport Board, an overseas concern who was no stranger to former London Buses having previously operated a large number of RTs, RTLs, RTWs and RFWs and whose predecessor, South Western Omnibus Co. of Colombo had purchased ex.London D-class Daimlers, G-class Guy Arabs, C & CR-class Leyland Cubs in the early 1950s. The RMs were all prepared for their new owner by BEL at Chiswick Works prior to shipping in December 1988, including their repainting into full London Buses red livery and the fitting of full-depth sliding windows. Despite a Routemaster having been successfully operated by Sri Lanka Transport Board since December 1985, it took almost three years to negotiate the deal for the additional 40!

Entering a new decade, despite the Routemaster continuing to create attention amongst operators both at home and overseas, Western Scottish by whom Clydeside Scottish had been absorbed in May 1989 had already begun to withdraw its large Routemaster fleet (to which 30ft.long RML900 had been added in 1988), completing this process in April 1990 to leave only RML900 and a forward entrance ex.British Airways example still in service. Both these were to be retained and ultimately passed to the newly created Clydeside 2000 upon privatisation of the Scottish Bus Group, although shortly afterwards this decision was reversed and both were offered for sale with the RML quickly finding a new owner. Meanwhile, a new company trading as Green Rover of Watford puchased an ex.British Airways Routemaster for use on tours to rallies and in July 1990 began a Saturday-only commercial service in Watford upon which this vehicle was employed while on the fringe of London, North Mymms Coaches introduced a standard

Routemaster to its fleet. Other operators such as Bygone Buses of Biddenham, Haven Bus of Newhaven and Black Prince of Morley also flirted with the Routemaster, albeit in tiny numbers, being followed during the next few years by several other independent concerns including Midway of Manchester who purchased several for operation under its Mancunian Bus Company banner on the 143 service which had once been maintained by Greater Manchester Buses RMs, Time of Thornton Heath, Rotherham & District and Routemaster, Watford.

As the withdrawal by London Buses of its Routemasters continued, so too did the regular sight of buses of this type, mostly on suspended tow, travelling northwards along the M1 motorway to their final destination, the Carlton yard of the largest of the Yorkshire breakers, PVS. Although the vast majority made this one-way journey, a few were more fortunate by being sold by London Buses sales department to companies both at home and overseas for future use in either passenger carrying or non PSV roles whilst the number purchased by preservationists was also steadily increasing as each year went by.

By now, however, although the Routemaster still remained popular with independent operators, it was starting to lose favour amongst the larger concerns and following the withdrawal by Southampton Citybus of its fleet of this type, Kelvin and Strathtay Scottish began to progressively take their Routemasters out of service as did Southend Transport, Cumberland, United Counties and Burnley & Pendle. Magicbus sold its examples along with its Glasgow-based services to Kelvin Central Buses in April 1992 and despite East Yorkshire adding more buses of this type to its fleet in 1994, it too withdrew a number during the spring of 1995 following service revisions in the Hull area. During this period of time, however, two new major Routemaster operators emerged - one in Bournemouth early in 1993, the other in Reading in the summer of 1994. In the event, the former was to last for little more than a year before finding itself in financial difficulties which resulted in its ceasing to trade whilst on a happier note, Greater Reading Omnibus has gone from strength to strength and has continued to increase its Routemaster fleet. Another less fortunate operator of the type was White Rose of Glasshoughton, near Castleford in West Yorkshire who purchased five Iveco-engined examples and placed them in service in December 1994. As a consequence of intense pressure from West Riding, the established operator in that area, White Rose abandoned its operation in May 1995 after which it resold its five immaculate Routemasters to whence they came - PVS at Carlton.

As well as attracting interest from companies all around Britain, the Routemaster became much sought after by overseas concerns who wanted 'genuine London buses' for a variety of uses. Whilst some were employed in passenger carrying roles, mainly on tourist services, others were converted into restaurants, boutiques or were used for promotional purposes. Some were bought for inclusion in museums and a tiny handful were acquired by preservationists. In addition to the 40 despatched to Sri-Lanka for continued use in the role for which they had originally been constructed, others were despatched to Canada and the USA for tourist work whilst the large number exported to Japan were mainly employed in non-passenger carrying roles. Indeed, the Routemaster has now found new homes in no less than 38 different countres around the world, thus proving its popularity in places far removed from its native shores.

Prior to many of these events, London Buses had embarked upon a massive re-engining and refurbishment programme under which numerous RMs and RMLs had their original engines replaced by new Iveco and Cummins units in order to overcome a growing shortage of AEC spares. Additionally, almost all the RMLs were contracted out during the period 1993-1995 to South Yorkshire Transport or West Midlands-based Tube Investments for major refurbishment in order to extend their lives and in 1993 upon Kentish Bus winning the tender for crew-operated central London route 19, a total of 22 RMLs were leased to that company for its operation. Similarly, in December 1993 upon the gaining of the contract to operate service 13 by BTS of Borehamwood, 19 RMLs were leased to that company for its operation. In both instances the buses concerned were repainted into the liveries of their respective temporary new owners and adorned with their fleet names etc.

Upon the privatisation of London Buses in the autumn of 1994, all its operational Routemasters passed to the new owners of its various subsidiaries whilst all but 30 of those held by the Sales Department were disposed of to PVS of Carlton. Despite several being cannibalised for spares by their new South Yorkshire owner, the majority were offered for resale via the joint

PVS-Wigley dealership at nearby Cudworth where they quickly attracted new owners both at home and overseas. Meanwhile, the 30 which were retained by London Buses were transferred from Fulwell to University Bus at Hatfield for storage pending possible future use by the privatised London Buses subsidiaries.

Despite now being an elderly bus in terms of age, the Routemaster has undoubtedly become a cult vehicle during the past ten years, a bus which has grown in popularity both at home and overseas and one which has enjoyed a far greater life span than was ever originally expected. Who would have believed when the withdrawal programme began in 1982 that the Routemaster would gain such a stay of execution or would, thirteen years later, still be used in every day service in the area for which they were designed? Indeed, many of those still operating in the capital now seem likely to survive the turn of the century with their current owners whilst elsewhere it will not be surprising if examples of this well-loved type continue to be seen for even more years.

Seen in Watford town centre in October 1994 in service with Timebus, RM2180 had previously been operated by Burnley & Pendle Transport. (P.Lamb)

ROUTEMASTER
Disposals

Correct at August 1995

In the following list :

Column 1 shows the RM London, BEA or Northern General fleet number
Column 2 shows the original registration number
Column 3 shows subsequent re-registration numbers
Column 4 shows the date first licensed for passenger-carrying service
Column 5 shows the initial London depot allocation
Column 6 shows the LT number of the final body carried
Column 7 shows the date withdrawn from service by LT, British Airways or Northern General
Column 8 shows the final London depot allocation
Column 9 shows the date sold by LT, British Airways or Northern General
Column 10 shows to whom originally sold and all subsequent owners

 # indicates buses stored by W.Norths on behalf of Clydeside Scottish

Vehicles shown *'for scrap'* or *'for resale'* were still extant in August 1995

The London Transport body numbers for RM1 - RML2760 when new were 1 - 2760 respectively, thus corresponding with the fleet number.

RM

1	SLT56		2.56	W	1	10.72	Dt	4.73	Lockheed Hydraulics, Leamington Spa 7.81 London Transport (not used) 2.86 London Transport Museum (preserved).
2	SLT57		5.57	RG	2	4.72	HTt	8.86	London Transport Museum (preserved) On permanent loan to Oxford Bus Museum
3	SLT58		6.57	AC	3	4.72	CTt	2.74	London Bus Preservation Group (preserved), Cobham
4	SLT59		7.57	RE	4	3.69	HF	1.70	London Country RMC4 9.86 London Country South West RMC4 2.93 London & Country RMC4
5	VLT5		6.59	AC	319	9.94	CT	9.94	Leaside Buses, London RM5
6	VLT6	VLT192 *NMB576*	11.59	WH	159	6.87	CT	10.87	Heddson, Helsingborg, Sweden
7	VLT7		6.59	AC	542	8.85	Q	10.85	Hurley, Bradford 2.92 Unknown (preserved), Doncaster
8	VLT8		3.76	SP	8	3.85	SP	5.84	RM8 Group (preserved), Sidcup LT Garage 1.88 Barratt (preserved), Sidcup
9	VLT9	OYM374A	11.59	WH	868	10.94	Q	10.94	London Central Buses, London RM9
10	VLT10	 XFF528	8.59	W	37	5.85	AL	2.86	Watson (preserved), Chesterfield 1.95 Pegg, Rotherham
11	VLT11		11.59	WH	12	12.86	T	3.87	PVS (breaker), Carlton - scrapped
12	VLT12	OYM413A	11.59	WH	510	9.87	E	9.88	Southend Transport 101 8.93 Martin (dealer), Middlewich 3.94 BTS, Borehamwood 3.95 scrapped by BTS, Borehamwood
13	VLT13	KGJ83A	11.59	WH	249	5.91	BN	10.94	PVS (breaker), Carlton - *for scrap*
14	VLT14	OYM424A	6.59	R	23	2.94	Q	9.94	PVS (breaker), Carlton - *for scrap*
15	VLT15	KGH602A	11.59	WH	72	12.90	AF	5.92	PVS (breaker), Carlton - scrapped
16	VLT16		3.60	WW	1888	9.84	AG	10.84	Potter & Lewer (preserved), Edgware
17	VLT17	 LDS214A WLT675	3.60	WH	547	5.85	AC	10.85	Clydeside Scottish 251 (RM17) 5.89 Western Scottish C11 8.90 PVS (breaker), Carlton 9.90 Harlott (preserved), Ipswich
18	VLT18		6.59	B	1075	12.94	BN	12.94	South London Transport, London RM18
19	VLT19		6.59	W	1111	9.87	GM	11.88	PVS (breaker), Carlton - scrapped
20	VLT20	OYM378A	11.59	WH	70	4.87	Q	6.87	PVS (breaker), Carlton - scrapped
21	VLT21		11.59	WH	619	7.84	NX	8.84	PVS (breaker), Carlton 8.84 Wigley (breaker), Carlton - scrapped

22	VLT22	EDS111A	7.59	AC	26	4.85	X	4.86	Kelvin Scottish RM22 (1901)
									4.89 Kelvin Central Buses 1901
									10.90 Dunsmore (breaker), Larkhall
23	VLT23	LGH31T	11.59	WH	1166	9.90	FWt	11.94	PVS (breaker), Carlton
									2.95 Greater Reading Omnibus, Reading 23
24	VLT24		6.59	AC	56	3.87	X	5.87	Walby Combustion Engines, Stevenage
									5.93 Kilby, Corfe Mullen
25	VLT25		7.59	AC	1138	12.94	BN	12.94	South London Transport, London RM25
26	VLT26	XSL220A	11.59	PR	1047	10.86	AC	3.87	SBG Engineering, Kilmarnock
									3.87 Strathtay Scottish SR21 (621)
									6.94 Greater Reading Omnibus, Reading
27	VLT27	KGH934A	11.59	WH	1104	6.91	AK	5.92	PVS (breaker), Carlton
									6.92 Wigley (breaker), Carlton - scrapped
28	VLT28		7.59	AC	343	11.85	TH	12.85	Clydeside Scottish (for spares)
29	VLT29	OYM453A	7.59	R	1134	10.94	HT	10.94	London Northern Bus Co., London RM29
30	VLT30		7.59	W	13	10.87	X	1.90	PVS (breaker), Carlton - scrapped
31	VLT31	OYM611M	7.59	W	11	2.92	TL	7.92	PVS (breaker), Carlton - scrapped
32	VLT32	XYJ428	7.59	R	1055	5.94	CT	*3.95*	*London Transport Buses reserve fleet*
33	VLT33		7.59	R	1071	2.87	CT	6.87	Clydeside Scottish (for spares)
									3.88 PVS (breaker), Carlton - scrapped
34	VLT34		7.59	R	627	5.87	NX	10.87	PVS (breaker), Carlton
									10.87 Wigley (breaker), Carlton - scrapped
35	VLT35		7.59	W	34	1.85	NX	6.85	PVS (breaker), Carlton
									6.86 Rollinson (breaker), Carlton - scrapped
36	VLT36		8.59	V	315	4.85	N	6.85	PVS (breaker), Carlton - scrapped
37	VLT37		7.59	R	270	10.85	WH	2.86	Clydeside Scottish 253 (RM37)
		LDS173A							5.89 Western Scottish C12
									8.90 PVS (breaker), Carlton
									10.90 Wigley (breaker), Carlton - scrapped
38	VLT38		9.59	W	669	10.86	ED	2.88	Strathtay Scottish (for spares)
									7.93 Scrapped by Strathtay Scottish
39	VLT39		7.59	W	32	4.85	AL	8.85	PVS (breaker), Carlton - scrapped
40	VLT40		8.59	H	728	5.87	BW	5.88	Darby & Mercer (preserved), London E12
41	VLT41		8.59	W	917	3.85	NX	4.85	PVS (breaker), Carlton - scrapped
42	VLT42	WTS97A	7.59	W	108	1.86	Q	4.86	Strathtay Scottish SR13
									4.90 Kelbie (dealer), Turriff
									5.90 Ripley (breaker), Carlton - scrapped
43	VLT43	EDS247A	8.59	H	693	6.87	SW	11.87	Magicbus, Glasgow
									5.89 Lamming, Coulsdon (for spares)
									3.90 Scrapped by Lamming
44	VLT44		9.59	AR	1890	5.84	AF	3.85	Walton Hall, Walton, Warwicks.
									2.88 Brakell (dealer), Cheam
									7.88 Broadhurst & Bingley, Shepherds Bush
									3.89 Brakell (dealer), Cheam
									10.89 Spence (dealer), Southend
									3.90 Ireland (dealer), Hull
									11.91 Southend Transport 122
									2.94 Clydeside 2000 (dealer), Paisley
									2.94 Greater Reading Omnibus, Reading 7
45	VLT45	AST415A	9.59	AR	105	6.87	St	2.88	Strathtay Scottish SR23
									6.94 Greater Reading Omnibus, Reading 12
46	VLT46	OYM580A	8.61	WW	25	7.93	GM	3.94	PVS (breaker), Carlton - scrapped
47	VLT47	GVS492	9.59	H	5	8.92	BN	12.92	Allmey (dealer), Eastcote
									9.93 Lamming (preserved), Coulsdon
48	VLT48		9.59	AR	186	6.86	AG	9.86	Clydeside Scottish RM48
		LDS199A							5.89 Western Scottish C13
									8.90 Lister (dealer), Bolton
									8.90 Brakell (dealer), Cheam
									6.93 Mendi, Hayange, France
49	VLT49		9.59	AR	69	4.91	WD	4.91	Lamming, Coulsdon
									4.91 PVS (breaker), Carlton - scrapped
50	VLT50		11.59	PR	1746	3.73	WL	2.74	Scrapped by LTE at Aldenham
51	VLT51	HVS936	9.59	AR	695	11.87	V	1.88	United Counties Omnibus Co. 709

52	VLT52		9.59	R	41	4.85	N	6.85	PVS (breaker), Carlton - scrapped
53	VLT53	OYM582A	11.59	PR	1013	1.94	RA	10.94	PVS (breaker), Carlton
									12.94 Pickett, Glasshoughton RM53
									5.95 PVS (breaker), Carlton - *for resale*
54	VLT54		9.59	H	31	8.85	PM	12.85	Clydeside Scottish 255 (RM54)
									5.89 Western Scottish C14
		LDS279A							9.90 PVS (breaker), Carlton
									3.92 Nadin, York
									10.93 Holmes (preserved), Blackburn
55	VLT55	EDS128A	9.59	H	49	8.85	WN	3.86	Kelvin Scottish RM55 (1902)
									4.89 Kelvin Central Buses 1902
									2.93 Regal (dealer), Kirkintilloch
		YVS289							2.93 BHT Buses, Parkstone 289
									8.94 BPTA, Bournemouth 289
56	VLT56		9.59	AR	1205	5.87	T	8.89	PVS (breaker), Carlton - scrapped
57	VLT57		9.59	V	972	11.87	HT	2.88	PVS (breaker), Carlton - scrapped
58	VLT58		11.59	WH	33	12.82	HT	7.83	Rollestone & Partners, Orpington
									1.84 Brakell (dealer), Cheam
		9149SQ72							12.90 Le Musee de L'Auto, Le Mans, France
59	VLT59		11.59	PR	1076	11.89	Q	12.89	PVS (breaker), Carlton - scrapped
60	VLT60	KGJ65A	11.59	PR	24	1.91	GM	6.91	PVS (breaker), Carlton - scrapped
61	VLT61		11.59	PR	14	5.85	SF	10.86	PVS (breaker), Carlton
									10.86 scrapped by Wigley (breaker), Carlton
62	VLT62		11.59	PR	567	6.84	CT	8.84	PVS (breaker), Carlton - scrapped
63	VLT63		11.59	PR	68	8.85	SP	9.85	PVS (breaker), Carlton - scrapped
64	VLT64		11.59	WH	64	4.85	ED	5.85	PVS (breaker), Carlton
									6.85 Rollinson (breaker), Carlton - scrapped
65	VLT65		11.59	PR	402	5.85	SF	6.85	PVS (breaker), Carlton - scrapped
66	VLT66		11.59	PR	475	5.87	NX	7.87	Lamming (preserved), Coulsdon
									.87 conv'td to single deck tow bus by Lamming
									4.90 Allmey (dealer), Eastcote
									4.94 BTS, Borehamwood
67	VLT67		11.59	PR	394	6.85	WL	8.85	PVS (breaker), Carlton
									8.85 Wigley (breaker), Carlton - scrapped
68	VLT68		11.59	PR	15	4.91	WD	4.91	Lamming, Coulsdon
									8.91 PVS (breaker), Carlton - scrapped
69	VLT69		11.59	PR	157	6.86	TH	9.86	PVS (breaker), Carlton - scrapped
70	VLT70		11.59	WH	644	10.94	Wt	10.94	Metroline Travel, London RM70
71	VLT71		11.59	PR	52	10.94	NXt	10.94	London Central Buses, London RM71
72	VLT72		11.59	PR	1611	11.84	NX	4.85	PVS (breaker), Carlton - scrapped
73	VLT73		11.59	PR	43	11.85	V	2.86	Clydeside Scottish 273 (RM73)
		LDS334A							5.89 Western Scottish C15
									9.90 PVS (breaker), Carlton
									8.92 East Yorkshire Motor Ser's (for spares)
									9.94 PVS (breaker), Carlton - scrapped
74	VLT74		11.59	PR	701	8.86	Q	9.86	PVS (breaker), Carlton - scrapped
75	VLT75		9.59	V	74	1.86	EM	6.86	PVS (breaker), Carlton
									7.86 Wigley (breaker), Carlton - scrapped
76	VLT76		11.59	PR	79	8.85	SP	11.85	PVS (breaker), Carlton
									11.85 Wigley (breaker), Carlton - scrapped
77	VLT77	OYM503A	11.59	PR	189	7.92	BN	11.92	PVS (breaker), Carlton - scrapped
78	VLT78		11.59	PR	60	5.85	AC	8.85	PVS (breaker), Carlton - scrapped
79	VLT79		11.59	PR	455	7.85	SW	8.85	PVS (breaker), Carlton - scrapped
80	VLT80		11.59	PR	86	5.92	WD	5.92	London Coaches, London ERM80
81	VLT81		11.59	PR	85	11.85	B	2.86	Clydeside Scottish 281 (RM81)
		LDS335A							5.89 Western Scottish C16
									9.90 PVS (breaker), Carlton
									6.92 East Yorkshire Motor Services 813
82	VLT82		11.59	PR	615	9.82	NX	4.83	Berry (bkr), Leicester - scrapped at Aldenham
83	VLT83		11.59	PR	482	11.88	HT	1.90	Keric, Yugoslavia
84	VLT84		11.59	HT	95	5.92	WD	5.92	London Coaches, London ERM84

85	VLT85		11.59	PR	921	5.87	BW	10.87	Pegg, Rotherham
									11.87 Ridgeway Record Tools, Sheffield
									9.94 PVS (breaker), Carlton
									2.95 Wright (dealer), Rainham
86	VLT86		10.59	AC	150	5.87	Q	8.87	Booth (breaker), Rotherham - scrapped
87	VLT87		11.59	PR	92	12.84	BW	7.85	Combined Industrial Services, Southend
									1.88 Spence (dealer), Thorpe Bay
									5.88 Brakell (dealer), Cheam
									10.91 Video Techn'y Marketing, London
									6.92 Plusbus, Bristol
									6.93 Acamex, Wandsworth
88	VLT88	OYM432A	11.59	PR	89	11.88	HT	6.90	Gunter Lenke, Germany
									6.91 Heidelberg Pilsner Brewery, Germany
89	VLT89	VYJ893	10.59	V	90	3.94	RA	7.94	McGills, Barrhead
90	VLT90		11.59	PR	93	5.92	WD	5.92	London Coaches, London ERM90
91	VLT91		11.59	PR	156	8.85	WN	8.85	PVS (breaker), Carlton - scrapped
92	VLT92		11.59	PR	194	8.85	NB	9.85	PVS (breaker), Carlton - scrapped
93	VLT93	WTS109A	11.59	PR	98	3.86	CA	7.86	Strathtay Scottish SR17
									5.93 Cosgrove (breaker), Dundee - scrapped
94	VLT94		10.59	V	416	5.92	WD	5.92	London Coaches, London ERM94
95	VLT95		10.59	V	97	8.83	PM	7.84	PVS (breaker), Carlton - scrapped
96	VLT96		10.59	V	501	5.85	WH	8.85	PVS (breaker), Carlton
									8.85 Wigley (breaker), Carlton - scrapped
97	VLT97		11.59	PR	461	4.85	UX	6.85	PVS (breaker), Carlton - scrapped
98	VLT98	KGJ28A	11.59	PR	169	8.92	AFt	11.93	SudbadenBus GmbH, Rheinhousen, Germany
99	VLT99		10.59	H	489	1.85	SF	2.85	PVS (breaker), Carlton - scrapped
100	VLT100	ALA814A	11.59	PR	51	8.85	WL	10.86	PVS (breaker), Carlton - scrapped
101	VLT101		10.59	V	188	9.85	AD	11.85	PVS (breaker), Carlton
									11.85 Wigley (breaker). Carlton - scrapped
102	VLT102		11.59	PR	437	4.85	BW	9.85	DPR International, Bromley
103	VLT103		11.59	PR	225	8.83	AK	7.84	PVS (breaker), Carlton - scrapped
104	VLT104		11.59	PR	39	8.85	AF	11.85	Clydeside Scottish 256 (RM104)
		LDS280A							5.89 Western Scottish C17
									8.90 Lister (dealer), Bolton
									8.90 Southend Transport 119
									8.93 Martin (dealer), Middlewich
									3.94 BTS, Borehamwood
105	VLT105		11.59	PR	506	4.85	CT	8.85	PVS (breaker), Carlton - scrapped
106	VLT106		11.59	PR	45	4.85	TH	6.85	PVS (breaker), Carlton
									6.86 Wigley (breaker), Carlton - scrapped
107	VLT107		11.59	PR	536	3.87	AL	4.87	PVS (breaker), Carlton - scrapped
108	VLT108		11.59	PR	1609	6.84	ED	9.84	Tibbett (preserved), Swindon
									5.91 Lowings (preserved), Amersham
109	VLT109		11.59	PR	216	8.86	Q	8.87	Matsui & Co., (agent), London
									8.87 Unknown, Japan
110	VLT110		159	PR	553	8.85	N	11.85	Clydeside Scottish 257 (RM110)
									5.89 Western Scottish C18
									8.90 PVS (breaker), Carlton
									8.90 Wright (dealer), Rainham
		XMD79A							8.90 Almeroth (preserved), Romford
		RSK572							11.91 Smoke City Wheelers, Tottenham

Restored to 'Showbus' condition and re-registered OYM424A, RM14 is seen still hard at work for London Buses subsidiary London Central in the heart of the capital in the summer of 1993.

Still wearing the corporate-style NBC green livery as it undertakes its duties as a driver training bus for London Transport is RMC1516 seen here in Vauxhall Bridge Road on 13 October 1986 followed by RM2124. (K.A.Jenkinson)

Stagecoach East London has introduced superb gold fleet names on its Routemasters as illustrated by this March 1995 view of refurbished RML2723. (J.A.Godwin)

159
BAKER STREET STN
OYM 424A

24
PIMLICO
INSURANCE
All London in your hand
Get a Red Bus Rover ticket for a day.
UNDER INSTRUCTION
328
THE SANDWICH BOUTIQ
ESPRESSO
516 CLT

PRAED STREET
HEEL BAR
HARVEY NICHOLS
15
VIA TOWER
UPTON PARK
Stagecoach
SMK 723F

111	VLT111		11.59	PR	21	7.87	BW	12.87	Almeroth (preserved), Romford 4.95 Wright (dealer), Rainham - scrapped
112	VLT112		11.59	PR	1886	1.84	WH	7.84	PVS (breaker), Carlton 7.84 Rollinson (breaker), Carlton - scrapped
113	VLT113	LLF881	11.59	PR	200	1.88	BW	5.88	Ketteridge (preserved), Bowthorpe 10.94 Hodgson (preserved), Collier Row 10.94 Adler (preserved), Clacton
114	VLT114		11.59	PR	546	11.85	TH	2.86	Clydeside Scottish 264 (RM114) 5.89 Western Scottish C19 8.90 PVS (breaker), Carlton 11.91 MTL Engineering, Liverpool for RML refurbishment project 4.92 PVS (breaker), Carlton - scrapped
115	VLT115		11.59	PR	76	4.85	MH	5.85	PVS (breaker), Carlton - scrapped
116	VLT116		11.59	PR	143	7.87	V	2.88	Lamming (preserved), Coulsdon 3.88 Nicholson et al (preserved), Coulsdon
117	VLT117		11.59	PR	132	8.85	V	8.85	PVS (breaker), Carlton 8.85 Wigley (breaker), Carlton - scrapped
118	VLT118		12.59	PR	607	11.84	NX	2.85	PVS (breaker), Carlton 3.85 Rollinson (breaker), Carlton - scrapped
119	VLT119		11.59	PR	532	8.85	HT	9.85	PVS (breaker), Carlton - scrapped
120	VLT120		11.59	PR	444	8.85	ED	9.85	High Life Advertising, Maidstone 1.88 London Bus Preservation Group, Cobham
121	VLT121		11.59	PR	1627	6.84	TL	8.84	LT Sports Association, LT Holloway garage 3.88 London Bus Preservation Group, Cobham
122	VLT122		11.59	PR	467	5.85	Q	6.85	PVS (breaker), Carlton 7.85 Rollinson (breaker), Carlton - scrapped
123	VLT123		11.59	PR	228	3.85	AL	5.85	PVS (breaker), Carlton - scrapped
124	VLT124		12.59	PR	120	12.83	CT	12.83	W.Norths (dealer), Sherburn - scrapped
125	VLT125		11.59	PR	502	5.87	BW	10.88	City of Birmingham Local Authority (not used) 9.89 WRVS, London SW9 (playbus) 7.92 Wealden (dealer), Five Oaks Green 8.92 Allmey (dealer), Eastcote
126	VLT126		12.59	PR	211	8.86	GM	10.86	PVS (breaker), Carlton - scrapped
127	VLT127		12.59	PR	254	8.85	E	9.85	PVS (breaker), Carlton - scrapped
128	VLT128		12.59	PR	144	8.85	CA	10.85	PVS (breaker), Carlton - scrapped
129	VLT129		2.60	PR	167	3.85	NX	5.85	PVS (breaker), Carlton 7.85 Rollinson (breaker), Carlton - scrapped
130	VLT130		11.59	PR	434	4.85	WD	6.85	PVS (breaker), Carlton - scrapped
131	VLT131		12.59	PR	261	11.87	BW	12.87	PVS (breaker), Carlton - scrapped
132	VLT132		12.59	PR	509	8.85	EM	8.85	PVS (breaker), Carlton 8.85 Wigley (breaker), Carlton - scrapped
133	VLT133		12.59	PR	505	4.85	V	5.85	PVS (breaker), Carlton 7.85 Rollinson (breaker), Carlton - scrapped
134	VLT134		12.59	PR	508	8.85	TH	9.85	PVS (breaker), Carlton - scrapped
135	VLT135		12.59	PR	110	9.85	AR	11.85	PVS (breaker), Carlton 11.85 Wigley (breaker), Carlton - scrapped
136	VLT136	OYM583A	2.60	WH	2214	5.91	GM	5.92	PVS (breaker), Carlton 6.92 Wigley (breaker), Carlton - scrapped
137	VLT137		11.59	WH	1899	4.84	AL	6.84	Lister (dealer), Bolton 6.84 Rollinson (breaker), Carlton - scrapped
138	VLT138		2.60	WH	513	3.89	X	3.91	PVS (breaker), Carlton - scrapped
139	VLT139		2.60	WW	17	8.85	Q	8.85	PVS (breaker), Carlton 8.85 Wigley (breaker), Carlton - scrapped
140	VLT140		2.60	WW	158	10.84	CT	2.85	Gale (preserved), Diptford
141	VLT141		2.60	WW	122	12.86	CT	4.87	PVS (breaker), Carlton 6.87 Wigley (breaker), Carlton - scrapped
142	VLT142		4.60	WW	40	4.85	BW	5.85	PVS (breaker), Carlton - scrapped
143	VLT143		2.60	WW	183	5.92	WD	5.92	London Coaches, London ERM143
144	VLT144		2.60	WW	124	8.85	U	9.85	PVS (breaker), Carlton - scrapped
145	VLT145		2.60	WW	570	8.85	CT	9.85	PVS (breaker), Carlton - scrapped
146	VLT146		2.60	WW	1893	7.84	Q	1.85	PVS (breaker), Carlton - scrapped
147	VLT147		4.60	WH	651	10.86	E	7.87	PVS (breaker), Carlton - scrapped

148	VLT148		2.60	WW 50	7.85	TC	8.85	PVS (breaker), Carlton
								8.85 Wigley (breaker), Carlton - scrapped
149	VLT149	EDS117A	2.60	WW 397	3.85	WH	4.86	Kelvin Scottish RM149 (1903)
								4.89 Kelvin Central Buses 1903
								1.93 Ripley (breaker), Carlton
								2.93 Mancunian Bus Co. Manchester RM149
								2.94 Ripley (breaker), Carlton
								2.94 Wright (dealer), Rainham
								2.94 Wright & Biddell, Rainham
								5.94 East Yorkshire Motor Services 818
								5.95 PVS (breaker), Carlton
								7.95 Unknown, Germany
150	VLT150		2.60	WW 35	1.86	T	6.86	PVS (breaker), Carlton - scrapped
151	VLT151		2.60	WW 245	11.85	NX	6.86	PVS (breaker), Carlton
								6.86 Wigley (breaker), Carlton - scrapped
152	VLT152	*60-Sri-6613*	2.60	WW 1063	6.87	WD	12.88	Sri Lanka Transport Board
153	VLT153		2.60	WW 88	10.85	S	9.86	PVS (breaker), Carlton
154	VLT154		2.60	WW 104	10.85	WH	2.86	Clydeside Scottish 258 (RM154)
		LDS232A						5.89 Western Scottish C20
								8.90 PVS (breaker), Carlton
								3.92 Pinewood Studios, Iver Heath
								4.92 PVS (breaker), Carlton - scrapped
155	VLT155		2.60	WW 538	8.85	Q	8.85	PVS (breaker), Carlton
								9.85 scrapped by Wigley (breaker), Carlton
156	VLT156		2.60	WW 166	1.85	AL	8.85	PVS (breaker), Carlton - scrapped
157	VLT157		2.60	WW 145	12.86	E	1.87	PVS (breaker), Carlton
								2.87 Wigley (breaker), Carlton - scrapped
158	VLT158		2.60	WW 423	4.85	AC	7.85	Brakell (dealer), Cheam
								11.91 Huckle (preserved), Edgbaston
								5.93 Huckle (preserved), Sutton Coldfield
159	VLT159		2.60	WW 1565	4.84	AR	9.84	PVS (breaker), Carlton - scrapped
160	VLT160		2.60	WW 61	8.85	CT	7.86	PVS (breaker), Carlton - scrapped
161	VLT161		2.60	WW 47	8.85	AL	8.85	PVS (breaker), Carlton - scrapped
162	VLT162		4.60	WW 290	4.85	AL	10.85	Clydeside Scottish (for spares)
								6.87 W.Norths (dealer), Sherburn - scrapped
163	VLT163		2.60	WW 71	5.92	WD	5.92	London Coaches, London ERM163
164	VLT164		2.60	WW 653	11.87	BW	4.88	PVS (breaker), Carlton
								6.88 Wigley (breaker), Carlton - scrapped
165	VLT165		4.60	WW 273	7.83	AD	7.84	PVS (breaker), Carlton - scrapped
166	VLT166		2.60	WW 625	11.85	Q	4.86	Clydeside Scottish 266 (RM166)
		LDS336A						5.89 Western Scottish C21
								8.90 PVS (breaker), Carlton - scrapped
167	VLT167		2.60	WW 1069	1.88	BW	3.88	United Counties Omnibus Co. (for spares)
								5.89 Smith (breaker), Bedford - scrapped at UCOC Bedford depot
168	VLT168		2.60	WW 206	11.88	WN	1.89	PVS (breaker), Carlton
								2.89 Wigley (breaker), Carlton - scrapped
169	VLT169		2.60	WW 586	9.85	SF	11.85	PVS (breaker), Carlton
								11.85 Wigley (breaker), Carlton - scrapped

Next page

Purchased by Sri Lanka Transport Board for evaluation in December 1985, former RM499 was painted in an advertising livery for Singapore Airlines as seen here in Colombo. (Colombo South Regional Transport Board).

It was not until December 1988 that any further Routemasters were exported to Sri Lanka Transport Board when a total of 40 such buses were purchased. Prepared at BEL's Chiswick Works before shipping from Sheerness and repainted into standard London red livery, three of this batch - RM1851, 2207 & 1243 - are seen here after being fitted with full-depth sliding windows in preparation for their new home. (K.A.Jenkinson)

Both owned by Strathtay Scottish, Perth City Transport liveried YTS973A passes revised standard liveried WTS186A in Mill Street, Perth whilst working city services in 1990. (K.A.Jenkinson)

NOW SINGAPORE AIRLINES TO
MANCHESTER
A great way to fly.
COLOMBO
SINGAPORE
AIRLINES

40
CHISWICK
SHEERNESS
COLOMBO
CUV 207C
243 CLT

4
Upper Letham
CITY TRANSPORT
1
DRESS FABRICS • CU
YTS 973A

BUS
PRIVATE
SNACKS
Hot Food
DRINKS
495 CLT

THE Bio GARDEN BUS
Bio
GARDEN
CARE
Bio
GARDEN
CARE
C682 MJX

3
Hoeford
JUKI
Daisywheel Printer
Electronic Portable Typewriter

170	VLT170		2.60	WW 1059	3.83	HT	7.83	Wombwell Diesels (breaker), Wombwell - scrapped
171	VLT171		2.60	WW 176	2.85	WL	4.85	PVS (breaker), Carlton - scrapped
172	VLT172	WYJ857	2.60	WW 20	11.87	AF	8.88	Southend Transport 102 2.94 Lister (dealer), Bolton 6.94 Greater Reading Omnibus, Reading 10
173	VLT173	KGH856A	2.60	WW 616	12.90	AK	12.90	PVS (breaker), Carlton - scrapped
174	VLT174		2.60	WW 420	5.85	WN	6.85	PVS (breaker), Carlton 6.85 Rollinson (breaker), Carlton - scrapped
175	VLT175		2.60	WW 1072	9.82	NSt	10.82	W.Norths (dealer), Sherburn - scrapped
176	VLT176		2.60	WW 160	2.85	MH	5.85	PVS (breaker), Carlton - scrapped
177	VLT177	EDS130A	2.60	WW 275	5.86	Q	8.86	Kelvin Scottish RM177 (1904) 4.89 Kelvin Central Buses 1904 4.93 Regal (dealer), Kirkintilloch 1.95 PVS (breaker), Carlton 1.95 Wigley (breaker), Carlton
178	VLT178		2.60	WW 257	1.86	TH	6.86	PVS (breaker), Carlton - scrapped
179	VLT179	KGJ61A	2.60	WW 551	1.91	AFt	6.91	PVS (breaker), Carlton - scrapped
180	VLT180	XVS830	2.60	WW 564	12.93	X	11.94	PVS (breaker), Carlton 2.95 Greater Reading Omnibus, Reading 20
181	VLT181		2.60	WW 171	11.87	WN	12.87	PVS (breaker), Carlton - scrapped
182	VLT182		2.60	WW 559	12.86	BN	2.87	PVS (breaker), Carlton - scrapped
183	VLT183	WTS101A	2.60	WW 274	4.86	CT	7.86	Strathtay Scottish SR12 11.92 Cosgrove (breaker), Dundee - scrapped
184	VLT184		2.60	WW 587	9.82	A	12.83	Booth (breaker), Rotherham 12.83 Goodwin (breaker), Carlton - scrapped
185	VLT185		2.60	WW 134	12.86	AF	2.87	PVS (breaker), Carlton - scrapped
186	VLT186		2.60	WH 116	9.82	PR	10.82	W.Norths (dealer), Sherburn - scrapped
187	VLT187		2.60	WH 53	12.86	AR	3.87	SBG Engineering, Kilmarnock 3.87 Clydeside Scottish RM187 5.89 Western Scottish C22 8.90 Lister (dealer), Bolton 9.90 Brakell (dealer), Cheam 2.94 Beach Bus Co., Kittyhawk, USA
188	VLT188		2.60	WH 572	8.87	E	5.88	Coster, Hull 3.89 Kingston upon Hull City Trans. (not used) 7.89 East Yorkshire Motor Services 808
189	VLT189		2.60	WH 1061	8.87	E	10.88	PVS (breaker), Carlton - scrapped
190	VLT190		2.60	WH 99	12.86	WD	4.87	PVS (breaker), Carlton 5.87 Wigley (breaker), Carlton - scrapped
191	VLT191	AST416A	2.60	WH 515	12.86	AL	3.87	Strathtay Scottish SR22 6.94 Greater Reading Omnibus, Reading 11
192	VLT192	VLT6	2.60	WH 6	1.95	BN	1.95	South London Transport, London RM6
193	VLT193		2.60	WH 115	3.85	WL	5.85	PVS (breaker), Carlton 8.85 Rollinson (breaker), Carlton - scrapped
194	VLT194	*60-Sri-6625*	2.60	WH 174	5.87	NX	12.88	Sri Lanka Transport Board
195	VLT195		2.60	WH 223	4.85	TH	6.85	PVS (breaker), Carlton 6.85 Wigley (breaker), Carlton - scrapped
196	VLT196		2.60	WH 162	11.87	GM	10.88	Brown (preserved), Muswell Hill, London

Previous page

Having found a new life as a mobile fast food bar, former Green Line RMC1495 is seen performing its new duties at Apps Court, Surrey in 1994. (P.T.Stokes)

Owned by Pan Britannica Industries, former RM2178 now frequently travels all round Britain as a promotional vehicle for Bio garden products.

Resting at Gosport Ferry in March 1987 is London Transport RM1145 which was loaned to Provincial for fou weeks for evaluation purposes following the return to London of RM831 which had been on loan for a week. Given Provincial fleet names for the duration of its brief stay, its loan sadly did not persuade the Hoeford-based company to purchase any vehicles of this type. (E.C.Churchill)

197	VLT197		2.60	WH 175	11.88	AD	1.90	PVS (breaker), Carlton
								2.90 Wigley (breaker), Carlton - scrapped
198	VLT198		2.60	WH 155	7.90	Xt	8.90	PVS (breaker), Carlton - scrapped
199	VLT199		2.60	WH 54	12.87	Q	1.88	PVS (breaker), Carlton - scrapped
200	VLT200		2.60	WH 660	12.86	SF	5.87	SBG Engineering, Kilmarnock
								5.87 Clydeside Scottish (for spares)
								1.89 Brydon & Perrett (pres'd), Cowdenbeath
								6.94 Hulks (preserved), Ollerton
								12.94 PVS (breaker), Carlton
								12.94 Punta Prava, Argentine
201	VLT201		2.60	WH 453	8.87	AR	12.87	PVS (breaker), Carlton - scrapped
202	VLT202		2.60	WH 520	10.94	NX	10.94	London Central Buses, London RM202
203	VLT203		2.60	WH 1865	8.84	WH	6.85	PVS (breaker), Carlton - scrapped
204	VLT204		2.60	WH 363	6.86	N	8.86	Clydeside Scottish RM204
		LDS233A						5.89 Western Scottish C23
								3.90 Scott (Mint Packaging), Midhurst
								7.90 Unknown, Japan
205	VLT205		2.60	WH 944	3.87	Q	11.88	Southend Transport (for spares)
								8.90 PVS (breaker), Carlton - scrapped
206	VLT206		2.60	WH 292	6.86	SF	8.86	Clydeside Scottish RM206
		LDS255A						5.89 Western Scottish C24
								8.90 PVS (breaker), Carlton
								8.92 European Bus Centre (dealer), Bruges, Belgium
								10.92 Gullegem, Belgium
207	VLT207		2.60	WH 1650	6.84	T	11.84	PVS (breaker), Carlton
								12.84 Rollinson (breaker), Carlton - scrapped
208	VLT208		4.60	WW 107	8.85	S	8.65	PVS (breaker), Carlton
								8.85 Wigley (breaker), Carlton - scrapped
209	VLT209		4.60	WW 239	9.82	Mt	8.83	De Dubbeldekkers (dealer), Schilde, Belgium
210	VLT210		3.60	WH 114	7.85	EM	8.85	PVS (breaker), Carlton
								8.85 Wigley (breaker), Carlton - scrapped
211	VLT211		4.60	WW 549	7.85	HT	8.85	PVS (breaker), Carlton
								8.85 Wigley (breaker), Carlton - scrapped
212	VLT212		4.60	WW 471	5.85	AR	6.85	PVS (breaker), Carlton - scrapped
213	VLT213		4.60	WW 464	11.85	AF	7.86	PVS (breaker), Carlton - scrapped
214	VLT214		4.60	WW 1921	5.84	AR	6.84	Wigley (breaker), Carlton - scrapped
215	VLT215		4.60	WW 121	5.85	HT	8.85	PVS (breaker), Carlton
								9.85 Wigley (breaker), Carlton - scrapped
216	VLT216		2.60	WH 585	10.81	CSx	11.83	Stamford Hill LT garage Social Club
								12.89 Cadogan (preserved), Newnham
								1.90 London Bus Export Co. (dlr), Chepstow
								11.90 GEC Marconi Dynamics Ltd., Stanmore
217	VLT217	WTS131A	4.60	WW 231	4.86	Q	9.86	Strathtay Scottish SR9
								4.90 Kelbie (breaker), Turriff
								5.90 Ripley (breaker), Carlton
								7.90 Black Prince, Morley
								9.90 Ripley (breaker), Carlton - scrapped
218	VLT218		2.60	WW 1908	10.84	B	6.85	PVS (breaker), Carlton - scrapped
219	VLT219		2.60	WW 465	6.85	Q	10.85	Clydeside Scottish 254 (RM219)
		LDS281A						5.89 Western Scottish C25
								5.90 Kelvin Central Buses 1941
								2.93 Regal (dealer), Kirkintilloch
		YVS291						2.93 BHT Buses, Parkstone 291
								8.94 BPTA, Bournemouth 291
220	VLT220		4.60	WW 1648	4.84	WH	6.84	Lister (dealer), Bolton
								6.84 J.Sykes (breaker), Carlton
								6.84 Barraclough (breaker), Carlton - scrapped
221	VLT221	WTS128A	4.60	WW 430	3.86	E	9.86	Strathtay Scottish SR19
								6.92 Lister (dealer), Bolton
								6.92 Brakell (dealer), Cheam
								9.93 Wallis, Wanaka, New Zealand
222	VLT222		4.60	WW 81	9.85	EM	11.85	PVS (breaker), Carlton
								11.85 Wigley (breaker), Carlton - scrapped

Still wearing its original Strathtay Scottish livery, SR19 (WTS128A) fitted with coloured destination blinds picks up its passengers in Mill Street, Perth in August 1988. (S.A.Jenkinson)

Painted in the revised livery adopted by Strathtay Scottish is SR24 (WTS186A) which began life in London numbered RM1143. When photographed in August 1989 it was operating a Perth city service. (S.K.Jenkinson)

e only rear-engined Routemaster to be built was FRM1 (KGD4D) which entered service in 1967 and is now eserved by the London Transport Museum. (J.A.Godwin)

ntreWest's refurbished RML2623 with a solid panel replacing the ventilators below its front destination play and carrying Gold Arrow fleet names is seen in London sunshine in the autumn of 1994 immediately er the sale of the company by London Buses to the private sector. (C.Morrison)

223	VLT223	WTS177A	4.60	WW 193	9.87	E	11.87	Magicbus, Glasgow 601
								7.89 Unknown, Norway
224	VLT224		4.60	WW 514	8.85	U	11.85	PVS (breaker), Carlton
								11.85 Wigley (breaker), Carlton - scrapped
225	VLT225		4.60	WW 202	5.86	Q	9.86	PVS (breaker), Carlton
								10.86 Wigley (breaker), Carlton - scrapped
226	VLT226		4.60	WW 663	12.85	NX	9.86	Clydeside Scottish RM226
		LDS234A						5.89 Western Scottish C26
								8.90 PVS (breaker), Carlton
								10.91 Octobus SARL, Paris, France
227	VLT227		4.60	WW 217	4.85	TC	6.85	PVS (breaker), Carlton - scrapped
228	VLT228		4.60	WW 230	2.87	E	5.87	PVS (breaker), Carlton - scrapped
229	VLT229	EDS134A	4.60	WW 670	2.86	CF	4.86	Kelvin Scottish RM229 (1905)
								4.89 Kelvin Central Buses 1905
								2.93 Regal (dealer), Kirkintilloch
		YVS294						3.93 BHT Buses, Parkstone 294 (not used)
								8.94 BPTA, Bournemouth 294
230	VLT230		4.60	WW 118	10.87	X	11.87	PVS (breaker), Carlton
								11.87 Wigley (breaker), Carlton - scrapped
231	VLT231		4.60	WW 589	9.85	AR	10.85	PVS (breaker), Carlton - scrapped
232	VLT232		4.60	WW 640	3.91	AR	5.91	LT International (dealer), London SW1
								5.91 Nilsen, Solberg B.I., Skien, Norway
233	VLT233		4.60	WW 622	10.85	GM	7.86	Clydeside Scottish (for spares)
								11.87 W.Norths (dealer), Sherburn
								11.87 PVS (breaker), Carlton - scrapped
234	VLT234		4.60	WW 628	11.85	X	4.86	Clydeside Scottish RM234
		LDS235A						5.89 Western Scottish C27
								9.90 PVS (breaker), Carlton
								6.91 European Bus Centre (dealer), Bruges, Belgium
								10.91 McDonalds Restaurants, Belgium
235	VLT235		4.60	WW 259	5.92	WD	5.92	London Coaches, London ERM235
236	VLT236		4.60	WW 978	5.86	X	10.86	PVS (breaker), Carlton - scrapped
237	VLT237		4.60	WW 334	5.92	WD	5.92	London Coaches, London ERM237
238	VLT238		3.60	WH 133	12.86	TH	4.89	Bucks Free Press, Amersham
239	VLT239		4.60	WW 152	8.85	TC	8.85	PVS (breaker), Carlton - scrapped
240	VLT240	PSK823	4.60	WW 269	6.92	SW	7.92	PVS (breaker), Carlton
								7.92 Wigley (breaker), Carlton - scrapped
241	VLT241		4.60	WW 649	10.86	AC	2.87	PVS (breaker), Carlton
								2.87 Wigley (breaker), Carlton - scrapped
242	VLT242		4.60	WH 480	5.92	WD	5.92	London Coaches, London ERM242
243	VLT243		4.60	WW 128	7.86	X	6.87	PVS (breaker), Carlton - scrapped
244	VLT244	XVS839	4.60	WW 689	6.93	N	11.94	PVS (breaker), Carlton
								2.95 Greater Reading Omnibus, Reading 19
245	VLT245		4.60	WH 704	6.86	ED	9.86	Clydeside Scottish RM245
		LDS282A						5.89 Western Scottish C28
								5.90 Kelvin Central Buses 1944
								1.93 Ripley (breaker), Carlton
								2.93 Mancunian Bus Co., Manchester RM245
								2.94 Ripley (breaker), Carlton
								2.94 Wright & Biddell, Rainham
								9.94 Wright (dealer), Rainham
								11.94 Double Vision, Sevenoaks
246	VLT246		4.60	WW 676	10.85	NB	2.86	PVS (breaker), Carlton - scrapped
247	VLT247		4.60	WW 804	4.86	TH	6.86	PVS (breaker), Carlton
								7.86 Wigley (breaker), Carlton - scrapped
248	VLT248		4.60	WW 207	2.86	MH	5.86	PVS (breaker), Carlton - scrapped
249	VLT249		3.60	WH 555	8.85	MH	11.85	PVS (breaker), Carlton
								11.85 Wigley (breaker), Carlton - scrapped
250	VLT250	EDS157A	3.60	WH 756	5.86	Q	8.86	Kelvin Scottish RM250 (1951)
								12.87 scrapped by Kelvin Scottish
251	VLT251		4.60	WH 1880	6.84	AG	9.84	PVS (breaker), Carlton - scrapped
252	VLT252		4.60	WH 314	4.85	AL	6.85	PVS (breaker), Carlton - scrapped

253	VLT253		3.60	WH 581	3.88	AD	6.90	PVS (breaker), Carlton - scrapped
254	VLT254		4.60	WH 718	8.85	NB	8.85	Norbiton LT garage Sports Club (preserved)
								9.91 Fennell & Rixon (pres'd), East Molesey
255	VLT255	HVS935	4.60	WH 764	11.87	AF	1.88	United Counties Omnibus Co. 710
256	VLT256		4.60	WH 78	8.85	TC	11.85	PVS (breaker), Carlton
								11.85 Wigley (breaker), Carlton - scrapped
257	VLT257		4.60	WH 219	8.86	CA	9.86	PVS (breaker), Carlton
								10.86 Wigley (breaker), Carlton - scrapped
258	VLT258		4.60	WH 191	3.87	X	5.87	PVS (breaker), Carlton - scrapped
259	VLT259		4.60	WH 714	1.88	BW	8.88	Brakell (dealer), Cheam
								4.92 Brewis (preserved), Sudbury, Suffolk
260	VLT260		4.60	WH 260	9.85	MH	11.85	PVS (breaker), Carlton - scrapped
261	VLT261		11.60	WW432	3.85	AF	7.85	PVS (breaker), Carlton - scrapped
262	VLT262		4.60	WH 361	2.86	WN	5.86	PVS (breaker), Carlton
								7.86 Wigley (breaker), Carlton - scrapped
263	VLT263		4.60	WH 321	4.87	Q	5.87	PVS (breaker), Carlton - scrapped
264	VLT264		4.60	WH 481	12.93	FY	*3.95*	*London Transport Buses reserve fleet*
265	VLT265		4.60	WH 284	6.86	X	9.86	Clydeside Scottish (for spares)
								11.87 W.Norths (dealer), Sherburn
								11.87 PVS (breaker), Carlton - scrapped
266	VLT266		4.60	WH 213	10.86	SF	1.87	PVS (breaker), Carlton
								2.87 Wigley (breaker), Carlton - scrapped
267	VLT267		4.60	WH 221	6.86	TC	9.86	PVS (breaker), Carlton
								10.86 Wigley (breaker), Carlton - scrapped
268	VLT268		4.60	WH 493	10.94	HT	10.94	London Northern Bus Co., London RM268
269	VLT269		4.60	WH 1866	2.85	NX	5.85	PVS (breaker), Carlton
								5.85 Wigley (breaker), Carlton - scrapped
270	VLT270		4.60	WH 123	2.86	AD	10.86	PVS (breaker), Carlton - scrapped
271	VLT271		4.60	WH 173	4.88	HT	2.89	PVS (breaker), Carlton - scrapped
272	VLT272		4.60	WH 180	8.85	BW	11.85	Clydeside Scottish 259 (RM272)
		LDS236A						5.89 Western Scottish C29
								8.90 Lister (dealer), Bolton
								8.90 Cound, Gloucester (not used)
								9.90 London Bus Export Co. (dlr), Chepstow
273	VLT273		4.60	WH 626	5.87	WD	7.87	PVS (breaker), Carlton - scrapped
274	VLT274		4.60	WH 179	5.86	Q	6.86	PVS (breaker), Carlton
								7.86 Wigley (breaker), Carlton - scrapped
275	VLT275		4.60	WH 117	1.95	BN	1.95	South London Transport, London RM275
276	VLT276		4.60	WH 705	11.87	GM	1.89	PVS (breaker), Carlton - scrapped
277	VLT277	GVS497	4.60	WW232	7.92	SW	1.93	PVS (breaker), Carlton - scrapped
278	VLT278		4.60	WH 299	9.82	NSt	7.84	PVS (breaker), Carlton - scrapped
279	VLT279		4.60	WH 242	11.86	GM	3.87	PVS (breaker), Carlton - scrapped
280	VLT280		4.60	WH 691	4.86	WD	7.86	Kelvin Scottish RM280
								9.87 PVS (breaker), Carlton - scrapped
281	VLT281		4.60	WH 518	5.92	WD	5.92	London Coaches, London ERM281
282	VLT282		4.60	WH 182	10.85	WH	1.86	PVS (breaker), Carlton - scrapped

Next page

Blackpool Transport initially placed its newly-acquired Routemasters in service still wearing their London red livery as illustrated by 627DYE in April 1986. Soon afterwards this operator devised a new red & white livery for its buses of this type as worn by ALD966B seen in its home town in 1992. (K.A.Jenkinson)

Delicenced inside Clydeside's Greenock depot in August 1988 are 32CLT, WLT666, 731DYE, CUV208C, 703DYE & VLT187, all of which were originally purchased for spares but were later placed in service. The three repainted in London-style red were thus treated for use on routes serving the Glasgow Garden Festival and all received standard livery before re-entering service later in 1988. (K.A.Jenkinson)

After the merging of Kelvin Scottish and Central Scottish, the newly created Kelvin Central Buses adopted a new red & cream livery for its fleet. Several Routemasters were repainted into this new scheme including 1918 (EDS393A) seen here in central Glasgow in April 1992. (K.A.Jenkinson)

THERE'S ONE NUMBER THAT BRINGS OUT THE BEST IN OUR TYRES.
999
5
HALFWAY HOUSE

22
Beachroamer
BLACKPOOL TRANSPORT
529

623
CARNWADRIC
CARNWADRIC
624

RESTAU
TIVOLI
"THE WORLD'S MOST COMFORTABLE SHOES."
5
REHAB
1918

Leather in Asia –
the voice of the Asian Industry
88
RM120
VLT120

17
LARGS
OOR WULLIE'S SPECIAL
MEET ME EVERY WEEK IN
The Sunday Post
WLT900

404CLT
ALM18B
ALD889B

283	VLT283	*60-Sri-6623*	4.60	WH 736	1.88	NX	12.88	Sri Lanka Transport Board
284	VLT284	GVS447	4.60	WW 281	7.92	SW	11.92	PVS (breaker), Carlton - scrapped
285	VLT285		4.60	WH 250	5.87	Q	8.88	PVS (breaker), Carlton - scrapped
286	VLT286		4.60	WH 809	11.88	WN	4.89	Burgsport International (dealer), Harrow
								4.89 Bisso Iwai Corporation, Japan
								7.89 Unknown, Osaka, Japan
287	VLT287		4.60	WH 766	1.87	AF	3.87	PVS (breaker), Carlton - scrapped
288	VLT288	EDS125A	4.60	WH 654	11.85	Q	4.86	Kelvin Scottish RM288 (1906)
								4.89 Kelvin Central Buses 1906
								10.92 Dunsmore (breaker), Larkhall - scrap'd
289	VLT289		4.60	WW 283	10.86	AC	1.87	PVS (breaker), Carlton
								2.87 Wigley (breaker), Carlton - scrapped
290	VLT290	EDS120A	4.60	WW 724	4.86	Q	9.86	Kelvin Scottish RM290 (1907)
								4.89 Kelvin Central Buses 1907
								11.91 Lockhart (breaker), Shaws Hill
								- for scrap
291	VLT291		4.60	WH 304	10.85	EM	2.86	Clydeside Scottish 291 (RM291)
								5.89 Western Scottish C30
								8.90 PVS (breaker), Carlton
								8.90 Wright (dealer), Rainham
								6.92 McGowan (pres'd), Lewisham, London
292	VLT292		4.60	WH 113	8.85	NX	8.85	PVS (breaker), Carlton - scrapped
293	VLT293	EDS147A	4.60	WH 233	6.86	AD	9.86	Kelvin Scottish RM293 (1953)
								4.89 Kelvin Central Buses 1953 (not used)
								11.91 Lockhart (breaker), Shaws Hill
294	VLT294		11.61	HT 237	12.86	E	6.87	PVS (breaker), Carlton
								7.87 Wigley (breaker), Carlton - scrapped
295	VLT295		4.60	WH 313	1.94	AR	*3.95*	*London Transport Buses reserve fleet*
296	VLT296		4.60	WH 1898	8.84	NX	11.84	PVS (breaker), Carlton - scrapped
297	VLT297		4.60	WH 933	3.85	AR	5.85	PVS (breaker), Carlton
								5.85 Rollinson (breaker), Carlton - scrapped
298	VLT298	WTS245A	4.60	WH 165	3.86	NX	6.86	Strathtay Scottish SR2
								10.92 Walker, Paisley
								2.93 Mancunian Bus Co., Manchester RM298
								2.94 Ripley (breaker), Carlton
								2.94 Wright, Rainham
299	VLT299		4.60	WH 172	6.86	X	10.86	PVS (breaker), Carlton - scrapped
300	VLT300		4.60	WH 147	3.87	Q	10.87	PVS (breaker), Carlton
								10.87 Wigley (breaker), Carlton - scrapped
301	WLT301		4.60	WH 429	2.85	SP	4.85	PVS (breaker), Carlton - scrapped
302	WLT302		4.60	WH 1891	12.84	PM	2.85	PVS (breaker), Carlton
								2.85 Wigley (breaker), Carlton - scrapped
303	WLT303		4.60	WH 657	6.86	CF	9.86	Clydeside Scottish RM303
		LDS206A						5.89 Western Scottish C31
								8.90 PVS (breaker), Carlton - scrapped
304	WLT304		4.60	WH 246	11.71	V	2.74	Scrapped by LTE at Aldenham Works

---

Previous page

London Bus Preservation Trust's RM120 which has been converted to open-top configuration since its purchase in 1988 is seen here in Crawley bus station in June 1993 whilst working on loan to Leisurelink of Crawley on its 88 service from Horsted Keynes to Gatwick Airport. (J.A.Godwin)

The only RML to be sold for further service in Britain is RML900 which joined the fleet of Clydeside Scottish in 1988 and is seen here carrying extensive advertising for the Sunday Post. It has since travelled south of the border to join an Engiish independent operator.

Purchased by Southampton Citybus in October 1987 for use on the then proposed Red Admiral operations, 404CLT, ALM18B & ALD889B despite being repainted into an all-red livery were in the event never placed service and were all instead resold without being used. Ironically, all three found new owners in Japan.

305	WLT305		4.60	WW716	10.85	S	3.86	Clydeside Scottish RM305
		LDS256A						5.89 Western Scottish C32
								8.90 PVS (breaker), Carlton
								2.92 European Bus Centre (dealer), Bruges, Belgium
306	WLT306		4.60	WW251	8.85	TC	10.85	PVS (breaker), Carlton - scrapped
307	WLT307		6.60	WH 673	5.92	WD	5.92	London Coaches, London RM307
308	WLT308		6.60	WH 308	2.85	AR	4.85	Bamford (JCB) Ltd., Rocester, Staffs
								8.87 Woodward Plant Hire, Milton Keynes
								10.87 Morgan & Saunders (pres'd), London
309	WLT309		4.60	WW309	4.85	HT	6.85	PVS (breaker), Carlton
								6.85 Rollinson (breaker), Carlton - scrapped
310	WLT310		4.60	WW218	6.87	SW	10.87	PVS (breaker), Carlton
								10.87 Wigley (breaker), Carlton - scrapped
311	WLT311	KGJ142A	7.61	EM 617	12.94	BN	12.94	South London Transport, London RM311
312	WLT312		6.60	WH 101	11.88	WN	12.89	Burgsport International (dealer), Harrow
								12.89 Unknown, Tokyo, Japan
313	WLT313		7.60	S 681	5.92	WD	5.92	London Coaches, London RM313
314	WLT314		6.60	WH 235	10.86	V	2.87	PVS (breaker), Carlton - scrapped
315	WLT315		6.60	WH 16	5.85	Q	6.85	PVS (breaker), Carlton - scrapped
316	WLT316	WTS333A	6.60	WH 763	11.87	AK	2.88	Strathtay Scottish SR25
								7.94 Greater Reading Omnibus, Reading 14
317	WLT317		6.60	WH 692	2.94	NX	11.94	PVS (breaker), Carlton
								12.94 Punta Prava, Argentina
318	WLT318		6.60	WH 787	11.86	U%	3.93	Barham, Surrey, Canada
319	WLT319		11.60	WH 137	10.85	GM	9.86	PVS (breaker), Carlton - scrapped
320	WLT320		6.60	WH 142	5.86	PM	6.86	PVS (breaker), Carlton
								7.86 Wigley (breaker), Carlton - scrapped
321	WLT321	YTS824A	6.60	WH 694	5.86	GM	8.86	Kelvin Scottish RM321 (1908)
								4.89 Kelvin Central Buses 1908
								4.93 Regal (dealer), Kirkintilloch
								7.93 Lister (dealer), Bolton
								7.93 Brakell (dealer), Cheam *- for resale*
322	WLT322		6.60	WH 747	10.87	BW	12.87	PVS (breaker), Carlton - scrapped
323	WLT323		7.60	S 743	6.86	BW	9.86	PVS (breaker), Carlton
								9.86 Wigley (breaker), Carlton - scrapped
324	WLT324		7.60	S 503	4.94	S	*3.95*	*London Transport Buses reserve fleet*
325	WLT325		7.60	S 256	6.87	WD	8.87	Hardwick (breaker), Carlton - scrapped
326	WLT326		7.60	S 777	8.82	R	10.82	Portman, London W1
								12.82 Matsuda Collection (pres'd), Hakone, Japan
								Karuizawa Classic Car Mus., Nagano, Japan
327	WLT327	*60-Sri-6634*	7.60	S 161	11.87	AK	12.88	Sri Lanka Transport Board
328	WLT328		7.60	S 820	4.88	GM	2.89	PVS (breaker), Carlton - scrapped
329	WLT329	MFF578	7.60	S 323	7.94	St	11.94	PVS (breaker), Carlton
								6.95 Scotts Minibuses, Liverpool
330	WLT330		7.60	S 325	6.85	SW	8.85	PVS (breaker), Carlton - scrapped
331	WLT331		7.60	S 340	3.85	TH	5.85	PVS (breaker), Carlton
								5.85 Wigley (breaker), Carlton - scrapped
332	WLT332		7.60	S 330	7.85	N	8.85	PVS (breaker), Carlton
								8.85 Wigley (breaker), Carlton - scrapped
333	WLT333	*60-Sri-6612*	7.60	S 333	1.88	NX	12.88	Sri Lanka Transport Board
334	WLT334		7.60	S 682	11.87	AK	1.88	PVS (breaker), Carlton - scrapped
335	WLT335		7.60	S 797	3.87	Q	12.88	TPS Technitube, Rohrenwarke, Germany
336	WLT336		7.60	S 336	7.85	NB	8.85	PVS (breaker), Carlton
								8.85 Wigley (breaker), Carlton - scrapped
337	WLT337		7.60	S 48	7.85	HT	8.85	PVS (breaker), Carlton
								9.85 Wigley (breaker), Carlton - scrapped
338	WLT338		7.60	S 331	2.87	GM	6.87	PVS (breaker), Carlton - scrapped
339	WLT339	MFF582	7.60	S 760	7.94	St	11.94	PVS (breaker), Carlton
								2.95 Brakell (dealer), Cheam *- for resale*
340	WLT340		7.60	S 671	2.87	AG	4.87	PVS (breaker), Carlton
								4.87 Wigley (breaker), Carlton - scrapped

45
LEICESTER
CONFIDENCE
WLT 621

SERVICE
WALTON
CITYBUS
RM 429
XMD 81A

YOU'RE VERY CLOSE TO A McDONALD'S
THE ORIGINAL LONDON
SIGHTSEEING TOUR
CUV235C

341	WLT341		7.60	S	298	11.87	AG	12.88	PVS (breaker), Carlton - scrapped
342	WLT342	KFF277	7.60	S	812	9.94	AC	*3.95*	*London Transport Buses reserve fleet*
343	WLT343		7.60	S	662	1.85	B	6.85	PVS (breaker), Carlton - scrapped
344	WLT344	*60-Sri-6635*	7.60	S	758	3.87	Q	12.88	Sri Lanka Transport Board
345	WLT345		7.60	S	376	4.85	EM	5.85	PVS (breaker), Carlton
									5.85 Rollinson (breaker), Carlton - scrapped
346	WLT346	SVS615	7.60	S	352	9.93	AF	10.94	PVS (breaker), Carlton
									12.94 Pickett, Glasshoughton RM346
									5.95 PVS (breaker), Carlton - *for resale*
347	WLT347		7.60	S	347	8.85	AL	11.85	PVS (breaker), Carlton - scrapped
348	WLT348		7.60	S	348	1.95	BN	1.95	South London Transport, London RM348
349	WLT349		7.60	S	286	5.87	BN	8.87	Lamming (dealer), Coulsdon
									8.87 Goode (preserved), Croydon
350	WLT350		7.60	S	389	7.85	Q	8.85	PVS (breaker), Carlton
									8.85 Wigley (breaker), Carlton - scrapped
351	WLT351		7.60	S	377	10.85	N	6.86	PVS (breaker), Carlton - scrapped
352	WLT352		6.60	WH	765	5.87	Q	7.87	PVS (breaker), Carlton - scrapped
353	WLT353		7.60	S	778	12.84	CA	3.85	PVS (breaker), Carlton - scrapped
354	WLT354		7.61	EM	629	11.85	AG	12.85	Wahlin, Norrkopping, Sweden
355	WLT355		7.60	S	355	3.85	AL	5.85	PVS (breaker), Carlton
									5.85 Rollinson (breaker), Carlton - scrapped
356	WLT356		7.60	S	842	8.86	SF	6.87	PVS (breaker), Carlton
									7.87 Wigley (breaker), Carlton - scrapped
357	WLT357	EDS278A	7.60	S	357	2.86	E	5.86	Kelvin Scottish RM357 (1909)
									4.89 Kelvin Central Buses 1909
									2.93 Regal (dealer), Kirkintilloch
		YVS288							2.93 BHT Buses, Parkstone 288
									8.94 BPTA, Bournemouth 288
358	WLT358		7.60	S	439	8.82	PM	10.82	W.Norths (dealer), Sherburn - scrapped
359	WLT359		7.60	S	808	11.87	AK	4.89	Pepsi Cola, Oman (loan from LBL)
		6286RX59							5.89 Sollac Steel Works, Dunkirk, France
360	WLT360		7.60	S	391	2.85	WD	4.85	PVS (breaker), Carlton - scrapped
361	WLT361		7.60	S	879	5.86	TH	6.86	PVS (breaker), Carlton
									7.86 Wigley (breaker), Carlton - scrapped
362	WLT362		7.60	S	364	1.86	AD	6.86	PVS (breaker), Carlton
									9.86 Wigley (breaker), Carlton - scrapped
363	WLT363		7.61	EM	652	2.86	GM	6.86	PVS (breaker), Carlton - scrapped
364	WLT364		7.60	HT	382	5.86	SF	8.86	Clydeside Scottish RM364
		LDS337A							5.89 Western Scottish C33
									9.90 PVS (breaker), Carlton
									6.92 East Yorkshire Motor Services 815
									5.95 PVS (breaker), Carlton - *for resale*
365	WLT365		7.60	S	42	4.85	TH	6.85	PVS (breaker), Carlton
									7.85 Rollinson (breaker), Carlton - scrapped
366	WLT366		7.60	S	366	1.85	ED	2.85	PVS (breaker), Carlton
									2.85 Wigley (breaker), Carlton - scrapped

Leicestershire independent Confidence of Oadby purchased its first Routemaster in October 1985. Some seven months later, it was joined by WLT621 which is seen here in May 1987 operating students service 45 to Leicester. (S.A.Gill)

Capital Citybus XMD81A (RM429) looks striking in its predominantly yellow livery as it stand on display at the Cobham bus rally in April 1993. (J.A.Godwin)

Rebuilt to convertible open-top configuration and painted in an all-over advertising livery for McDonalds Restaurants is London Coaches former Green Line RCL2235 seen here in Whitehall, London whilst undertaking London Sightseeing duties. (K.A.Jenkinson)

367	WLT367		7.60	S	557	8.85	HT	2.86	Clydeside Scottish 267 (RM367)
		LDS317A							5.89 Western Scottish C34
									5.90 Kelvin Central Buses 1943
									4.93 Regal (dealer), Kirkintilloch
									11.93 Pegg (Rotherham & Dist.), Rotherham
									12.93 Wombwell Diesels (breaker), Wombwell
									3.94 Sykes (breaker), Carlton
368	WLT368		7.60	S	291	8.85	HT	8.85	PVS (breaker), Carlton - scrapped
369	WLT369		7.60	S	852	9.86	E	9.86	PVS (breaker), Carlton - scrapped
370	WLT370		7.60	S	354	1.88	BW	1.89	PVS (breaker), Carlton
									2.89 Wigley (breaker), Carlton - scrapped
371	WLT371	EDS281A	7.60	S	369	3.85	Q	2.86	Kelvin Scottish RM371 (1910)
		WLT371							4.89 Kelvin Central Buses 1910
									4.93 Roulston (preserved), Glasgow
372	WLT372	KGJ84A	7.60	S	279	4.91	BN	5.92	PVS (breaker), Carlton
									6.92 Wigley (breaker), Carlton - scrapped
373	WLT373		7.60	HT	675	11.84	BN	10.86	PVS (breaker), Carlton - scrapped
374	WLT374		7.60	HT	374	5.85	WN	6.85	PVS (breaker), Carlton
									6.85 Wigley (breaker), Carlton - scrapped
375	WLT375		11.60	HL	276	6.85	WL	8.85	PVS (breaker), Carlton - scrapped
376	WLT376		7.60	HT	665	11.87	AG	12.87	Banks, Crowland, Peterborough
377	WLT377		7.60	S	483	5.92	WD	5.92	London Coaches, London RM377
									4.93 Unknown (preserved), Coulsdon
378	WLT378		7.60	HT	378	3.87	X	8.88	Gtr Manchester Buses, Manchester 2206
									7.90 Pegg (Rotherham & Dist.), Rotherham
									8.90 Sykes (breaker), Carlton
									8.90 Allmey (dealer), Eastcote
									1.91 Southend Transport 115
									11.93 Spence (dealer), Thorpe Bay
									2.94 Dines, Boreham
379	WLT379	GVS479	7.60	HT	305	8.92	GM	7.93	PVS (breaker), Carlton - scrapped
380	WLT380		7.60	S	375	8.85	X	8.85	PVS (breaker), Carlton - scrapped
381	WLT381		7.60	HT	563	3.85	TC	6.85	PVS (breaker), Carlton
									7.85 Rollinson (breaker), Carlton - scrapped
382	WLT382		7.60	HT	380	5.85	S	6.85	PVS (breaker), Carlton
									7.85 Wigley (breaker), Carlton - scrapped
383	WLT383		7.60	HT	383	8.85	S	9.85	PVS (breaker), Carlton - scrapped
384	WLT384		7.60	HT	344	8.85	HT	8.85	PVS (breaker), Carlton
									9.85 Rollinson (breaker), Carlton - scrapped
385	WLT385		7.60	HT	494	10.93	Ut	*3.95*	*London Transport Buses reserve fleet*
386	WLT386		7.60	HT	839	5.85	PM	11.85	PVS (breaker), Carlton
									11.85 Wigley (breaker), Carlton - scrapped
387	WLT387		7.60	HT	387	3.85	PM	5.85	PVS (breaker), Carlton
									5.85 Wigley (breaker), Carlton - scrapped
388	WLT388	EDS300A	7.60	HT	55	2.86	AG	7.86	Kelvin Scottish RM388 (1911)
									4.89 Kelvin Central Buses 1911
									1.93 Regal (dealer), Kirkintilloch
									1.93 Lister (dealer), Bolton
									2.93 Brakell (dealer), Cheam
									5.94 Davies, Haxby, York
389	WLT389		7.60	S	717	7.85	TC	8.85	PVS (breaker), Carlton - scrapped
390	WLT390		7.60	HT	390	3.83	CF	8.84	PVS (breaker), Carlton
									8.84 Rollinson (breaker), Carlton - scrapped
391	WLT391		7.60	HT	80	11.85	WL	5.86	Clydeside Scottish RM391
									5.89 Western Scottish C35
									9.90 PVS (breaker), Carlton
		OKU34A							11.90 East Midland Motor Services (not used)
									7.91 PVS (breaker), Carlton - scrapped
392	WLT392		8.60	S	392	2.85	SW	8.85	PVS (breaker), Carlton - scrapped
393	WLT393		11.60	HL	287	11.88	THt	11.88	PVS (breaker), Carlton - scrapped
394	WLT394		7.60	S	496	8.85	AF	8.85	PVS (breaker), Carlton - scrapped

395	WLT395	VYJ892	7.60	S	529	1.94	RA	10.94	PVS (breaker), Carlton
									12.94 Pickett, Glasshoughton RM395
									5.95 PVS (breaker), Carlton - *for resale*
396	WLT396		8.60	S	46	3.85	BN	6.85	PVS (breaker), Carlton - scrapped
397	WLT397		11.60	HL	9986	5.85	WH	6.85	PVS (breaker), Carlton - scrapped
398	WLT398		11.60	WH	112	5.92	WD	5.92	London Coaches, London RM398
399	WLT399		11.60	HL	822	5.85	Q	6.85	PVS (breaker), Carlton - scrapped
400	WLT400	OYM518A	11.60	HL	400	2.92	TL	7.92	PVS (breaker), Carlton - scrapped
401	WLT401		11.60	HL	401	3.85	NB	5.85	PVS (breaker), Carlton
									5.85 Rollinson (breaker), Carlton - scrapped
402	WLT402		7.60	S	234	9.92	PM	12.93	PVS (breaker), Carlton - scrapped
403	WLT403		11.60	HL	168	12.85	S	6.86	PVS (breaker), Carlton - scrapped
404	WLT404		11.60	HL	574	7.92	PM	7.92	PVS (breaker), Carlton - scrapped
405	WLT405		11.60	HL	371	4.85	TH	6.85	PVS (breaker), Carlton
									6.85 Wigley (breaker), Carlton - scrapped
406	WLT406		11.60	HL	980	3.85	BN	9.85	Brakell (dealer), Cheam
									11.86 Gillespie (pres'd), Dunmurray, N.Ireland
									.88 McNeill (preserved), Ballyclare, N.Ireland
									11.92 Irish Commercials, Naas, Eire
407	WLT407		11.60	HL	407	7.85	SF	8.85	PVS (breaker), Carlton - scrapped
408	WLT408	EDS282A	11.60	HL	385	11.85	Q	7.86	Kelvin Scottish RM408 (1912)
									3.88 Kelvin Central Buses 1912
									1.93 Ripley (dealer), Carlton
		KVS599							1.93 Frontline Buses, Dordon (not used)
									3.93 Morris (preserved), Erdington
									8.93 Wealden PSV (dealer), Five Oaks Green
									7.94 Blackall (preserved), Ashford
									5.95 Lowings (preserved), Bagshot
409	WLT409		11.60	HL	783	6.86	HT	9.86	PVS (breaker), Carlton
									9.86 Wigley (breaker), Carlton
410	WLT410		11.60	HL	759	1.88	BW	3.88	United Counties Omnibus Co. (for spares)
									5.89 Smith (breaker), Bedford - scrapped at UCOC Bedford depot.
411	WLT411		11.60	HL	332	8.85	MH	11.85	PVS (breaker), Carlton - scrapped
412	WLT412		11.60	HL	341	4.85	X	5.85	PVS (breaker), Carlton
									5.85 Wigley (breaker), Carlton - scrapped
413	WLT413		11.60	HL	177	8.85	AG	10.85	Carai SRL, Cita Di Castello, Italy
414	WLT414		11.60	HL	426	4.85	NB	5.85	PVS (breaker), Carlton - scrapped
415	WLT415	EDS285A	11.60	HL	368	12.85	N	7.86	Kelvin Scottish RM415 (1913)
									4.89 Kelvin Central Buses 1913
									11.92 Dunsmore (breaker), Larkhall - scrapped
416	WLT416		11.60	HL	415	10.85	SW	3.86	Clydeside Scottish RM416
		LDS237A							5.89 Western Scottish C36
									9.90 PVS (breaker), Carlton
									6.92 East Yorkshire Motor Services 814
									5.95 PVS (breaker), Carlton - *for resale*
417	WLT417		11.60	HL	320	2.85	SP	5.85	PVS (breaker), Carlton
									5.85 Wigley (breaker), Carlton - scrapped
418	WLT418		11.60	HL	419	8.85	WD	9.85	PVS (breaker), Carlton
									9.85 Wigley (breaker), Carlton - scrapped
419	WLT419	EDS393A	11.60	HL	339	12.85	S	4.86	Kelvin Scottish RM419 (1914)
									4.89 Kelvin Central Buses 1914
									4.93 Regal (dealer), Kirkintilloch
									1.95 PVS (breaker), Carlton - *for scrap*
420	WLT420		11.60	HL	395	8.82	PM	10.82	W.Norths (dealer), Sherburn - scrapped
421	WLT421		11.60	HL	1815	3.84	AG	5.84	Tapanines, Kuopio, Finland
422	WLT422		2.61	HT	337	3.85	S	5.85	PVS (breaker), Carlton - scrapped
423	WLT423		11.60	HL	280	10.93	BW	11.94	PVS (breaker), Carlton - *for scrap*
424	WLT424		11.60	HL	317	9.88	Q	10.88	PVS (breaker), Carlton - scrapped
425	WLT425		11.60	HL	296	4.85	HT	5.85	PVS (breaker), Carlton
									5.85 Wigley (breaker), Carlton - scrapped
426	WLT426		11.60	HL	300	10.88	AD	11.88	PVS (breaker), Carlton - scrapped

427	WLT427	YTS867A	11.60	HL	428	5.86	BW	9.86	Strathtay Scottish SR10
									4.90 Kelbie (dealer), Turriff
									5.90 Ripley (breaker), Carlton - scrapped
428	WLT428		11.60	HL	631	5.92	WD	5.92	London Coaches, London RM428
429	WLT429		11.60	HL	360	3.87	E	9.88	Gtr Manchester Buses, Manchester 2207
		XMD81A							7.90 Pegg (Rotherham & Dist.), Rotherham
									11.90 J.Sykes (breaker), Carlton
									1.91 Allmey (dealer), Eastcote
									4.91 Frontrunner South East, Dagenham 429
									7.93 Capital Citybus, Dagenham 903
430	WLT430		2.61	HT	396	2.85	EM	5.85	PVS (breaker), Carlton
									7.85 Rollinson (breaker), Carlton - scrapped
431	WLT431		11.60	HL	595	11.85	X	6.86	PVS (breaker), Carlton - scrapped
432	WLT432	SVS617	11.60	HL	498	12.95	BN	1.95	South London Transport RM432
433	WLT433		11.60	HL	212	2.85	T	5.85	PVS (breaker), Carlton
									5.85 Rollinson (breaker), Carlton - scrapped
434	WLT434	OYM579A	11.60	HL	297	3.90	GM	6.90	PVS (breaker), Carlton - scrapped
435	WLT435	*60-Sri-6620*	11.60	HL	303	11.87	V	12.88	Sri Lanka Transport Board
436	WLT436		11.60	HL	358	10.94	NX	10.94	London Central Buses, London RM436
437	WLT437		11.60	HL	277	10.84	NB	12.84	PVS (breaker), Carlton
									12.84 Rollinson (breaker), Carlton - scrapped
438	WLT438		11.60	HL	578	5.92	WD	5.92	London Coaches, London RM438
439	WLT439	EDS392A	11.60	HL	381	4.85	N	3.86	Kelvin Scottish RM439 (1915)
									4.89 Kelvin Central Buses 1915
									11.92 Dunsmore (breaker), Larkhall - scrapped
440	WLT440		11.60	HL	418	7.85	SW	8.85	PVS (breaker), Carlton
									8.85 Wigley (breaker), Carlton - scrapped
441	WLT441		11.60	HL	209	10.85	Vt	3.86	Clydeside Scottish 241 (RM441)
		LDS341A							5.89 Western Scottish C37
									9.90 PVS (breaker), Carlton
									9.90 Ripley (breaker), Carlton
									9.90 Black Prince, Morley RM441
442	WLT442		11.60	HL	569	8.85	HT	8.85	PVS (breaker), Carlton
									8.85 Wigley (breaker), Carlton - scrapped
443	WLT443		11.60	HL	373	3.85	MH	5.85	PVS (breaker), Carlton - scrapped
444	WLT444		11.60	HL	351	3.85	UX	12.85	Clydeside Scottish 260 (RM444)
		LDS150A							5.89 Western Scottish C38
									2.90 Jakob, Schweinfurt, Germany
445	WLT445		11.60	HL	386	3.85	T	6.85	PVS (breaker), Carlton - scrapped
446	WLT446		11.60	HL	1791	10.94	HT	10.94	London Northern Bus Co., London RM446
447	WLT447		11.60	HL	702	8.86	CT	10.86	SBG Engineering, Kilmarnock
									11.86 Clydeside Scottish RM447
		LDS283A							5.89 Western Scottish C39
									5.90 Kelvin Central Buses 1945
									2.93 Regal (dealer), Kirkintilloch
		YVS293							2.93 BHT Buses, Parkstone 293
									8.94 BPTA, Bournemouth 293
448	WLT448		11.60	HL	127	12.85	CT	5.86	PVS (breaker), Carlton - scrapped
449	WLT449		11.60	HL	427	2.92	TL	9.92	PVS (breaker), Carlton - scrapped
450	WLT450		11.60	HL	609	5.92	WD	5.92	London Coaches, London RM450
451	WLT451		11.60	HL	537	7.85	WH	8.85	PVS (breaker), Carlton - scrapped
452	WLT452		11.60	HL	324	1.85	NX	6.85	PVS (breaker), Carlton
									6.85 Rollinson (breaker), Carlton - scrapped
453	WLT453		2.61	HT	406	8.85	N	9.85	PVS (breaker), Carlton - scrapped
454	WLT454		11.60	HL	288	2.86	E	6.86	PVS (breaker), Carlton
									7.86 Wigley (breaker), Carlton - scrapped
455	WLT455		11.60	HL	384	1.85	Q	6.85	PVS (breaker), Carlton
									6.85 Wigley (breaker), Carlton - scrapped
456	WLT456	XMC223A	11.60	HL	289	7.85	AG	10.85	PVS (breaker), Carlton - scrapped
457	WLT457		11.60	HL	356	3.85	Q	9.85	Boutique Lou-Lou, Beirut, Lebanon
									12.91 Faud Nassif, Beirut, Lebanon
458	WLT458		11.60	HL	295	5.87	NX	7.90	PVS (breaker), Carlton - scrapped
459	WLT459		11.60	HL	1797	4.91	ONt	3.93	Unknown, France

460	WLT460		2.61	HT	435	5.87	B	2.88	Worthington (preserved), Salford
461	WLT461	PSK820	11.60	HL	633	2.92	TL	7.92	PVS (breaker), Carlton - scrapped
462	WLT462		11.60	HL	1703	1.85	WH	3.85	PVS (breaker), Carlton - scrapped
463	WLT463	KGH899A	11.60	HL	316	5.93	AF	5.94	PVS (breaker), Carlton - scrapped
464	WLT464		11.60	HL	328	3.85	GM	6.85	PVS (breaker), Carlton - scrapped
465	WLT465		11.60	HL	850	11.85	AL	2.86	Clydeside Scottish 265 (RM465)
		LDS148A							5.89 Western Scottish C40
									8.90 PVS (breaker), Carlton
									9.90 Wigley (breaker), Carlton - scrapped
466	WLT466		11.60	HL	327	3.85	N	5.85	PVS (breaker), Carlton - scrapped
467	WLT467	XVS851	11.60	HL	227	1.95	BN	1.95	South London Transport, London RM467
468	WLT468		11.60	HL	312	2.86	CT	5.86	PVS (breaker), Carlton - scrapped
469	WLT469		11.60	HL	802	7.87	E	11.87	PVS (breaker), Carlton - scrapped
470	WLT470	MFF504	11.60	HL	301	2.94	RA	10.94	PVS (breaker), Carlton
									12.94 Unknown, Denmark
471	WLT471	EDS394A	11.60	HL	576	11.85	N	3.86	Kelvin Scottish RM471 (1916)
									4.89 Kelvin Central Buses 1916
									1.93 Ripley (breaker), Carlton
		KVS601							1.93 Frontline Buses, Dordon
									10.94 Dunkley (preserved), Croydon
472	WLT472		11.60	HL	642	11.85	SP	1.86	PVS (breaker), Carlton - scrapped
473	WLT473		11.60	HL	1764	3.87	BN	5.87	Clydeside Scottish (for spares)
									9.87 Strathtay Scottish (for spares)
									11.87 Scrapped by Strathtay Scottish
474	WLT474	GVS480	11.60	HL	594	7.92	SW	7.93	PVS (breaker), Carlton - scrapped
475	WLT475		11.60	HL	342	3.85	AV	4.85	PVS (breaker), Carlton - scrapped
476	WLT476		11.60	HL	353	10.88	AD	11.88	PVS (breaker), Carlton - scrapped
477	WLT477		11.60	HL	445	3.85	B	5.85	PVS (breaker), Carlton
									5.85 Wigley (breaker), Carlton - scrapped
478	WLT478		11.60	HL	605	10.94	NX	10.94	London Central Buses, London RM478
479	WLT479		11.60	HL	620	5.92	WD	5.92	London Coaches, London RM479
480	WLT480	EDS381A	11.60	HL	349	2.86	E	7.86	Kelvin Scottish RM480 (1917)
									4.89 Kelvin Central Buses 1917
									4.93 Regal (dealer), Kirkintilloch
									1.95 PVS (breaker), Carlton
									1.95 Wigley (breaker), Carlton *for scrap*
481	WLT481		2.61	HT	1848	12.84	AR	1.85	PVS (breaker), Carlton - scrapped
482	WLT482		2.61	HT	1882	1.85	NX	2.85	PVS (breaker), Carlton - scrapped
483	WLT483		11.60	HL	928	4.85	AG	6.85	PVS (breaker), Carlton
									6.85 Rollinson (breaker), Carlton - scrapped
484	WLT484		2.61	HT	1112	12.86	E	6.87	PVS (breaker), Carlton
									7.87 Wigley (breaker), Carlton - scrapped
485	WLT485		2.61	HT	1150	5.90	GM	8.90	PVS (breaker), Carlton - scrapped
486	WLT486		11.60	HL	1850	4.84	AK	6.84	Rollinson (breaker), Carlton - scrapped
487	WLT487	XVS827	2.61	HT	1074	12.93	FY	9.94	PVS (breaker), Carlton - *for scrap*
488	WLT488		11.60	HL	345	10.85	HT	9.86	PVS (breaker), Carlton
									9.86 Wigley (breaker), Carlton - scrapped
489	WLT489		11.60	HL	456	4.85	AC	8.85	PVS (breaker), Carlton - scrapped
490	WLT490		11.60	HL	740	8.85	SF	9.85	PVS (breaker), Carlton - scrapped
491	WLT491	PSK821	11.60	HL	519	2.92	TL	7.92	PVS (breaker), Carlton - scrapped
492	WLT492		2.61	HT	936	12.84	AL	1.85	PVS (breaker), Carlton
									1.85 Wigley (breaker), Carlton - scrapped
493	WLT493		2.61	HT	556	7.85	B	8.85	PVS (breaker), Carlton
									8.85 Wigley (breaker), Carlton - scrapped
494	WLT494		2.61	HT	1367	9.82	WH	8.83	De Dubbeldekkers (dealer), Schilde, Belgium
495	WLT495		2.61	HT	452	7.85	SW	3.86	Clydeside Scottish 295 (RM495)
		LDS136A							5.89 Western Scottish C41
									5.90 scrapped by Western Scottish
496	WLT496		2.61	HT	1342	8.82	K	10.82	Portman (dealer), London W1
									11.82 Karuizawa Classic Car Museum (preserved), Nagano, Japan
497	WLT497		2.61	HT	370	5.85	WN	6.85	PVS (breaker), Carlton - scrapped

498	WLT498	*ECW313*	1.60	HL	431	4.85	AL	6.85	Varkabinettet, Kolmarden, Sweden
									9.86 Sveriges Kyrkliga, Stockholm, Sweden
									8.91 Stift Tsgarden, Soraker, Sweden
499	WLT499	*60-Sri-2542*	2.61	HT	393	5.85	Q	12.85	Sri Lanka Transport Board
500	WLT500		2.61	HT	597	2.87	HT	4.87	PVS (breaker), Carlton - scrapped
501	WLT501		11.60	HL	405	10.85	NX	6.86	Clydeside Scottish RM501
		LDS153A							5.89 Western Scottish C42
									8.90 PVS (breaker), Carlton
502	WLT502		11.60	HL	915	3.85	MH	5.85	PVS (breaker), Carlton - scrapped
503	WLT503		11.60	HL	477	5.84	PR	6.84	W.Norths (dealer), Sherburn
									6.84 Parton & Allen (bkr), Carlton - scrapped
504	WLT504		11.60	HL	1846	3.85	SW	5.85	Stagecoach, Perth
		EDS48A							10.86 Magicbus, Glasgow
									4.88 United Counties Omnibus Co. 717
									10.91 Lister (dealer), Bolton
									11.91 Brakell (dealer), Cheam
									2.94 Beach Bus Co., Kittyhawk, USA
505	WLT505		11.60	HL	379	1.85	NX	4.85	PVS (breaker), Carlton
									4.85 Wigley (breaker), Carlton - scrapped
506	WLT506		11.60	HL	1818	3.84	V	5.84	West Midlands Probation Service, Birmingham
									11.88 Vintage Vehicle Society, (preserved), Birmingham
507	WLT507		2.61	HT	484	9.87	FY	10.88	PVS (breaker), Carlton - scrapped
508	WLT508		2.61	HT	442	4.85	T	6.85	PVS (breaker), Carlton - scrapped
509	WLT509		2.61	HT	1884	6.84	B	9.84	PVS (breaker), Carlton - scrapped
510	WLT510		3.61	HT	1524	6.83	T	9.83	PVS (breaker) Carlton - scrapped
511	WLT511		2.61	HT	1370	9.82	AR	12.83	Booth (breaker), Rotherham
									12.83 Goodwin (breaker), Carlton - scrapped
512	WLT512	HVS710	7.61	EM	698	11.87	V	1.88	United Counties Omnibus Co. 701
513	WLT513		2.61	HT	526	4.85	WL	6.85	PVS (breaker), Carlton
									6.85 Wigley (breaker), Carlton - scrapped
514	WLT514		2.61	HT	1307	9.82	NX	4.83	Berry (bkr), Leicester - scrapped at Aldenham
515	WLT515		2.61	HT	414	4.85	N	6.85	PVS (breaker), Carlton - scrapped
516	WLT516	MFF518	2.61	HT	872	1.94	NX	11.94	PVS (breaker), Carlton
									1.95 Daly (agent), London
									1.95 Exported
517	WLT517		2.61	HT	417	4.85	NB	6.85	PVS (breaker), Carlton
									6.85 Rollinson (breaker), Carlton - scrapped
518	WLT518		4.61	WN	1377	4.84	NX	6.84	Hartwood Finance (breaker), Birdwell
									6.84 Morris (breaker), Carlton - scrapped
519	WLT519		2.61	HT	65	4.85	X	6.85	PVS (breaker), Carlton - scrapped
520	WLT520		2.61	HT	473	3.85	CA	5.85	PVS (breaker), Carlton
									5.85 Rollinson (breaker), Carlton - scrapped
521	WLT521		4.61	WN	524	3.89	X	8.90	Mars Confectionery, Slough
									9.90 Mars Confectionery, Turkey
									2.91 Mars Confectionery, Dubai
									12.91 Mars Confect'y, Riyadh, Saudi Arabia
522	WLT522		11.60	HL	443	5.92	PM	12.93	PVS (breaker), Carlton - scrapped
523	WLT523		2.61	HT	408	3.85	BN	4.85	PVS (breaker), Carlton
									4.85 Wigley (breaker), Carlton - scrapped
524	WLT524		4.61	WN	523	2.84	U	1.85	PVS (breaker), Carlton - scrapped
525	WLT525		12.60	HL	815	5.87	BW	9.87	Redbridge Truck & Bus (dealer), Wakefield
									9.87 Unknown, USA
526	WLT526		11.60	HL	734	2.86	WD	5.86	Clydeside Scottish RM526
		LDS152A							5.89 Western Scottish C43
									8.90 PVS (breaker), Carlton
									9.90 Wigley (breaker), Carlton - scrapped
527	WLT527		12.60	HL	338	10.94	NX	10.94	London Central Buses, London RM527
528	WLT528	WSK219	12.60	HL	803	11.87	AK	1.88	United Counties Omnibus Co., 702
									10.92 Ribble Motor Services (not used)
529	WLT529		12.60	HL	190	4.86	AD	8.86	Dare (preserved), Caversham
530	WLT530		12.60	HL	458	2.85	E	5.85	PVS (breaker), Carlton - scrapped
531	WLT531		12.60	HL	855	1.95	BN	1.95	South London Transport, London RM531

532	WLT532	GVS483	12.60	HL	854	7.92	SW	11.92	PVS (breaker), Carlton - scrapped
533	WLT533		12.60	HL	264	2.85	EM	6.85	PVS (breaker), Carlton - scrapped
534	WLT534		12.60	HL	470	5.85	S	6.85	PVS (breaker), Carlton
									6.85 Wigley (breaker), Carlton - scrapped
535	WLT535		12.60	HL	521	6.86	ED	9.86	PVS (breaker), Carlton - scrapped
536	WLT536		12.60	HL	1802	3.85	AG	4.85	PVS (breaker), Carlton - scrapped
537	WLT537		12.60	HL	271	2.87	E	6.87	PVS (breaker), Carlton - scrapped
538	WLT538		12.60	HL	1917	11.85	TC	5.86	Kelvin Scottish RM538 (1918)
		EDS395A							4.89 Kelvin Central Buses 1918
									4.93 Regal (dealer), Kirkintilloch
									1.95 PVS (breaker), Carlton - *for scrap*
539	WLT539		12.60	HL	412	11.85	NX	1.86	PVS (breaker), Carlton
									2.86 Wigley (breaker), Carlton - scrapped
540	WLT540		12.60	HL	1838	6.83	BN	11.83	Ensign (dealer), Purfleet
541	WLT541		12.60	HL	593	10.94	NX	10.94	London Central Buses, London RM541
542	WLT542		12.60	HL	918	11.85	SP	1.86	PVS (breaker), Carlton
									2.86 Wigley (breaker), Carlton - scrapped
543	WLT543		12.60	HL	359	4.85	AL	6.85	PVS (breaker), Carlton
									6.85 Rollinson (breaker), Carlton - scrapped
544	WLT544		12.60	HL	253	11.85	V	2.86	PVS (breaker), Carlton
									2.86 Wigley (breaker), Carlton - scrapped
545	WLT545		12.60	HL	441	5.92	WD	5.92	London Coaches, London RM545
546	WLT546		12.60	HL	421	8.85	Q	12.85	Clydeside Scottish 261 (RM546)
		LDS284A							5.89 Western Scottish C44
									9.90 PVS (breaker), Carlton
									10.90 Southend Transport 120
									2.94 Lister (dealer), Bolton
									2.94 Brakell (dealer), Cheam - *for resale*
547	WLT547		12.60	HL	362	3.85	AC	4.85	PVS (breaker), Carlton - scrapped
548	WLT548	SVS618	12.60	HL	409	7.93	GM	9.94	PVS (breaker), Carlton
									12.94 Pickett, Glasshoughton RM548
									5.95 PVS (breaker), Carlton - *for resale*
549	WLT549	*AA29300*	12.60	HL	1832	4.84	Q	1.85	Halden-Trafikk, Halden, Norway
550	WLT550		12.60	HL	388	3.85	B	4.86	Clydeside Scottish 250 (RM550)
		LDS184A							5.89 Western Scottish C45
									4.90 Brakell (dealer), Cheam
									8.92 Grimm, Plauen, Germany
551	WLT551		12.60	HL	1847	6.84	GM	9.84	PVS (breaker), Carlton - scrapped
552	WLT552	*586-JEW-75*	12.60	HL	1681	10.82	MH	11.83	Brakell (dealer), Cheam
									12.83 Octobus SARL, Paris, France
553	WLT553		12.60	HL	491	5.80	HT	7.83	Wombwell Diesels (breaker), Wombwell - scrapped
554	WLT554	KGH883A	12.60	HL	613	6.91	AKt	7.93	PVS (breaker), Carlton - scrapped
555	WLT555		12.60	HL	1803	11.87	AK	8.88	D.T.G.Schwerlner, Bornheim, Germany
556	WLT556		12.60	HL	1535	2.85	SW	6.85	PVS (breaker), Carlton - scrapped
557	WLT557		12.60	HL	436	4.85	T	5.86	PVS (breaker), Carlton - scrapped
558	WLT558		12.60	HL	424	7.85	Q	9.85	PVS (breaker), Carlton - scrapped
559	WLT559		12.60	HL	539	6.85	AV	8.85	PVS (breaker), Carlton
									8.85 Wigley (breaker), Carlton - scrapped
560	WLT560		12.60	HL	1879	11.84	WH	5.85	Stagecoach, Perth
		EDS50A							10.86 Magicbus, Glasgow 602
									10.90 Stagecoach, Perth 602
									10.94 Bluebird Buses 602
561	WLT561		12.60	HL	469	3.85	EM	5.85	PVS (breaker), Carlton
									5.85 Wigley (breaker), Carlton - scrapped
562	WLT562		12.60	HL	577	5.92	WD	5.92	London Coaches, London RM562
									4.93 Lamming (dealer), Coulsdon
									11.94 Unknown, Missouri, USA
563	WLT563		12.60	HL	404	3.85	WL	5.85	PVS (breaker), Carlton - scrapped
564	WLT564		12.60	HL	1869	5.84	WH	5.87	Southampton Citybus 406
									9.89 Amex Trading (dealer), Buxton
									10.89 Nomas Co., Tokyo, Japan
									1.90 Unknown, Osaka, Japan

565	WLT565		12.60	HL	447	8.85	HT	8.85	PVS (breaker), Carlton - scrapped
566	WLT566		12.60	HL	410	7.85	NX	10.85	PVS (breaker), Carlton - scrapped
567	WLT567		12.60	HL	433	3.89	X	1.90	PVS (breaker), Carlton - scrapped
568	WLT568		12.60	HL	462	3.85	SP	11.85	PVS (breaker), Carlton - scrapped
569	WLT569		12.60	HL	1793	2.85	ED	4.85	PVS (breaker), Carlton - scrapped
570	WLT570		12.60	HL	346	2.85	B	4.85	PVS (breaker), Carlton - scrapped
571	WLT571		12.60	HL	398	5.85	Q	8.85	PVS (breaker), Carlton - scrapped
572	WLT572		11.60	HL	367	4.91	WD	4.91	Lamming (dealer), Coulsdon
									10.91 PVS (breaker), Carlton - scrapped
573	WLT573		12.60	HL	446	4.85	T	6.85	PVS (breaker), Carlton - scrapped
574	WLT574		12.60	HL	486	3.85	CT	5.85	PVS (breaker), Carlton
									6.85 Wigley (breaker), Carlton - scrapped
575	WLT575	PSK822	2.61	HT	545	2.92	TL	7.92	PVS (breaker), Carlton
									7.92 Wigley (breaker), Carlton - scrapped
576	WLT576		2.61	HT	403	4.85	Q	5.85	PVS (breaker), Carlton - scrapped
577	WLT577		2.61	HT	664	9.87	GM	8.88	Southend Transport 103
									2.94 Clydeside 2000 (dealer), Paisley
									2.94 Greater Reading Omnibus, Reading 6
578	WLT578		2.61	HT	448	4.85	HT	5.85	PVS (breaker), Carlton - scrapped
579	WLT579		2.61	HT	1330	9.82	ED	11.82	Berry (breaker), Leicester - scrapped
580	WLT580		2.61	HT	497	3.89	X	10.90	PVS (breaker), Carlton - scrapped
581	WLT581		2.61	HT	504	5.85	WH	9.85	Stephen Austin Newspapers, Hertford
582	WLT582		2.61	HT	478	7.85	NX	8.85	PVS (breaker), Carlton
									8.85 Wigley (breaker), Carlton - scrapped
583	WLT583	*BA4 846*	2.61	HT	66	1.87	CT	4.87	Double Deck Tours, Niagara, Canada
584	WLT584		2.61	HT	149	11.87	V	6.88	Record Tools, Sheffield
									1.89 Pegg (Rotherham & Dist.), Rotherham
									4.91 Jamieson (breaker), Dunscroft
									4.91 Cound, Gloucester
									7.91 London Bus Export Co. (dlr), Chepstow
585	WLT585		2.61	HT	488	7.85	MH	8.85	PVS (breaker), Carlton - scrapped
586	WLT586		2.61	HT	603	9.85	AR	10.86	PVS (breaker), Carlton
									10.86 Wigley (breaker), Carlton - scrapped
587	WLT587		2.61	HT	457	8.85	ED	8.85	PVS (breaker), Carlton - scrapped
588	WLT588		2.61	HT	511	11.87	AF	8.88	Clydeside Scottish (for spares)
									1.89 Kelvin Scottish (for spares)
									3.89 Dunsmore (breaker), Larkhall -scrapped
589	WLT589		2.61	HT	472	8.85	NX	11.85	PVS (breaker), Carlton - scrapped
590	WLT590		2.61	HT	772	9.88	AR	2.89	PVS (breaker), Carlton - scrapped
591	WLT591		2.61	HT	59	7.86	NX	9.86	PVS (breaker), Carlton - scrapped
592	WLT592		2.61	HT	522	1.87	SW	9.88	Nissho Iwai Corporation (dealer), Japan
593	WLT593		2.61	HT	548	7.85	V	8.85	PVS (breaker), Carlton
									8.85 Wigley (breaker), Carlton - scrapped
594	WLT594		2.61	HT	533	8.85	WL	11.85	PVS (breaker), Carlton
									11.85 Wigley (breaker), Carlton - scrapped
595	WLT595		2.61	HT	454	7.85	TH	8.85	PVS (breaker), Carlton
									9.85 Wigley (breaker), Carlton - scrapped
596	WLT596	*60-Sri-6632*	2.61	HT	516	10.87	AR	12.88	Sri Lanka Transport Board
597	WLT597		2.61	HT	544	5.87	B	3.88	Loughborough University Students Union
									7.91 National Playbus Assoc'n (dlr), Creaton
									2.92 Spooner (preserved), Sanderstead
									8.93 Dyba (pres'd), Upper Norwood, London
									12.94 Lowings (preserved), Bagshot
598	WLT598	MFF510	2.61	HT	19	3.94	U	9.94	PVS (breaker), Carlton
									12.94 Pickett, Glasshoughton RM598
									5.95 PVS (breaker), Carlton - *for resale*
599	WLT599	MFF503	2.61	HT	1798	2.94	RA	10.94	PVS (breaker), Carlton
									12.94 Tuckett Bros.
600	WLT600		4.61	WN	163	5.88	AK	6.92	Kuwahara (agent), London NW7
									12.92 Matsugi, Japan
601	WLT601		2.61	HT	399	8.85	TL	11.85	PVS (breaker), Carlton
									11.85 Wigley (breaker), Carlton - scrapped

602	WLT602		2.61	HT	540	8.85	AF	8.85	PVS (breaker), Carlton - scrapped
603	WLT603		2.61	HT	490	6.87	PM	10.87	PVS (breaker), Carlton
									10.87 Wigley (breaker), Carlton - scrapped
604	WLT604		1.61	HL	372	8.85	EM	8.85	PVS (breaker), Carlton - scrapped
605	WLT605		2.61	HT	531	8.85	V	3.86	Kelvin Scottish RM605
									7.87 PVS (breaker), Carlton
									9.87 Wigley (breaker), Carlton - scrapped
606	WLT606	EDS320A	2.61	HT	28	5.86	X	8.86	Kelvin Scottish RM606 (1919)
									4.89 Kelvin Central Buses 1919
									8.94 Regal (dealer), Kirkintilloch
									1.95 Unknown (preserved), Glasgow
607	WLT607		1.61	HL	1854	5.84	NX	8.84	PVS (breaker), Carlton
									8.84 Rollinson (breaker), Carlton - scrapped
608	WLT608		2.61	HT	58	9.85	WH	10.85	PVS (breaker), Carlton - scrapped
609	WLT609		2.61	HT	307	11.85	V	9.86	PVS (breaker), Carlton
									9.86 Wigley (breaker), Carlton - scrapped
610	WLT610	WTS316A	2.61	HT	612	3.86	E	7.86	Strathtay Scottish SR16
									7.90 Ripley (breaker), Carlton
									9.90 Black Prince, Morley
									2.91 Wigley (breaker), Carlton - scrapped
611	WLT611		4.61	HT	1800	1.88	BW	5.89	Sollac Steel Works, Nantes, France
612	WLT612		2.61	HT	451	8.85	AD	9.85	PVS (breaker), Carlton - scrapped
613	WLT613		2.61	HT	198	9.94	U	9.94	Stagecoach East London RM613
614	WLT614		4.61	HT	119	8.85	T	9.85	PVS (breaker), Carlton
									9.85 Wigley (breaker), Carlton - scrapped
615	WLT615		2.61	HT	1885	6.84	AP	6.85	PVS (breaker), Carlton - scrapped
616	WLT616		2.61	HT	151	9.88	WN	11.88	PVS (breaker), Carlton - scrapped
617	WLT617		4.61	EM	801	8.85	X	8.85	PVS (breaker), Carlton - scrapped
618	WLT618		2.61	HT	440	8.85	TH	8.85	PVS (breaker), Carlton - scrapped
619	WLT619		2.61	HT	623	10.85	ED	9.86	PVS (breaker), Carlton - scrapped
620	WLT620		2.61	HT	84	7.85	NX	10.85	PVS (breaker), Carlton
									2.86 Wigley (breaker), Carlton - scrapped
621	WLT621		4.61	WN	1920	10.85	N	5.86	Williams (Confidence), Oadby
									4.92 Brierley Hill Salvage (bkr), Brierley Hill
									4.92 Wacton (dealer), Bromyard
									4.92 Brown, Motcombe
									9.94 Greater Reading Omnibus, Reading 16
622	WLT622		2.61	HT	1521	9.82	CT	4.83	Berry (bkr), Leicester - scrapped at Aldenham
623	WLT623		2.61	HT	666	8.92	X	8.92	PVS (breaker), Carlton - scrapped
624	WLT624		4.61	WN	131	5.85	AR	8.85	PVS (breaker), Carlton - scrapped
625	WLT625	XYJ419	4.61	WN	139	2.94	NX	11.94	PVS (breaker), Carlton
									3.95 Chester Bus & Boat, Chester
626	WLT626	*NEL88*	2.61	HT	579	9.82	BW	1.83	Silerinne, Espo, Finland
627	WLT627		2.61	HT	82	8.85	TC	8.85	PVS (breaker), Carlton
									8.85 Wigley (breaker), Carlton - scrapped
628	WLT628		2.61	HT	1415	9.82	BN	12.82	Berry (bkr), Leicester - scrapped at Aldenham
629	WLT629		2.61	HT	178	9.86	ED	2.87	PVS (breaker), Carlton
									2.87 Wigley (breaker), Carlton - scrapped
630	WLT630		2.61	HT	1814	8.84	AR	12.84	PVS (breaker), Carlton - scrapped
631	WLT631		2.61	HT	602	11.84	PM	11.85	PVS (breaker), Carlton
									11.85 Wigley (breaker), Carlton - scrapped
632	WLT632		6.61	HL	773	11.88	WN	10.89	Burgsport International (dealer), Harrow
									Unknown, Tokyo, Japan
633	WLT633		4.61	WN	630	9.82	AK	5.83	Berry (bkr), Leicester - scrapped at Aldenham
634	WLT634		4.61	WN	130	8.85	FY	9.85	PVS (breaker), Carlton - scrapped
635	WLT635		4.61	WN	9	1.87	SW	3.87	SBG Engineering, Kilmarnock (for spares)
									4.87 scrapped by SBG Engineering
636	WLT636		4.61	WN	1896	9.84	PM	12.84	PVS (breaker), Carlton
									12.84 Rollinson (breaker), Carlton - scrapped
637	WLT637		4.61	WN	575	11.88	PM	1.90	PVS (breaker), Carlton - scrapped
638	WLT638		4.61	WN	618	7.87	N	1.90	Burgsport International (dealer), Harrow
									5.92 Shiseido, Tokyo, Japan
639	WLT639		4.61	WN	29	11.83	WD	7.84	PVS (breaker), Carlton - scrapped
640	WLT640		4.61	WN	2195	8.85	AD	9.85	PVS (breaker), Carlton - scrapped

641	WLT641		4.61	WN 244	6.86	GM	9.86	Clydeside Scottish RM641
								5.89 Western Scottish C46
								8.90 Lister (dealer), Bolton
								8.90 Brakell (dealer), Cheam
								2.95 Unknown, Menden, Germany
642	WLT642		4.61	WN 784	11.87	BW	7.88	Morgan (preserved), Fleet
								6.91 Allmey (dealer), Eastcote
								11.91 Simmonds (preserved), Morden
643	WLT643		4.61	WN 604	8.85	B	9.85	PVS (breaker), Carlton - scrapped
644	WLT644		4.61	WN 690	10.94	EW	10.94	Metroline Travel, London RM644
645	WLT645		4.61	WN 745	7.86	TH	9.86	PVS (breaker), Carlton - scrapped
646	WLT646	KFF257	4.61	WN 236	10.94	HT	10.94	London Northern Bus Co., London RM646
647	WLT647		4.61	HT 1712	10.84	AR	2.85	PVS (breaker), Carlton - scrapped
648	WLT648	XVS826	4.61	WN 793	12.93	X	11.94	PVS (breaker), Carlton *- for resale*
649	WLT649	*60-Sri-6641*	4.61	WN 140	9.87	GM	12.88	Sri Lanka Transport Board
650	WLT650		4.61	WN 584	10.84	AL	12.84	PVS (breaker), Carlton
								12.84 Wigley (breaker), Carlton - scrapped
651	WLT651		4.61	BN 1788	11.84	BN	6.85	PVS (breaker), Carlton - scrapped
652	WLT652		4.61	WN 598	1.85	SF	9.85	Clydeside Scottish 252 (RM652)
		LDS161A						5.89 Western Scottish C47
								8.90 PVS (breaker), Carlton
								11.90 East Midland Motor Services (not used)
		WLT652						4.91 Watson (preserved), Chesterfield
653	WLT653		4.61	WN 460	8.85	EM	8.85	PVS (breaker), Carlton
								8.85 Wigley (breaker), Carlton - scrapped
654	WLT654		4.61	WN 1897	5.84	AL	8.84	Hedingham & District Omnibuses (not used)
								8.84 Brakell (dealer), Cheam
								9.85 Cartmill (preserved), Belfast
								6.91 Cartmill & Begley (preserved), Belfast
655	WLT655		4.61	WN 1883	7.84	WH	10.85	Williams (Confidence), Oadby 15
656	WLT656		4.61	WN 1795	10.84	W	12.84	PVS (breaker), Carlton - scrapped
657	WLT657		4.61	WN 582	8.85	EM	8.85	PVS (breaker), Carlton
								8.85 Wigley (breaker), Carlton - scrapped
658	WLT658		4.61	WN 661	2.91	WD	2.91	Lamming (dealer), Coulsdon
								4.91 PVS (breaker), Carlton - scrapped
659	WLT659	KFF239	4.61	WN 920	5.94	X	*3.95*	*London Transport Buses reserve fleet*
660	WLT660		6.61	HL 83	3.88	Q	1.90	PVS (breaker), Carlton - scrapped
661	WLT661		4.61	HT 1911	11.84	AF	2.85	PVS (breaker), Carlton - scrapped
662	WLT662		4.61	HT 94	8.85	ED	8.85	PVS (breaker), Carlton
								9.85 Wigley (breaker), Carlton - scrapped
663	WLT663	*A11 963*	4.61	HT 788	4.87	PM	7.88	Camp Edphy, Valmoria, Quebec, Canada
664	WLT664		6.61	HT 1214	12,94	BN	12.94	South London Transport, London RM664
665	WLT665		6.61	HL 512	9.85	ED	11.85	PVS (breaker), Carlton
								11.85 Wigley (breaker), Carlton - scrapped
666	WLT666		4.61	HT 875	10.86	ED	2.87	SBG Engineering, Kilmarnock (for spares)
								3.87 Clydeside Scottish RM666
		LDS257A						5.89 Western Scottish C48
								8.90 Lister (dealer), Bolton
								8.90 Cound, Gloucester (not used)
								10.90 London Bus Export Co. (dlr), Chepstow
								10.90 Bevan et al (preserved), Newport,
667	WLT667		4.61	HT 580	5.85	AR	5.86	Stagecoach, Perth
		EDS143A						10.86 Magicbus, Glasgow
								4.88 Cumberland Motor Serv's (driver trainer)
								5.89 Watson, Chesterfield (for spares)
								9.90 PVS (breaker), Carlton - scrapped
668	WLT668		4.61	WN 1626	12.84	N	3.85	PVS (breaker), Carlton
								8.85 Rollinson (breaker), Carlton - scrapped
669	WLT669		4.61	EM 949	2.87	BW	7.87	PVS (breaker), Carlton - scrapped
670	WLT670		4.61	EM 837	6.87	AK	8.87	Goodwin (breaker), Carlton - scrapped
671	WLT671		4.61	WN 67	8.85	NX	8.85	PVS (breaker), Carlton - scrapped
672	WLT672		4.61	EM 535	7.85	NB	8.85	PVS (breaker), Carlton - scrapped
673	WLT673		4.61	WN 583	8.85	NB	8.85	PVS (breaker), Carlton
								8.85 Wigley (breaker), Carlton - scrapped

'4	WLT674		4.61	EM 1662	7.86	TC	9.86	PVS (breaker), Carlton - scrapped
5	WLT675		4.61	WN 1913	3.84	AK	7.84	Southwark Women's Action Group, London
								10.90 Taffell (preserved), Ruislip
		ALC338A						9.93 Harlott, Ipswich (for spares)
'6	WLT676		4.61	EM 517	12.94	BN	12.94	South London Transport, London RM676
'7	WLT677	WTS164A	4.61	WN 87	2.86	CT	7.86	Kelvin Scottish RM677 (1920)
								4.89 Kelvin Central Buses 1920
								4.93 Regal (dealer), Kirkintilloch
								1.95 PVS (breaker), Carlton - *for scrap*
8	WLT678	EDS293A	4.61	WN 713	5.86	AV	8.86	Kelvin Scottish RM678 (1921)
								4.89 Kelvin Central Buses 1921
								3.91 Dunsmore (breaker), Larkhall - *for scrap*
'9	WLT679		4.61	WN 621	9.85	CA	11.85	PVS (breaker), Carlton - scrapped
0	WLT680		4.61	WN 302	6.86	BW	8.86	Strathtay Scottish (for spares)
								.88 Cosgrove (breaker), Dundee - scrapped
1	WLT681		4.61	WN 111	9.85	MH	11.85	PVS (breaker), Carlton - scrapped
2	WLT682	HVS937	4.61	WN 248	11.87	V	1.88	United Counties Omnibus Co. 703
3	WLT683		4.61	EM 813	11.85	X	6.86	PVS (breaker), Carlton - scrapped
4	WLT684		4.61	EM 38	11.84	V	12.84	PVS (breaker), Carlton - scrapped
5	WLT685		4.61	EM 648	11.85	TC	6.86	PVS (breaker), Carlton
								7.86 Wigley (breaker), Carlton - scrapped
6	WLT686		4.61	EM 492	3.86	MH	5.86	PVS (breaker), Carlton
								7.86 Wigley (breaker), Carlton - scrapped
7	WLT687		4.61	EM 738	10.94	NX	10.94	London Central Buses, London RM687
8	WLT688		4.61	WN 824	10.94	NX	10.94	London Central Buses, London RM688
9	WLT689		4.61	EM 601	9.85	SF	11.85	PVS (breaker), Carlton - scrapped
0	WLT690		4.61	EM 96	10.85	HT	2.86	PVS (breaker), Carlton - scrapped
1	WLT691		4.61	WN 100	10.86	HT	4.87	PVS (breaker), Carlton - scrapped
2	WLT692		4.61	EM 262	12.85	EM	9.86	PVS (breaker), Carlton - scrapped
3	WLT693		4.61	EM 153	3.87	PM	4.87	PVS (breaker), Carlton
								6.87 Wigley (breaker), Carlton - scrapped
4	WLT694		4.61	WN 634	8.85	X	12.85	Clydeside Scottish 253 (294 - RM694)
								5.89 Western Scottish C49
								9.90 PVS (breaker), Carlton
		RSK605						2.92 East Yorkshire Motor Serv's (for spares)
								4.92 PVS (breaker), Carlton - scrapped
5	WLT695		4.61	EM 688	8.85	WN	8.85	PVS (breaker), Carlton
								9.85 Hardwick (breaker), Carlton - scrapped
6	WLT696	XVS829	4.61	EM 830	4.93	AF	11.94	PVS (breaker), Carlton
								2.95 Daly (agent), London
								2.95 Exported
7	WLT697		4.61	EM 647	1.86	WN	4.86	Clydeside Scottish 297 (RM697)
		LDS238A						5.89 Western Scottish C50
								8.90 Lister (dealer), Bolton
								8.90 Cound, Gloucester (not used)
								10.90 London Bus Export Co. (dlr), Chepstow
								12.90 Rampage Hospitality, Enstone
								8.93 Prestwold Estates, Prestwold
8	WLT698		4.61	EM 614	3.87	Q	9.88	Gtr Manchester Buses, Manchester 2208
								7.90 Pegg (Rotherham & Dist.), Rotherham
								12.90 J.Sykes (breaker), Carlton
								3.92 Lister (dealer), Bolton
								3.92 Brakell (dealer), Cheam
								1.95 Unknown, Buenos Aires, Argentine
9	WLT699	WTS887A	4.61	EM 624	11.87	AF	2.88	Strathtay Scottish SR26
		PAN696						4.90 Bjork, Ljunskile, Sweden
0	WLT700		4.61	EM 75	1.87	GM	3.87	PVS (breaker), Carlton - scrapped
1	WLT701		4.61	EM 109	3.94	Q	11.94	PVS (breaker), Carlton - *for scrap*
2	WLT702	WTS404A	4.61	EM 611	4.85	X	7.86	Strathtay Scottish SR5
								6.92 Lister (dealer), Bolton
								6.92 Brakell (dealer), Cheam
								.94 Vannier, Toulouse, France

703	WLT703		4.61	EM	588	2.85	TL	5.85	Stagecoach. Perth
									3.86 used for spares by Stagecoach
									1.89 Dunsmore (breaker), Larkhall - scrapped
704	WLT704		4.61	EM	103	5.92	WD	5.92	London Coaches, London RM704
705	WLT705		4.61	EM	1728	2.84	SF	7.84	PVS (breaker), Carlton
									7.84 Wigley (breaker), Carlton - scrapped
706	WLT706		4.61	EM	832	6.86	BW	8.86	Kelvin Scottish RM706
									8.87 Stagecoach, Perth (not used)
		TSK269							10.87 Cumberland Motor Services 905
707	WLT707		4.61	EM	672	8.86	TC	10.86	PVS (breaker), Carlton
									10.86 Wigley (breaker), Carlton - scrapped
708	WLT708		4.61	EM	196	2.92	TL	7.92	PVS (breaker), Carlton - scrapped
709	WLT709		4.61	EM	721	7.90	Vt	1.91	Hans-grd, Vastert, Germany
710	WLT710		4.61	EM	596	5.92	WD	5.92	London Coaches, London RM710
711	WLT711		4.61	EM	282	11.85	TC	6.86	PVS (breaker), Carlton
									7.86 Wigley (breaker), Carlton - scrapped
712	WLT712		4.61	EM	908	1.87	E	9.89	PVS (breaker), Carlton - scrapped
713	WLT713		4.61	EM	958	2.87	AL	5.87	Stagecoach, Perth (not used)
		TSK270							10.87 Cumberland Motor Services 900
714	WLT714		4.61	EM	656	9.84	BN	11.84	PVS (breaker), Carlton - scrapped
715	WLT715		4.61	EM	468	11.88	AD	4.89	Burgsport International (dealer), Harrow
									4.89 Nissho Iwai Corporation (agent), Japan
									8.89 Unknown, Osaka, Japan
716	WLT716		4.61	EM	684	3.86	E	8.86	Kelvin Scottish (for spares)
									7.87 PVS (breaker), Carlton - scrapped
717	WLT717		4.61	EM	201	12.86	AF	2.87	PVS (breaker), Carlton - scrapped
718	WLT718		4.61	EM	725	6.87	SW	8.87	Benninck, Vijmen, Holland
		BS-04-96							2.95 British Transp't & Promo's, Arnhem, Holla
719	WLT719		4.61	EM	794	1.95	BN	1.95	South London Transport, London RM719
720	WLT720		4.61	EM	138	11.85	X	4.86	Clydeside Scottish 298 (RM720)
		LDS258A							5.89 Western Scottish C51
									8.90 Lister (dealer), Bolton
									8.90 Brakell (dealer), Cheam
									1.93 Londag, Wadenswil, Zurich, Switzerland
721	WLT721		4.61	EM	591	8.84	AL	12.84	PVS (breaker), Carlton
									1.85 Rollinson (breaker), Carlton - scrapped
722	WLT722		4.61	EM	590	12.84	PM	6.85	PVS (breaker), Carlton - scrapped
723	WLT723		4.61	EM	735	12.86	E	2.87	PVS (breaker), Carlton - scrapped
724	WLT724		4.61	EM	102	7.86	WD	8.86	Clydeside Scottish (for spares)
									3.88 # W.Norths (dealer), Sherburn
									3.88 PVS (breaker), Carlton - scrapped
725	WLT725		4.61	EM	678	1.85	CF	6.85	PVS (breaker), Carlton
									6.85 Wigley (breaker), Carlton - scrapped
726	WLT726		4.61	EM	848	8.86	ED	9.86	PVS (breaker), Carlton - scrapped
727	WLT727		4.61	EM	655	5.86	AD	9.86	Clydeside Scottish RM727
		LDS239A							5.89 Western Scottish C52
									8.90 PVS (breaker), Carlton
									8.92 East Yorkshire Motor Services 817
728	WLT728		4.61	EM	639	4.84	BW	7.84	Wombwell Diesels (breaker), Wombwell - scrapped
729	WLT729		4.61	EM	554	11.86	AC	1.87	PVS (breaker), Carlton - scrapped
730	WLT730	*60-Sri-6624*	4.61	HT	146	11.87	AF	12.88	Sri Lanka Transport Board
731	WLT731	*60-Sri-6639*	4.61	EM	106	2.87	AL	12.88	Sri Lanka Transport Board
732	WLT732	NRH801A	4.61	HT	322	11.87	BW	4.88	East Yorkshire Motor Services 801
733	WLT733		4.61	HT	610	9.82	NX	10.82	W.Norths (dealer), Sherburn - scrapped
734	WLT734		4.61	HT	703	12.86	AV	1.87	PVS (breaker), Carlton - scrapped
735	WLT735	XYJ417	4.61	HT	677	2.94	NX	11.94	PVS (breaker), Carlton
									11.94 de la Parra, Vargas, Mexico City
736	WLT736	XYJ418	4.61	EM	185	2.94	NX	*3.95*	*London Transport Buses reserve fleet*
737	WLT737		4.61	HT	730	4.83	HD	11.83	LT Sports Association, LT HD Garage
									.88 RM737 Group (preserved), Harrow
738	WLT738		4.61	HT	210	8.86	CA	1.89	PVS (breaker), Carlton - scrapped
739	WLT739		4.61	HT	643	4.84	SW	12.84	PVS (breaker), Carlton
									1.85 Rollinson (breaker), Carlton - scrapped

740	WLT740		4.61	HT	258	12.86	TH	9.89	PVS (breaker), Carlton - scrapped
741	WLT741	EDS295A	4.61	HT	136	12.85	NX	4.86	Kelvin Scottish RM741 (1922) 4.89 Kelvin Central Buses 1922 11.91 Lockhart (breaker), Shaws Hill - *for scrap*
742	WLT742		4.61	HT	148	11.86	AC	3.87	Yorkshire Evening Press, York
743	WLT743	WTS268A	4.61	HT	606	11.85	TH	7.86	Strathtay Scottish SR11 10.91 Cosgrove (breaker), Dundee - scrapped
744	WLT744		4.61	HT	91	8.86	SF	10.86	PVS (breaker), Carlton - scrapped
745	WLT745		4.61	HT	927	11.87	AK	9.89	PVS (breaker), Carlton - scrapped
746	WLT746	*60-Sri-6611*	4.61	EM	7	11.87	AG	12.88	Sri Lanka Transport Board
747	WLT747		4.61	HT	638	10.86	CA	1.87	PVS (breaker), Carlton - scrapped
748	WLT748		4.61	EM	706	3.87	PM	6.87	PVS (breaker), Carlton 7.87 Wigley (breaker), Carlton - scrapped
749	WLT749		4.61	EM	204	10.85	SW	2.86	PVS (breaker), Carlton 2.86 Wigley (breaker), Carlton - scrapped
750	WLT750		4.61	EM	181	3.85	WN	5.85	PVS (breaker), Carlton - scrapped 5.85 Rollinson (breaker), Carlton - scrapped
751	WLT751	KGH889A	4.61	EM	957	7.91	Nt	2.93	Hafner-u-Fliesen-Legergwerbe, Wilhelmsberg, Austria
752	WLT752		4.61	EM	857	5.92	WD	5.92	London Coaches, London RM752
753	WLT753		4.61	WG	646	5.92	WD	5.92	London Coaches, London RM753
754	WLT754		4.61	WG	135	2.87	AL	3.87	SBG Engineering, Kilmarnock (for spares) 4.87 Scrapped by SBG Engineering
755	WLT755		4.61	WG	715	3.86	NX	7.86	PVS (breaker), Carlton 8.86 Wigley (breaker), Carlton - scrapped
756	WLT756		4.61	WG	750	11.86	GM	3.87	PVS (breaker), Carlton - scrapped
757	WLT757 NVS855		4.61	WG	779	8.86	Q	12.86	Gash, Newark RM21 5.89 Lincolnshire Road Car Co. 1121 7.89 East Yorkshire Motor Services 810
758	WLT758		4.61	EM	823	10.94	NX	10.94	London Central Buses, London RM758
759	WLT759	WTS329A WLT759	4.61	EM	635	4.86	Q	7.86	Strathtay Scottish SR3 5.92 Roulston (preserved), Glasgow
760	WLT760	EDS297A	4.61	EM	187	5.86	SF	8.86	Kelvin Scottish RM760 (1924) 4.89 Kelvin Central Buses 1924 11.92 Scrapped by Kelvin Central Buses
761	WLT761		4.61	EM	696	1.87	CT	2.87	PVS (breaker), Carlton - scrapped
762	WLT762		4.61	EM	214	5.92	WD	5.92	London Coaches, London RM762 4.93 Scrapped by London Coaches at WD
763	WLT763		4.61	EM	129	5.86	AD	6.86	PVS (breaker), Carlton 9.86 Wigley (breaker), Carlton - scrapped
764	WLT764		4.61	EM	742	12.84	PM	1.85	PVS (breaker), Carlton - scrapped
765	WLT765		4.61	EM	699	10.94	HT	10.94	London Northern Bus Co., London RM765
766	WLT766		4.61	EM	170	8.84	PM	1.85	PVS (breaker), Carlton - scrapped
767	WLT767		4.61	EM	658	4.85	NX	5.85	PVS (breaker), Carlton - scrapped
768	WLT768		4.61	EM	709	5.87	PM	10.87	PVS (breaker), Carlton 10.87 Wigley (breaker), Carlton - scrapped
769	WLT769		4.61	EM	329	1.92	EWt	6.92	Zadian SRL, Terano, Italy
770	WLT770	EDS277A	4.61	EM	608	12.85	SP	4.86	Kelvin Scottish RM770 (1925) 4.89 Kelvin Central Buses 1925 5.91 Dunsmore (breaker), Larkhall - *for scrap*
771	WLT771		4.61	EM	776	11.84	WL	1.85	PVS (breaker), Carlton - scrapped
772	WLT772		4.61	EM	834	7.86	HT	9.86	PVS (breaker), Carlton - scrapped
773	WLT773		7.61	EM	659	11.85	TC	6.86	PVS (breaker), Carlton 7.86 Wigley (breaker), Carlton - scrapped
774	WLT774	EDS397A	7.61	EM	226	5.86	Q	9.86	Kelvin Scottish RM774 (1923) 4.89 Kelvin Central Buses 1923 1.91 Dunsmore (breaker), Larkhall - *for scrap*
775	WLT775		4.61	EM	184	12.86	TH	8.87	Ringsted Energy Centre, Ringsted, Denmark
776	WLT776		7.61	EM	680	10.84	BN	12.84	PVS (breaker), Carlton - scrapped
777	WLT777		7.61	EM	1605	9.82	T	4.83	Berry (bkr), Leicester - scrapped at Aldenham
778	WLT778		7.61	EM	851	6.89	WD	1.90	PVS (breaker), Carlton - scrapped
779	WLT779		7.61	EM	650	8.86	GM	10.86	PVS (breaker), Carlton - scrapped

780	WLT780		7.61	EM	1889	4.89	HT	3.91	PVS (breaker), Carlton - scrapped
781	WLT781		7.61	EM	125	11.87	GM	4.89	Pepsi Cola, Oman
		6295-RX-59							5.89 Sollac Steel Works, Dunkirk, France
782	WLT782		7.61	SF	707	10.94	NX	10.94	London Central Buses, London RM782
783	WLT783		7.61	SF	737	2.87	AR	6.87	PVS (breaker), Carlton - scrapped
784	WLT784	YTS565A	7.61	SF	164	6.86	PD	8.86	Strathtay Scottish (for spares)
									5.88 PVS (breaker), Carlton - scrapped
785	WLT785		7.61	SF	723	5.87	B	1.88	Nomas Co. (agents),Osaka, Japan
									2.88 Samwa Co., Osaka, Japan
									10.91 Scrapped at Osaka, Japan
786	WLT786		7.61	SF	272	4.85	EM	6.85	PVS (breaker), Carlton - scrapped
787	WLT787		7.61	SF	199	10.94	NX	10.94	London Central Buses, London RM787
788	WLT788		7.61	SF	710	7.85	N	12.85	Ernst, Dortmund, Germany
789	WLT789		7.61	SF	192	10.94	NX	10.94	London Central Buses, London RM789
790	WLT790		7.61	SF	685	6.87	AK	11.87	Gagg, Bunny
									8.89 Crick Commercials (dealer), Daventry
									9.90 Imperial Engineering, Cheshunt
									5.93 Wright (dealer), Rainham
									5.94 Greater Reading Omnibus, Reading 9
791	WLT791		7.61	SF	775	6.86	V	9.86	PVS (breaker), Carlton
									9.86 Wigley (breaker), Carlton - scrapped
792	WLT792		7.61	SF	1918	5.85	BN	8.85	PVS (breaker), Carlton - scrapped
793	WLT793		7.61	SF	843	12.86	HT	2.87	PVS (breaker), Carlton
									2.87 Wigley (breaker), Carlton - scrapped
794	WLT794		7.61	SF	955	7.86	AG	9.86	Clydeside Scottish RM794
		LDS162A							5.89 Western Scottish C53
									9.90 Lister (dealer), Bolton
									9.90 Brakell (dealer), Cheam
		BF6 690							6.92 Burkitt, Niagara, Canada
		BF7 312							11.92 Holiday VIP Tours, Niagara, Canada
795	WLT795		7.61	SF	727	11.86	SF	5.87	Marley Extrusions, Lenham
									1.93 Carr (preserved), Pluckley
796	WLT796		7.61	SF	2103	2.87	WD	6.87	PVS (breaker), Carlton - scrapped
797	WLT797	VYJ542	7.61	SF	285	12.86	AC	8.88	Southend Transport 104
									1.94 Beach Bus Co., Kittyhawk, USA
798	WLT798	NRH802A	7.61	SF	751	11.87	BW	4.88	East Yorkshire Motor Services 802
799	WLT799	EDS312A	7.61	SF	796	5.86	S	8.86	Kelvin Scottish RM799 (1926)
									4.89 Kelvin Central Buses 1926
									1.93 Ripley (breaker), Carlton
									1.93 Mancunian Bus Co., Manchester RM79
									2.94 Ripley (breaker), Carlton
									2.94 Wright & Biddell, Rainham
									7.94 Wright (dealer), Rainham
									10.94 Sweetingham-Clarke, Maidenhead
800	WLT800	*60-Sri-6628*	7.61	SF	722	11.87	AG	12.88	Sri Lanka Transport Board
801	WLT801		7.61	SF	241	6.92	PM	12.93	PVS (breaker), Carlton - scrapped
802	WLT802		7.61	EM	731	6.86	Q	9.86	PVS (breaker), Carlton - scrapped
803	WLT803	KGJ24A	7.61	EM	719	8.92	GM	7.93	PVS (breaker), Carlton - scrapped
804	WLT804	MFF581	7.61	EM	220	7.94	St	11.94	PVS (breaker), Carlton
									1.95 Armitage, Barnsley
805	WLT805		7.61	EM	1790	2.85	WH	10.86	PVS (breaker), Carlton - scrapped
806	WLT806		7.61	EM	1811	11.87	HT	2.88	PVS (breaker), Carlton - scrapped
807	WLT807	KGJ69A	7.61	EM	771	3.91	AKt		PVS (breaker), Carlton - scrapped
808	WLT808		7.61	EM	240	3.87	Q	6.87	PVS (breaker), Carlton - scrapped
809	WLT809	EDS396A	7.61	EM	1052	8.86	Q	10.86	SBG Engineering, Kilmarnock
									11.86 Kelvin Scottish RM809 (1927)
									4.89 Kelvin Central Buses 1927
									1.93 Regal (dealer), Kirkintilloch
		YVS286							2.93 BHT Buses, Parkstone 286
									8.94 BPTA, Bournemouth 286
810	WLT810		7.61	EM	831	10.86	HT	3.87	PVS (breaker), Carlton - scrapped
811	WLT811		7.61	EM	720	8.89	WD	8.89	London Underground Distrib'n Serv's, London
									3.93 Shepherd, Somerset

812	WLT812		7.61	EM	1810	12.86	AV	1.89	S.A.Au Vieux Moulin, Boullion, Belgium
		LAN558							1.93 Roisin, Chatelet, Belgium
813	WLT813		7.61	EM	224	6.86	V	9.86	PVS (breaker), Carlton
									9.86 Wigley (breaker), Carlton - scrapped
814	WLT814		7.61	SF	976	8.86	GM	10.86	PVS (breaker), Carlton - scrapped
815	WLT815		7.61	EM	44	10.94	NX	10.94	London Central Buses, London RM815
816	WLT816		7.61	SF	268	8.86	NX	10.86	PVS (breaker), Carlton
									11.86 Wigley (breaker), Carlton - scrapped
817	WLT817		7.61	SF	828	11.86	SF	1.87	PVS (breaker), Carlton
									2.87 Wigley (breaker), Carlton - scrapped
818	WLT818	KGJ41A	7.61	EM	474	8.92	GM	3.93	PVS (breaker), Carlton - scrapped
819	WLT819		7.61	SF	768	7.90	ADt	6.91	PVS (breaker), Carlton - scrapped
820	WLT820		7.61	SF	632	2.87	SW	9.87	Southampton Citybus 414
									5.90 Unknown, Japan
821	WLT821		7.61	SF	674	11.84	CA	11.84	PVS (breaker), Carlton - scrapped
822	WLT822		7.61	SF	247	5.87	HT	8.87	Sibbons (preserved), Billericay
823	WLT823		7.61	SF	795	1.86	Q	6.86	PVS (breaker), Carlton
									7.86 Wigley (breaker), Carlton - scrapped
824	WLT824		7.61	EM	243	5.86	AF	8.86	Kelvin Scottish RM824
									8.87 Stagecoach, Perth (not used)
		TSK271							10.87 Cumberland Motor Services 907
825	WLT825		1.62	X	992	5.90	GM	6.90	PVS (breaker), Carlton
									6.90 Wigley (breaker), Carlton - scrapped
826	WLT826	KFF252	7.61	SF	826	6.94	AC	12.94	PVS (breaker), Carlton
									12.94 Punta Prava, Argentina
827	WLT827		8.61	EM	798	1.87	S	4.87	PVS (breaker), Carlton - scrapped
828	WLT828		7.61	SF	686	10.84	CT	5.85	Jensen, Oslo, Norway
									8.92 Halden Traffik, Halden, Norway
829	WLT829		7.61	SF	1384	2.85	B	4.85	PVS (breaker), Carlton - scrapped
830	WLT830		7.61	SF	767	7.86	HT	9.86	Clydeside Scottish RM830
		LDS248A							5.89 Western Scottish C54
									8.90 Lister (dealer), Bolton
									8.90 Southend Transport (for spares)
									2.92 Hardwick (breaker), Carlton - scrapped
831	WLT831		7.61	SF	741	2.87	CT	5.87	Stagecoach, Perth (not used)
		EDS341A							10.87 Magicbus, Glasgow 603
									6.90 Cumberland Motor Services (for spares)
									5.92 Willowholme Recoveries, Carlisle
832	WLT832		7.61	SF	861	11.88	HT	12.88	Balloon Stables, Bath
		BHU987A							10.91 Webbs Haulage (dealer), Stratford upon Avon
									10.91 Unknown, Germany
833	WLT833		7.61	SF	800	11.86	CF	10.87	PVS (breaker), Carlton - scrapped
834	WLT834		7.61	EM	791	12.86	TH	2.87	PVS (breaker), Carlton - scrapped
835	WLT835		7.61	SF	238	7.86	X	9.86	Clydeside Scottish RM835
									5.89 Western Scottish C55
									8.90 PVS (breaker), Carlton
									8.90 Wright (dealer), Rainham
									11.90 Clydemaster Pres'n Group, Brentwood
836	WLT836		7.61	SF	744	1.87	BW	2.87	PVS (breaker), Carlton - scrapped
837	WLT837	KGJ62A	7.61	SF	757	12.93	FY	11.94	PVS (breaker), Carlton
									2.95 Daly (agent), London
									2.95 Exported
838	WLT838	XYJ440	7.61	SF	990	4.94	NXt	11.94	PVS (breaker), Carlton
									3.95 Greater Reading Omnibus, Reading 22
839	WLT839		7.61	SF	1812	2.85	GM	4.85	PVS (breaker), Carlton - scrapped
840	WLT840		7.61	SF	252	12.86	E	1.87	PVS (breaker), Carlton - scrapped
841	WLT841		7.61	EM	265	12.86	SF	2.87	PVS (breaker), Carlton - scrapped
842	WLT842		7.61	EM	799	10.86	S	4.87	PVS (breaker), Carlton
									4.87 Wigley (breaker), Carlton - scrapped
843	WLT843	XVS828	7.61	SF	748	7.93	AC	1.94	Bravo Timewarp Television, Watford
844	WLT844		7.61	EM	906	5.86	X	9.86	PVS (breaker), Carlton
									9.86 Wigley (breaker), Carlton - scrapped

845	WLT845		7.61	EM	749	2.86	SF	5.86	PVS (breaker), Carlton
									7.86 Wigley (breaker), Carlton - scrapped
846	WLT846		7.61	EM	1805	1.88	PD	5.88	East Yorkshire Motor Services (for spares)
									7.89 PVS (breaker), Carlton - scrapped
847	WLT847		7.61	EM	762	12.86	SW	6.87	Clydeside Scottish (for spares)
									5.89 Western Scottish (for spares)
									8.90 Wombwell Diesels (breaker), Wombwell - scrapped
848	WLT848		7.61	EM	847	12.85	V	4.86	Blackpool Transport 522
849	WLT849		7.61	SF	679	9.82	AL	12.82	Berry (bkr), Leicester - scrapped at Aldenham
850	WLT850		7.61	SF	781	6.89	WD	1.90	PVS (breaker), Carlton - scrapped
851	WLT851		7.61	SF	278	11.88	AD	1.89	Burgsport International (dealer), Harrow
									4.89 Nissho Iwai Corporation (agent), Japan
									11.89 Unknown, Osaka, Japan
852	WLT852	*60-Sri-6610*	7.61	SF	810	6.87	AK	12.88	Sri Lanka Transport Board
853	WLT853		7.61	SF	687	8.86	TH	9.86	PVS (breaker), Carlton
									9.86 Wigley (breaker), Carlton - scrapped
854	WLT854		7.61	SF	970	11.87	AF	12.87	PVS (breaker), Carlton
									12.87 Wigley (breaker), Carlton - scrapped
855	WLT855		7.61	SF	293	6.86	CT	9.86	PVS (breaker), Carlton
									9.86 Wigley (breaker), Carlton - scrapped
856	WLT856		7.61	SF	263	6.86	GM	9.86	PVS (breaker), Carlton - scrapped
857	WLT857		7.61	SF	1819	12.84	CT	8.86	South Park Motors, Reigate
858	WLT858	EDS362A	7.61	SF	754	5.86	NX	9.86	Kelvin Scottish RM858 (1928)
									4.89 Kelvin Central Buses 1928
									11.90 Coutts, Glasgow
859	WLT859		7.61	SF	919	6.86	CF	9.86	Clydeside Scottish RM859
		LDS247A							5.89 Western Scottish C56
									8.90 PVS (breaker), Carlton
									2.92 European Bus Centre (dlr), Bruges, Belgi
860	WLT860		7.61	SF	774	6.86	N	10.86	PVS (breaker), Carlton - scrapped
861	WLT861		7.61	SF	726	12.84	SP	6.85	PVS (breaker), Carlton
									6.85 Rollinson (breaker), Carlton - scrapped
862	WLT862		8.61	SF	318	2.85	WL	5.85	PVS (breaker), Carlton - scrapped
863	WLT863		5.62	SE	1320	1.84	Q	2.84	Ensign (dealer), Purfleet
									3.84 PVS (breaker), Carlton - scrapped
864	WLT864		8.61	SF	1571	9.82	A	10.82	W.Norths (dealer), Sherburn - scrapped
865	WLT865		12.62	AE	1302	8.82	PM	10.82	W.Norths (dealer), Sherburn - scrapped
866	WLT866		5.62	SE	913	5.87	AK	6.87	PVS (breaker), Carlton - scrapped
867	WLT867		5.62	SE	1418	9.82	K	12.83	Booth (breaker), Rotherham
									12.83 Goodwin (breaker), Carlton - scrapped
868	WLT868		12.62	FY	422	10.94	NX	10.94	London Central Buses, London RM868
869	WLT869		1.62	FY	937	2.92	TL	7.92	PVS (breaker), Carlton - scrapped

Another operator to use a special livery for its Routemasters was Cumberland Motor Services who introduce eight buses of this type on its Carlislebus services in October 1987. ALD983B illustrated here had previously operated for Kelvin Scottish for ten months following its departure from London. (K.A.Jenkinson)

Despite its fleet being in the process of being repainted into Stagecoach corporate livery, United Counties retained its old green & orange scheme for its Routemasters. One of these, WLT682, with fixed front upper deck windows shows its 'Routemaster' fleet name to good effect whilst working the local 101 service in Bedford. (S.A.Jenkinson)

Having been transferred from Magicbus, Glasgow to Perth and given Stagecoach fleet names, 602 (EDS50A) which migrated to Stagecoach in October 1986 was still hard at work with that company in the summer of 1994. (K.A.Jenkinson)

61
HARRABY EAST
cms Carlislebus
SUN ALLIANCE
INSURANCE GROUP

Routemaster
101
WOODSIDE Church Lane
THE INSIDE OF THIS BUS IS A SMOKE FREE ZONE
TRAVEL IN CLEAN AIR COMFORT ON
RAISES A FEW EYEBRAUS.
Kellerbrau
Routemaster
Routemaster

1
Rannoch Road
Strathtay Road
Primrose Crescent
LETHAM-tulloch-CITY
STAGECOACH
602
STAGECOACH
EDS 50A

870	WLT870		9.61	HL	845	4.86	CF	10.86	Clydeside Scottish RM870
									5.89 Western Scottish C57
									8.90 PVS (breaker), Carlton
									8.90 Wright (dealer), Rainham
									5.91 Doggett, Purley
									5.91 Lamming (dealer), Coulsdon
									6.91 Frontrunner SE, Dagenham (not used)
									6.91 Citybus, Hong Kong (not used)
									3.93 Scrapped by Citybus, Hong Kong
871	WLT871	NRH803A	1.62	FY	909	11.87	AG	4.88	East Yorkshire Motor Services 803
									3.95 Greater Reading Omnibus, Reading 26
872	WLT872		1.62	FY	197	10.94	NX	10.94	London Central Buses, London RM872
873	WLT873		1.62	FY	914	8.87	GM	10.87	PVS (breaker), Carlton
									10.87 Wigley (breaker), Carlton - scrapped
874	WLT874		1.62	FY	876	5.86	V	8.86	Clydeside Scottish RM874
		LDS338A							5.89 Western Scottish C58
									9.90 PVS (breaker), Carlton - scrapped
875	WLT875		1.62	FY	910	5.86	HT	8.86	Kelvin Scottish RM875
									8.87 Stagecoach, Perth (not used)
		OVS940							10.87 Cumberland Motor Services 906
876	WLT876		11.61	FY	849	11.87	AF	9.89	PVS (breaker), Carlton - scrapped
877	WLT877		1.62	FY	1787	2.87	E	4.87	PVS (breaker), Carlton
									6.87 Wigley (breaker), Carlton - scrapped
878	WLT878		11.61	FY	1002	2.87	X	5.87	Clydeside Scottish (for spares)
									11.88 Kelvin Scottish (for spares)
									3.89 W.Norths (dealer), Sherburn
									3.89 PVS (breaker), Carlton - scrapped
879	WLT879		11.61	FY	1322	11.87	HT	4.88	Blackpool Transport 527

RML

880	WLT880		11.61	FY	897	11.94	S	11.94	London United Busways, London RML880
881	WLT881		11.61	FY	895	11.94	S	11.94	London United Busways, London RML881
882	WLT882		11.61	FY	889	9.94	CT	9.94	Leaside Bus Co., London RML882
883	WLT883		11.61	FY	892	10.94	Q	10.94	London Central Buses, London RML883
884	WLT884		11.61	FY	896	9.94	CT	9.94	Leaside Bus Co., London RML884
885	WLT885		11.61	FY	886	9.94	X	9.94	CentreWest, London RML885
886	WLT886		11.61	FY	893	9.94	U	9.94	Stagecoach East London, London RML886
887	WLT887		11.61	FY	880	10.94	AF	10.94	London General Transport, London RML887
888	WLT888		11.61	FY	881	9.94	CT	9.94	Leaside Bus Co., London RML888
889	WLT889		11.61	FY	882	10.94	AF	10.94	London General Transport, London RML889
890	WLT890	XFF814	11.61	FY	885	9.94	U	9.94	Stagecoach East London, London RML890
891	WLT891		11.61	FY	883	11.94	S	11.94	London United Busways, London RML891
892	WLT892		11.61	FY	888	1.95	BN	1.95	South London Transport, London RML892
893	WLT893	KFF276	11.61	FY	887	10.94	AC	10.94	Metroline Travel, London RML893
894	WLT894		11.61	FY	899	10.94	RA	10.94	London General Transport, London RML894
895	WLT895		12.61	FY	884	1.95	BN	1.95	South London Transport, London RML895
896	WLT896		12.61	FY	894	9.94	CT	9.94	Leaside Bus Co., London RML896
897	WLT897		12.61	FY	890	9.94	CT	9.94	Leaside Bus Co., London RML897
898	WLT898	XFF813	1.62	FY	898	9.94	BW	9.94	Stagecoach East London, London RML898
899	WLT899		1.62	FY	891	10.94	AF	10.94	London General Transport, London RML899
900	WLT900		1.62	FY	900	7.87	Q	2.88	Clydeside Scottish RML900
									5.89 Western Scottish C10
									10.91 Clydeside 2000 99
									1.95 Wright & Biddell, Rainham
901	WLT901		1.62	FY	901	9.94	CT	9.94	Leaside Bus Co., London RML901
902	WLT902	ALC464A	5.64	FY	902	10.94	AC	10.94	Metroline Travel, London RML902
903	WLT903		3.63	FY	903	10.94	HT	10.94	London Northern Bus Co., London RML903

904	WLT904		11.61	FY	530	8.86	SF	9.86	PVS (breaker), Carlton - scrapped
905	WLT905		11.61	FY	645	7.90	Wt		Pepsi Cola, Istanbul, Turkey
906	WLT906		11.61	FY	729	11.91	AGt	12.93	PVS (breaker), Carlton - scrapped
907	WLT907		11.61	FY	829	4.86	CA	5.86	PVS (breaker), Carlton - scrapped
908	WLT908	BMJ919A	11.61	FY	938	11.87	AG	1.88	United Counties Omnibus Co. 704
									10.91 Lister (dealer), Bolton
									2.93 PVS (breaker), Carlton - scrapped
909	WLT909	WTS418A	11.61	WN	912	6.87	SW	11.87	Magicbus, Glasgow
									4.89 East Midland Motor Services RM909
									10.91 Ireland (dealer), Hull
									10.91 Walker (preserved), Eastham, Wirral
910	WLT910	EDS288A	11.61	FY	861	5.86	NX	9.86	Kelvin Scottish RM910 (1929)
									4.89 Kelvin Central Buses 1929
									4.93 Regal (dealer), Kirkintilloch
									9.93 Lister (dealer), Bolton
									9.93 Brakell (dealer), Cheam - *for resale*
911	WLT911		11.61	WN	57	6.87	AK	10.87	PVS (breaker), Carlton - scrapped
912	WLT912		11.61	FY	732	10.94	HT	10.94	London Northern Bus Co., London RM912
913	WLT913		1.62	X	817	3.87	Q	11.88	PVS (breaker), Carlton - scrapped
914	WLT914		1.62	X	838	12.86	TH	1.87	PVS (breaker), Carlton
									2.87 Wigley (breaker), Carlton - scrapped
915	WLT915	EDS401A	11.61	WN	833	2.86	GM	4.86	Kelvin Scottish RM915 (1930)
									4.89 Kelvin Central Buses 1930
									8.91 Dunsmore (breaker), Larkhall - scrapped
916	WLT916	GVS491	11.61	WN	215	7.92	BN	7.93	PVS (breaker), Carlton - scrapped
917	WLT917	WTS102A	11.61	WN	326	4.86	N	8.86	Strathtay Scottish SR20 (620)
									6.94 Greater Reading Omnibus, Reading
918	WLT918	*NNY023*	11.61	WN	700	3.87	Q	6.88	Smulsen Sport, Visby, Sweden
									7.88 Haack, Gotland, Sweden
919	WLT919	LDS259A	11.61	WN	827	5.86	CA	9.86	Clydeside Scottish RM919
									5.89 Western Scottish C59
									9.90 PVS (breaker), Carlton - scrapped
920	WLT920	XVS876	11.61	WN	934	7.93	GM	5.94	PVS (breaker), Carlton - scrapped
921	WLT921	YTS892A	11.61	WN	780	6.86	Q	9.86	Strathtay Scottish SR8
									10.91 Cosgrove (breaker), Dundee - scrapped
922	WLT922		11.61	FY	6.83	2.86	AV	9.86	Kelvin Scottish (for spares)
									7.87 PVS (breaker), Carlton - scrapped
923	WLT923		11.61	FY	853	6.86	WD	9.86	PVS (breaker), Carlton
									9.86 Wigley (breaker), Carlton - scrapped
924	WLT924	LDS260A	11.61	FY	667	6.86	AL	10.86	Clydeside Scottish RM924
									5.89 Western Scottish C60
									8.90 PVS (breaker), Carlton
									6.91 European Bus Centre (dealer), Bruges, Belgium
									10.91 McDonalds Restaurants, Belgium
925	WLT925		11.61	FY	126	3.91	WD	4.91	Lamming (dealer), Coulsdon
									4.91 PVS (breaker), Carlton - scrapped
926	WLT926		11.61	NX	27	6.89	X	1.90	PVS (breaker), Carlton - scrapped
927	WLT927		11.61	NX	688	9.82	T	12.83	Booth (breaker), Rotherham - scrapped
928	WLT928		11.61	NX	782	10.94	NX	10.94	London Central Buses, London RM928
929	WLT929		11.61	NX	841	2.86	WD	9.86	PVS (breaker), Carlton
									10.86 Wigley (breaker), Carlton - scrapped
930	WLT930		11.61	NX	952	3.87	Q	6.87	PVS (breaker), Carlton
									7.87 Wigley (breaker), Carlton - scrapped
931	WLT931	MFF580	11.61	NX	1710	7.94	St	11.94	PVS (breaker), Carlton
									3.95 Greater Reading Omnibus, Reading 24
932	WLT932		11.61	NX	916	10.86	BW	2.87	PVS (breaker), Carlton - scrapped

Now preserved, former RM1262 is seen here whilst still in the ownership of the London Borough of Harrow who used it as a further education publicity vehicle for Harrow Teachers Centre. *(P.T.Stokes)*

Painted in Kelvin's revised livery which omitted the broad dark blue band is 1943 (LDS317A), one of six Routemasters acquired from neighbouring Clydeside/Western Scottish in May 1990. It is seen here in Glasg city centre in April 1992. (K.A.Jenkinson)

Painted in London-style livery and fitted with a specially designed logo on its side panels, Greater Manchester Buses 2201/RM1136 traverses Manchester's Mosley Street whilst working Piccadilly Line service 143 to West Didsbury. (K.A.Jenkinson)

Routemasters briefly returned to Manchester in 1993 when the Mancunian Bus Co. introduced them onto a service previously operated by Greater Manchester Buses RMs. Former Kelvin Scottish RM799 freshly repainted into Mancunian's pseudo London red livery is seen here on its first day in service on route 143. (R.Boardman)

933	WLT933		11.61	NX	911	5.86	NX	9.86	Clydeside Scottish RM933
									5.89 Western Scottish C61
									8.90 PVS (breaker), Carlton
									~~8.90 Wright (dealer), Rainham~~
									6.91 Haven Coaches, Newhaven RM933
									1.94 Wright & Biddell (Blue Triangle), Rainham
934	WLT934		11.61	NX	222	12.86	HT	1.87	PVS (breaker), Carlton - scrapped
935	WLT935		11.61	FY	733	2.87	HT	4.87	PVS (breaker), Carlton - scrapped
936	WLT936		11.61	NX	708	8.86	AF	10.86	SBG Engineering, Kilmarnock
									11.86 Clydeside Scottish RM936
									5.89 Western Scottish C62
									8.90 PVS (breaker), Carlton - scrapped
937	WLT937		11.61	NX	1796	2.87	HT	8.88	Southend Transport 105
									2.94 Clydeside 2000 (dealer), Paisley
									2.94 Greater Reading Omnibus, Reading 5
938	WLT938		11.61	NX	790	9.87	FY	11.87	Magicbus, Glasgow
									7.89 Hoskin (preserved), Mitcham
939	WLT939		11.61	WN	806	8.86	NX	10.86	PVS (breaker), Carlton - scrapped
940	WLT940		11.61	WN	905	12.93	FY	11.94	PVS (breaker), Carlton - *for scrap*
941	WLT941		11.61	WN	255	8.86	SW	2.87	PVS (breaker), Carlton - scrapped
942	WLT942		11.61	NX	746	2.85	HT	5.85	PVS (breaker), Carlton
									5.85 Rollinson (breaker), Carlton - scrapped
943	WLT943	WTS225A	11.61	WN	844	4.86	NX	6.86	Strathtay Scottish SR1
									10.92 Walker, Paisley
									12.92 Dewvale, Paisley
									2.93 Mancunian Bus Co., Manchester RM943
									2.94 Ripley (breaker), Carlton
									2.94 Wright (dealer), Rainham
944	WLT944		11.61	WN	943	11.93	FW	9.94	CentreWest, London RM944
945	WLT945		11.61	WN	835	9.82	X	10.82	W.Norths (dealer), Sherburn - scrapped
946	WLT946	MFF577	11.61	NX	1026	7.94	St	11.94	PVS (breaker), Carlton
									11.94 de la Parra, Vargas, Mexico City
947	WLT947		11.61	NX	870	2.87	AL	6.87	PVS (breaker), Carlton
									7.87 Wigley (breaker), Carlton - scrapped
948	WLT948		11.61	NX	860	3.87	Q	6.87	PVS (breaker), Carlton - scrapped
949	WLT949	XVS319	11.61	NX	755	11.87	GM	8.88	Southend Transport 106
									2.94 Clydeside 2000 (dealer), Paisley
									2.94 Greater Reading Omnibus, Reading 3
950	WLT950		11.61	NX	697	8.86	NX	9.86	PVS (breaker), Carlton
									9.86 Wigley (breaker), Carlton - scrapped
951	WLT951		11.61	NX	786	6.86	CA	9.86	Clydeside Scottish RM951
									5.89 Western Scottish C63
									8.90 Lister (dealer), Bolton
									8.90 Brakell (dealer), Cheam
									12.94 Kangaro International (agent), Colnbrook
									12.94 Unknown, South America
952	WLT952		11.61	NX	989	6.86	N	9.86	PVS (breaker), Carlton
									10.86 Wigley (breaker), Carlton - scrapped
953	WLT953		11.61	NX	1776	6.89	X	6.90	PVS (breaker), Carlton
									6.90 Wigley (breaker), Carlton - scrapped
954	WLT954	GVS490	11.61	NX	335	8.92	BN	10.92	PVS (breaker), Carlton - scrapped
955	WLT955		11.61	WN	858	3.87	WD	9.87	Wombwell Diesels (breaker), Wombwell - scrapped
956	WLT956		11.61	WN	205	5.86	CF	8.86	Clydeside Scottish RM956
		LDS261A							5.89 Western Scottish C64
									8.90 Lister (dealer), Bolton
									8.90 Cound, Gloucester (not used)
									8.90 London Bus Export Co. (dlr), Chepstow
									10.94 J.Sykes (breaker), Carlton
957	WLT957		11.61	WN	819	6.87	E	7.87	W.Norths (dealer), Sherburn - scrapped
958	WLT958		11.61	WN	310	6.87	AK	10.87	PVS (breaker), Carlton - scrapped
959	WLT959		11.61	WN	856	4.86	AC	10.86	PVS (breaker), Carlton
									10.86 Wigley (breaker), Carlton - scrapped

960	WLT960		11.61	WN 923	3.87	WD	5.87	Clydeside Scottish RM960
								5.89 Western Scottish C65
								9.90 PVS (breaker), Carlton
								4.91 Wright (dealer), Rainham
								9.91 Haven Coaches, Newhaven RM960/6
								6.92 Lamming (dealer), Coulsdon
								8.92 Gregory (preserved), Croydon
961	WLT961		11.61	WN 636	4.86	SW	9.86	PVS (breaker), Carlton
								9.86 Wigley (breaker), Carlton - scrapped
962	WLT962		11.61	WN 974	5.86	Q	6.86	PVS (breaker), Carlton - scrapped
963	WLT963		11.61	WN 941	7.87	AK	8.88	British & American Bingo, Albequerque, USA
964	WLT964		11.61	WN 821	10.86	N	3.87	PVS (breaker), Carlton - scrapped
965	WLT965		11.61	FY 811	11.85	X	1.86	Dunkley, Hayes
								11.89 scrapped at Yeading
966	WLT966		11.61	WN 753	9.93	BW	*3.95*	*London Transport Buses reserve fleet*
967	WLT967		11.61	WN 907	10.94	NX	10.94	London Central Buses, London RM967
968	WLT968		11.61	WN 925	3.87	E	4.87	PVS (breaker), Carlton
								4.87 Wigley (breaker), Carlton - scrapped
969	WLT969		11.61	WN 1813	2.85	AR	10.87	Southampton Citybus (not used)
		DFH806A						10.88 London Bus Export Co. (dlr), Chepstow
970	WLT970		11.61	WH 954	1.95	BN	1.95	South London Transport, London RM970
971	WLT971		1.62	SE 1264	9.82	E	3.83	Berry (bkr), Leicester - scrapped at Aldenham
972	WLT972		11.61	WN 988	7.85	WH	8.85	PVS (breaker), Carlton
								8.85 Wigley (breaker), Carlton - scrapped
973	WLT973		11.61	WN 770	2.92	TL	7.92	PVS (breaker), Carlton - scrapped
974	WLT974		11.61	WN 862	5.86	HT	8.86	Clydeside Scottish RM974
		LDS339A						5.89 Western Scottish C64
								9.90 PVS (breaker), Carlton
								12.92 East Yorkshire Motor Serv's (for spares)
								11.94 PVS (breaker), Carlton - scrapped
975	WLT975		11.61	WH 785	11.86	SF	1.87	PVS (breaker), Carlton - scrapped
976	WLT976		11.61	FY 836	6.86	NX	8.86	Kelvin Scottish (for spares)
								7.87 PVS (breaker), Carlton - scrapped
977	WLT977		11.61	FY 961	5.93	BW	7.93	Unknown, Belgium
978	WLT978		11.61	FY 975	8.86	SF	10.86	SBG Engineering, Kilmarnock
								11.86 Clydeside Scottish RM978
		LDS164A						5.89 Western Scottish C67
								8.90 PVS (breaker), Carlton
								4.91 Raven (preserved), London
								.92 Raven (preserved), Westcliff-on-Sea
979	WLT979		11.61	FY 752	8.86	X	10.86	PVS (breaker), Carlton - scrapped
980	WLT980		11.61	WH 266	11.87	X	1.88	United Counties Omnibus Co. 711
		USK625						5.89 East Midland Motor Services RM980
								10.92 Stagecoach, Perth 605
								10.94 Bluebird Buses 605
981	WLT981		11.61	FY 141	3.85	HT	5.85	PVS (breaker), Carlton
								5.85 Rollinson (breaker), Carlton - scrapped
982	WLT982	NVS804	11.61	FY 940	9.87	E	4.88	East Yorkshire Motor Sevices 804
								5.95 PVS (breaker), Carlton
								5.95 Wigley (breaker), Carlton
								5.95 Jenkinson (dealer), Queensbury
								5.95 Yorkshire Programmes, Farsley
983	WLT983		11.61	FY 979	5.86	GM	9.86	Kelvin Scottish RM983
								8.87 Clydeside Scottish (for spares)
								9.87 # W.Norths (dealer), Sherburn
								3.89 PVS (breaker), Carlton - scrapped

After spending several years as the Routemaster dedicated to BBC Television's soap 'East Enders', RM318 was donated to the London Transport Museum for auction to raise funds. Purchased by a Canadian, it was exported to his native country and is seen here in January 1994 at Surrey, British Columbia in full London livery.

Originally London Transport RM54 and later Clydeside Scottish 255, this bus was re-registered LDS279A whilst north of the border. Purchased for preservation in 1992, it has been restored by its present owner to Blackburn Transport livery as seen in this view taken in May 1994. (B.Newsome)

Former Northern General front entrance RCN699 spent five years with Stevenson of Spath, Uttoxeter before being purchased by Stagecoach of Perth in 1986. Now safely preserved, it has been restored to Northern General livery by its current owners, employees of that north-east based company. (G.R.Littlewood)

Seen in 1990, 403CLT which was converted to open-top for its owners, Benskins Brewery who purchased it in 984 was sold to a preservationist in 1992 after serving for eight years as a promotional vehicle. (P.T.Stokes)

984	WLT984		11.61	FY	985	6.86	BW	9.86	Kelvin Scottish RM984
									8.87 Clydeside Scottish (for spares)
		ALD959B							5.88 Clydeside Scottish RM1959
									5.89 Western Scottish C79
									9.90 PVS (breaker), Carlton
									3.91 Gallier, Dunnington
									8.91 Allmey (dealer), Eastcote
									9.91 Humphries, Willesden
									7.92 Humphries (Routemaster), Watford
985	WLT985		11.61	WH	769	11.87	AG	1.88	United Counties Omnibus Co. 712
									10.91 Lister (dealer), Bolton
									11.91 Whiting (bkr), Ferrybridge - *for scrap*
986	WLT986	*BE9 683*	11.61	FY	592	9.82	K	5.84	Piccadilly Bus Tours, Ottowa, Canada
987	WLT987	EDS352A	11.61	WH	792	5.86	ED	8.86	Kelvin Scottish RM987 (1931)
									4.89 Kelvin Central Buses 1931
									6.93 Regal (dealer), Kirkintilloch
									1.95 PVS (breaker), Carlton
									1.95 Wigley (breaker), Carlton - *for scrap*
988	WLT988		11.61	WH	641	2.87	AG	6.87	PVS (breaker), Carlton - scrapped
989	WLT989		11.61	WH	229	4.90	GM	6.90	PVS (breaker), Carlton
									6.90 Wigley (breaker), Carlton - scrapped
990	WLT990	XYJ443	11.61	WH	208	4.94	NXt	9.94	PVS (breaker), Carlton - *for scrap*
991	WLT991		11.61	WH	267	9.86	AL	1.87	Dickenson (preserved), Timperley
992	WLT992		1.62	W	1226	11.87	NX	1.88	PVS (breaker), Carlton - scrapped
993	WLT993		5.62	SE	930	11.87	V	8.88	Southend Transport 107
									2.94 Greater Reading Omnibus, Reading 2
994	WLT994	VLT89	3.62	HT	873	11.94	RA	11.94	London General Transport, London RM994
995	WLT995		5.62	SE	1103	4.94	AR	*3.95*	*London Transport Buses reserve fleet*
996	WLT996		5.62	SE	600	8.86	GM	9.86	PVS (breaker), Carlton
									9.86 Wigley (breaker), Carlton - scrapped
997	WLT997		5.62	SE	407	1.95	BN	1.95	South London Transport, London RM997
998	WLT998		1.62	X	864	2.87	TH	3.87	SBG Engineering, Kilmarnock (for spares)
									4.87 scrapped by SBG Engineering
999	WLT999		1.62	W	991	8.86	CA	4.87	Brakell (dealer), Cheam
									10.89 Ensign (dealer), Purfleet
									10.89 Kestrell Contracts & Leasing, London
		WVS423							5.93 Bole (preserved), Dover
									9.94 Greater Reading Omnibus, Reading 15
1000	100BXL		3.62	WH	1604	6.85	TC	6.87	RM1000 Group (preserved), LT TC garage
1001	1CLT		1.62	X	1037	6.86	HT	4.87	Smith (preserved), Billericay
1002	2CLT	OYM368A	1.62	X	711	2.94	NX	10.94	London Central Buses, London RM1002
1003	3CLT		3.62	SF	871	1.95	BN	1.95	South London Transport, London RM1003
1004	4CLT		1.62	X	1659	9.82	BW	3.83	Scrapped by LTE at Aldenham
1005	5CLT	ALC290A	3.62	HT	154	2.94	NX	*3.95*	*London Transport Buses reserve fleet*
1006	6CLT	EDS98A	1.62	X	926	5.86	Q	8.86	Kelvin Scottish RM1006 (1932)
									4.89 Kelvin Central Buses 1932
									1.93 Ripley (breaker), Carlton
									3.93 Mancunian Bus Co., Manchester RM1006
									2.94 Ripley (breaker), Carlton
									2.94 Wright (dealer), Rainham
1007	7CLT	KGJ43A	1.62	SE	1449	1.91	AK	6.91	PVS (breaker), Carlton - scrapped
1008	8CLT		1.62	X	986	6.86	HT	10.86	PVS (breaker), Carlton - scrapped
1009	9CLT		3.62	HL	1078	6.87	AK	10.87	Humphries (preserved), Dagenham
									6.91 Wright & Humphries, Rainham
1010	10CLT	EDS221A	1.62	SE	818	4.86	AG	9.86	Kelvin Scottish RM1010 (1933)
									4.89 Kelvin Central Buses 1933
									1.93 Ripley (breaker), Carlton
									2.93 Mancunian Bus Co., Manchester RM1010
									2.94 Ripley (breaker), Carlton
									2.94 Wright & Biddell (Blue Triangle), Rainham
									6.94 East Yorkshire Motor Services 819
1011	11CLT		1.62	SE	449	11.86	SF	2.87	PVS (breaker), Carlton - scrapped
1012	12CLT		1.62	X	805	5.86	GM	10.86	PVS (breaker), Carlton - scrapped

1013	13CLT		5.62	SE	1032	6.86	AR	9.86	Clydeside Scottish RM1013
		LDS253A							5.89 Western Scottish C68
									8.90 PVS (breaker), Carlton
									9.90 Wright (dealer), Rainham
									9.91 Soucek, Brighton
									8.93 Soucek, Prague, Czeck Republic
1014	14CLT		1.62	SE	947	7.85	SF	8.85	PVS (breaker), Carlton - scrapped
1015	15CLT		1.62	SE	1574	2.87	AG	3.87	PVS (breaker), Carlton - scrapped
1016	16CLT		3.62	SE	1197	3.87	Q	6.87	PVS (breaker), Carlton
									7.87 Wigley (breaker), Carlton - scrapped
1017	17CLT	WTS973A	1.62	SE	950	4.86	Q	8.86	Strathtay Scottish SR4
									9.92 Walker, Paisley
									2.93 Mancunian Bus Co., Manchester RM1017
									2.94 Ripley (breaker), Carlton
									2.94 Wright (dealer), Rainham
									2.94 Wright & Biddell (Blue Triangle), Rainham
									7.94 Greater Reading Omnibus, Reading 8
1018	18CLT	PVS828	1.62	W	931	4.93	GM	11.94	PVS (breaker), Carlton
									3.95 Greater Reading Omnibus, Reading 18
1019	19CLT	PVS829	5.62	SE	1039	4.93	GM	10.94	PVS (breaker), Carlton - *for scrap*
1020	20CLT	PVS830	1.62	SE	939	4.93	GM	11.94	PVS (breaker), Carlton
									2.95 Dunstan, Middleton
1021	21CLT		1.62	SE	922	6.86	X	6.87	PVS (breaker), Carlton
									6.87 Wigley (breaker), Carlton - scrapped
1022	22CLT		1.62	SE	984	3.83	AK	6.83	Scrapped by LTE at Aldenham
1023	23CLT	KGH956A	1.62	SE	959	11.90	GMt	11.94	PVS (breaker), Carlton - *for scrap*
1024	24CLT		5.62	SE	2164	2.87	CA	6.87	PVS (breaker), Carlton
									7.87 Wigley (breaker), Carlton - scrapped
1025	25CLT		1.62	SE	878	12.84	X	1.85	PVS (breaker), Carlton - scrapped
1026	26CLT		1.62	X	1641	6.86	CF	10.86	Producciones Ciceron, Madrid, Spain
1027	27CLT		5.62	SE	1251	1.87	E	7.87	PVS (breaker), Carlton
									7.87 Wigley (breaker), Carlton - scrapped
1028	28CLT		5.62	SE	1220	8.82	AR	10.82	W.Norths (dealer), Sherburn - scrapped
1029	29CLT	*60-Sri-6626*	1.62	X	1210	5.88	GM	12.88	Sri Lanka Transport Board
1030	30CLT		1.62	X	945	8.86	GM	9.86	PVS (breaker), Carlton - scrapped
1031	31CLT		12.62	W	1296	11.83	ED	8.84	PVS (breaker), Carlton - scrapped
1032	32CLT		1.62	W	977	12.86	E	2.87	SBG Engineering, Kilmarnock
									5.87 Clydeside Scottish RM1032
		LDS254A							5.89 Western Scottish C69
									8.90 PVS (breaker), Carlton
									8.92 W.Norths (dealer), Sherburn
		YVS292							2.93 BHT Buses, Parkstone 292
									8.94 BPTA, Bournemouth 292
									4.95 Pegg, Rotherham
1033	33CLT		1.62	X	1030	10.94	Q	10.94	London Central Buses, London RM1033
1034	34CLT		12.62	W	1719	9.82	AG	2.83	Berry (bkr). Leicester - scrapped at Aldenham
1035	35CLT		1.62	X	1083	6.85	NB	8.85	PVS (breaker), Carlton - scrapped
1036	36CLT		1.62	SE	935	10.86	E	4.87	PVS (breaker), Carlton - scrapped
037	37CLT		1.62	W	1269	12.86	HT	2.87	PVS (breaker), Carlton - scrapped
038	38CLT		1.62	SE	1378	6.84	EM	1.85	PVS (breaker), Carlton - scrapped
039	39CLT		1.62	SE	562	6.89	X	1.90	PVS (breaker), Carlton - scrapped
040	40CLT	EDS109A	1.62	W	1096	2.86	NB	4.86	Kelvin Scottish RM1040 (1934)
									4.89 Kelvin Central Buses 1934
									12.91 Dunsmore (breaker), Larkhall - *for scrap*
041	41CLT	NRH805A	1.62	W	962	11.87	AG	4.88	East Yorkshire Motor Services 805
									4.95 Lister (dealer), Bolton
									4.95 Brakell (dealer), Cheam - *for resale*
042	42CLT		1.62	W	952	9.87	T	11.87	PVS (breaker), Carlton
									11.87 Wigley (breaker), Carlton - scrapped
043	43CLT		1.62	W	968	6.86	AF	9.86	PVS (breaker), Carlton - scrapped
044	44CLT		1.62	W	869	8.86	X	9.86	PVS (breaker), Carlton - scrapped
045	45CLT		1.62	W	1022	12.86	WN	6.87	PVS (breaker), Carlton - scrapped
046	46CLT	EGF282B	1.62	W	1004		GM	5.94	PVS (breaker), Carlton - scrapped

One of a pair of former British Airways front entrance Routemasters purchased by Magicbus, Glasgow, NMY634E like its sister was at first placed in service lacking front destination equipment as illustrated by t. 1988 view at Stagecoach's Perth depot. (K.A.Jenkinson)

Acquired by Green Rover of Watford in January 1990, ex.British Airways/London Transport front entrance KGJ602D is seen here wearing its new owner's attractive livery. (P.T.Stokes)

Its body extended in length by the fitting of an additional bay removed from a scrap Routemaster, London Coaches open-top ERM84 is seen here on sightseeing duties at London's Trafalgar Square in June 1993.

Originally a red central area bus, 183CLT was sold to Southend Transport in August 1988 before passing to London & Country in 1993. Initially painted in its new owner's standard livery for use on the Surrey Leisure Sunday services, it has more recently been restored to the dark green & cream London Transport country area colour scheme. It is seen here in 1994 operating the 408 service to Guildford. (J.A.Godwin)

1047	47CLT		1.62	W	956	11.87	AK	4.88	Vorlander GMBH, Ruppichferath, Germany
1048	48CLT		1.62	W	964	1.88	NX	7.88	Strathtay Scottish (for spares)
									8.89 Cosgrove (breaker), Dundee
									10.89 Dunsmore (breaker), Larkhall - scrapped
1049	49CLT	PSK819	1.62	W	761	2.92	TL	7.92	PVS (breaker), Carlton - scrapped
1050	50CLT		1.62	W	1177	10.86	N	5.87	PVS (breaker), Carlton
									6.87 Wigley (breaker), Carlton - scrapped
1051	51CLT		1.62	SE	904	12.86	SW	1.87	PVS (breaker), Carlton
									2.87 Wigley (breaker), Carlton - scrapped
1052	52CLT		1.62	SE	1562	9.82	BN	12.82	Berry (bkr), Leicester - scrapped at Aldenham
1053	53CLT	EDS107A	1.62	SE	983	6.86	BW	9.86	Kelvin Scottish RM1053 (1935)
									4.89 Kelvin Central Buses 1935
									2.93 Regal (dealer), Kirkintilloch
		YVS287							2.93 BHT Buses, Parkstone 287
									8.94 BPTA, Bournemouth 287
1054	54CLT		1.62	SE	987	6.86	ED	9.86	Clydeside Scottish RM1054
		LDS285A							5.89 Western Scottish C70
									8.90 Reinheimer Autoteile, Krickenbach, Germany
1055	55CLT	NVS405	1.62	SE	1117	8.92	X	10.92	PVS (breaker), Carlton - scrapped *(collected by PVS from Nottingham)*
1056	56CLT		1.62	SE	1131	5.87	NX	6.87	Hampshire Bus (not used)
		LDS68A							11.87 Magicbus, Glasgow 604
									6.90 Dunsmore (breaker), Larkhall - scrapped
1057	57CLT		1.62	SE	965	5.85	SF	6.85	PVS (breaker), Carlton - scrapped
1058	58CLT		5.62	FW	599	10.94	NX	10.94	London Central Buses, London RM1058
1059	59CLT		1.62	SE	1554	4.84	AL	9.84	PVS (breaker), Carlton - scrapped
1060	60CLT		1.62	SE	1551	9.82	HW	3.83	Berry (bkr), Leicester - scrapped at Aldenham
1061	61CLT		1.62	SE	1021	6.87	AK	8.88	Southend Transport 108
									1.94 Beach Bus Co., Kittyhawk, USA
1062	62CLT		1.62	SE	739	10.94	NX	10.94	London Central Buses, London RM1062
1063	63CLT		1.62	SE	1154	3.87	N	8.87	Wycombe Youth Council, High Wycombe
									3.90 Ward Jones (preserved), High Wycombe
									4.91 Ladd (preserved), Richings Park
1064	64CLT		1.62	SE	1107	2.86	WN	5.86	PVS (breaker), Carlton
									6.86 Wigley (breaker), Carlton - scrapped
1065	65CLT		1.62	SE	1017	1.87	E	6.87	PVS (breaker), Carlton - scrapped
1066	66CLT		1.62	SE	981	8.86	CT	6.87	PVS (breaker), Carlton - scrapped
1067	67CLT	*60-Sri-6633*	1.62	SE	982	12.86	AR	12.88	Sri Lanka Transport Board
1068	68CLT	ABD892A	1.62	SE	969	11.87	AF	1.88	United Counties Omnibus Co. 705
1069	69CLT		1.62	SE	1001	12.86	NX	2.87	Sullivan (preserved), Leytonstone
									1.92 Sullivan (preserved), Harrow
1070	70CLT	XYJ430	1.62	SE	1211	5.94	CT	7.94	Unknown
1071	71CLT		1.62	AR	1594	9.82	CT	3.83	Berry (bkr), Leicester - scrapped at Aldenham
1072	72CLT	*BD7873*	1.62	HL	932	3.89	X	1.90	Kent, Mississauga, Ontario, Canada
1073	73CLT		5.62	AV	1564	11.82	NX	7.83	Wombwell Diesels (breaker), Wombwell - scrapped
1074	74CLT		2.62	SE	1094	7.88	Q	2.89	PVS (breaker), Carlton - scrapped
1075	75CLT		1.62	EM	1018	9.82	Mt	12.83	Booth (breaker), Rotherham - scrapped
1076	76CLT		1.62	HT	1006	8.87	E	9.87	PVS (breaker), Carlton
									9.87 Wigley (breaker), Carlton - scrapped
1077	77CLT	KGH26A	1.62	SF	1041	3.87	WD	8.87	Brakell (dealer), Cheam
									2.90 Handelsbolaget Rode Orm, Aland Is., Finland
1078	78CLT	KGH925A	1.62	WH	1095	5.94	AC	*3.95*	*London Transport Buses reserve fleet*
1079	79CLT		1.62	SF	1742	1.88	Q	1.88	PVS (breaker), Carlton
									1.88 Wigley (breaker), Carlton - scrapped
1080	80CLT	*60-Sri-6621*	1.62	SE	1014	5.88	GM	12.88	Sri Lanka Transport Board
1081	81CLT		2.62	SE	1025	12.93	BW	*3.95*	*London Transport Buses reserve fleet*
1082	82CLT		1.62	SE	1300	10.94	NX	10.94	London Central Buses, London RM1082
1083	83CLT	XVS850	1.62	SE	1024	5.94	AF	10.94	PVS (breaker), Carlton
									10.94 Time, Thornton Heath
1084	84CLT		1.62	SE	1008	5.87	AK	6.87	PVS (breaker), Carlton
									8.87 Wigley (breaker), Carlton - scrapped

1085	85CLT		1.62	NX	1038	10.86	AD	3.87	PVS (breaker), Carlton - scrapped
1086	86CLT		5.62	FW	479	12.86	N	3.87	Sejthen, Krusas, Denmark
1087	87CLT		5.62	FW	1178	2.87	AL	5.87	Hampshire Bus (not used)
									11.87 Magicbus, Glasgow 605
									10.89 Lister (dealer), Bolton
									10.89 Brakell (dealer), Cheam - *for resale*
1088	88CLT		5.62	FW	1340	9.82	U	8.83	De Dubbeldekkers (dealer), Schilde, Belgium
1089	89CLT	ALC179A	5.62	FW	1183	12.93	FY	3.94	PVS (breaker), Carlton - scrapped
1090	90CLT		5.62	FW	1066	11.88	PM	4.89	Nissho Iwai Corporation (agent), Japan
1091	91CLT		5.62	FW	203	11.86	WD	2.87	PVS (breaker), Carlton - scrapped
1092	92CLT		5.62	FW	1387	6.84	NX	8.84	PVS (breaker), Carlton
									8.84 Wigley (breaker), Carlton - scrapped
1093	93CLT		5.62	FW	1087	5.87	NX	8.87	Ripley (breaker), Carlton - scrapped
1094	94CLT		1.62	NX	1011	8.87	E	9.87	PVS (breaker), Carlton
									9.87 Wigley (breaker), Carlton - scrapped
1095	95CLT		5.62	AV	1160	10.86	HT	4.87	PVS (breaker), Carlton - scrapped
1096	96CLT		2.62	FY	1070	12.86	BN	1.87	PVS (breaker), Carlton - scrapped
1097	97CLT		2.62	SE	859	10.94	NX	10.94	London Central Buses, London RM1097
1098	98CLT		5.62	AV	840	7.90	GM	8.90	PVS (breaker), Carlton - scrapped
1099	99CLT		2.62	SE	966	8.86	Q	10.86	PVS (breaker), Carlton - scrapped
1100	100CLT		5.62	FW	1366	9.82	H	3.83	Berry (bkr), Leicester - scrapped at Aldenham
1101	101CLT	KGH969A KFF367	5.62	FW	1089	3.94	U	9.94	PVS (breaker), Carlton
									9.94 Ashworth, Birkenhead 20
1102	102CLT		5.62	FW	942	2.94	FY	11.94	PVS (breaker), Carlton
									11.94 Ensign (dealer), Rayleigh
1103	103CLT		2.62	SE	1029	6.89	X	1.90	PVS (breaker), Carlton - scrapped
1104	104CLT		5.62	AV	1051	10.94	NX	10.94	London Central Buses, London RM1104
1105	105CLT		5.62	FW	1045	2.85	BN	4.85	PVS (breaker), Carlton
									4.85 Wigley (breaker), Carlton - scrapped
1106	106CLT		5.62	FW	1028	9.82	AL	4.83	Berry (bkr), Leicester - scrapped at Aldenham
1107	107CLT		5.62	AV	789	12.86	Q	4.87	PVS (breaker), Carlton
									6.87 Wigley (breaker), Carlton - scrapped
1108	108CLT		2.62	SE	306	11.87	SF	12.87	PVS (breaker), Carlton
									12.87 Wigley (breaker), Carlton - scrapped
1109	109CLT		5.62	AV	1067	2.87	AL	5.87	Pulfrey, Great Gonnerby
									11.87 Pegg (Rotherham & Dist.), Rotherham
									4.91 Jamieson (breaker), Dunscroft
									4.91 Cound, Gloucester
									7.91 London Bus Export Co. (dlr), Chepstow
1110	110CLT		5.62	AV	874	6.85	TH	7.85	PVS (breaker), Carlton - scrapped
1111	111CLT		5.62	AV	1015	1.86	CF	12.87	Haltmayr, Auseberg, Germany
1112	112CLT		5.62	AV	807	4.86	BW	6.86	PVS (breaker), Carlton - scrapped
1113	113CLT		5.62	FW	1056	4.86	NX	10.86	PVS (breaker), Carlton - scrapped
1114	114CLT		5.62	FW	1184	6.89	X	6.90	PVS (breaker), Carlton - scrapped
1115	115CLT	*60-Sri-6609*	5.62	FW	1124	11.87	SF	12.88	Sri Lanka Transport Board
1116	116CLT		5.62	FW	1064	11.86	SF	3.87	PVS (breaker), Carlton
									3.87 Wigley (breaker), Carlton - scrapped
1117	117CLT		5.62	FW	1347	11.82	X	7.83	Potter, London
									8.83 Unknown, Spain
1118	118CLT		5.62	FW	1158	3.87	X	6.87	PVS (breaker), Carlton - scrapped
1119	119CLT		5.62	FW	1242	10.94	NX	10.94	London Central Buses, London RM1119
1120	120CLT		5.62	FW	1123	12.86	E	4.87	PVS (breaker), Carlton - scrapped
1121	121CLT	*60-Sri-6622*	5.62	FW	1122	11.87	AK	12.88	Sri Lanka Transport Board
1122	122CLT		5.62	FW	1101	3.87	S	10.87	PVS (breaker), Carlton - scrapped
1123	123CLT		5.62	FW	507	11.86	V	6.87	Burtons Biscuits, Blackpool
									12.89 Blackpool Transport 534
									4.94 Burtons Biscuits, Blackpool
1124	124CLT	VYJ806	5.62	FW	1120	1.95	BN	1.95	South London Transport, London RM1124
1125	125CLT	KGH858A	5.62	FW	1206	1.95	BN	1.95	South London Transport, London RM1125
1126	126CLT		5.62	FW	1215	2.89	X	9.89	PVS (breaker), Carlton - scrapped
1127	127CLT		5.62	FW	1262	9.82	BN	1.83	Berry (bkr), Leicester - scrapped at Aldenham

Preserved and restored in London General livery, former Northern General FPT603C is seen here in store at East Midland's Chesterfield depot in June 1991. (K.A.Jenkinson)

Repainted into Black Prince of Morley's attractive livery is former RM441 which was re-registered LDS341A by its previous owner, Western Scottish. Its body with fixed glazed front upper deck windows was originally fitted to RM209. (K.A.Jenkinson)

1128	128CLT		5.62	FW	1161	3.90	GM	6.90	PVS (breaker), Carlton
									6.90 Wigley (breaker), Carlton - scrapped
1129	129CLT		5.62	FW	1060	10.86	HT	4.87	PVS (breaker), Carlton - scrapped
1130	130CLT		5.62	FW	1174	10.88	HT	1.89	PVS (breaker), Carlton
									1.89 Wigley (breaker), Carlton - scrapped
1131	131CLT		5.62	FW	1127	10.88	HT	8.90	Burgsport International (agent), Harrow
									9.90 Shiesido, Tokyo, Japan
1132	132CLT		5.62	FW	1191	12.86	AC	2.87	PVS (breaker), Carlton - scrapped
1133	133CLT	KFF240	5.62	FW	1217	6.94	X	11.94	PVS (breaker), Carlton
									11.94 Unknown, France
1134	134CLT		5.62	AV	973	8.86	AL	9.86	Clydeside Scottish RM1134
		LDS475A							5.89 Western Scottish C71
									5.90 Kelvin Central Buses 1946
									2.93 Regal (dealer), Kirkintilloch
		YVS285							2.93 BHT Buses, Parkstone 285
									8.94 BPTA, Bournemouth 285
1135	135CLT		5.62	FW	1219	9.92	HT	1.93	PVS (breaker), Carlton - scrapped
1136	136CLT		5.62	FW	1187	3.87	Q	8.88	Gtr Manchester Buses, Manchester 2201
									11.90 Lister (dealer), Bolton
									5.91 Brakell (dealer), Cheam
									4.94 Unknown, Buenos Aires, Argentina
1137	137CLT		5.62	FW	550	6.87	PD	6.87	PVS (breaker), Carlton - scrapped
1138	138CLT		5.62	AV	2151	5.94	S	*3.95*	*London Transport Buses reserve fleet*
1139	139CLT		5.62	FW	1132	12.87	Q	2.88	PVS (breaker), Carlton - scrapped
1140	140CLT		5.62	AV	1430	9.82	NX	10.82	W.Norths (dealer), Sherburn - scrapped
1141	141CLT		5.62	AV	998	4.93	GM	3.94	PVS (breaker), Carlton - scrapped
1142	142CLT		5.62	FW	1042	9.87	E	11.88	PVS (breaker), Carlton - scrapped
1143	143CLT	WTS186A	5.62	AV	637	11.87	X	2.88	Strathtay Scottish SR24 (624)
									7.94 Greater Reading Omnibus, Reading 13
1144	144CLT		7.62	SE	1253	5.88	AK	1.90	PVS (breaker), Carlton - scrapped
1145	145CLT	LDS402A	5.62	AV	558	11.86	AV	5.87	Magicbus, Glasgow 606
									4.92 Kelvin Central Buses 1921
									10.93 Regal (dealer), Kirkintilloch
									11.93 Pegg (Rotherham & Dist.), Rotherham
									11.94 J.Sykes (breaker), Carlton
1146	146CLT		5.62	AV	1046	5.87	HT	4.88	PVS (breaker), Carlton
									6.88 Wigley (breaker), Carlton - scrapped
1147	147CLT		5.62	AV	1149	9.88	Q	10.88	PVS (breaker), Carlton - scrapped
1148	148CLT		5.62	AV	1301	1.88	BW	2.89	PVS (breaker), Carlton - scrapped
1149	149CLT		5.62	AV	929	8.86	NX	10.86	SBG Engineering, Kilmarnock
		WTS163A							11.86 Kelvin Scottish RM1149 (1936)
									4.89 Kelvin Central Buses 1936
									2.93 Regal (dealer), Kirkintilloch
		YVS290							3.93 BHT Buses, Parkstone 290
									8.94 BPTA, Bournemouth 290
1150	150CLT	*60-Sri-6619*	5.62	AV	1248	1.88	BW	12.88	Sri Lanka Transport Board
1151	151CLT		5.62	AV	1675	8.84	SW	11.84	PVS (breaker), Carlton - scrapped
1152	152CLT		5.62	AV	1040	9.86	TC	5.87	Clydeside Scottish RM1152
									5.89 Western Scottish C72
									9.90 PVS (breaker), Carlton
									7.91 Elsdon (pres'd), Thornton-in-Lonsdale
									3.94 Pryer (preserved), Sandbach
1153	153CLT		5.62	AV	1097	8.86	Q	9.86	PVS (breaker), Carlton
									9.86 Wigley (breaker), Carlton - scrapped
1154	154CLT		5.62	AV	1009	10.86	V	8.87	Brown (preserved), Romford
									1.88 Brakell (dealer), Cheam
									3.89 Coppard, Great Dunford
									7.89 Williams, Ashford
									8.89 Nichioh Trade Services, Kobe, Japan
1155	155CLT		12.62	AE	1102	11.85	CT	9.87	PVS (breaker), Carlton - scrapped
1156	156CLT		12.62	AE	1036	11.87	AG	4.88	London Regeneration Consortium, London
									6.94 Unknown, Bedford

1157	157CLT		12.62	RL	1208	9.82	T	7.83	Gallagher International, Benin, West Africa 9.83 Spoexci, Cotonou, Benin, West Africa
1158	158CLT		5.62	NB	1654	10.94	HT	10.94	London Northern Bus Co., London RM1158
1159	159CLT		5.62	SE	1916	6.86	GM	10.86	Kent County Council, Aylesford 12.89 Goodman, Herne Bay
1160	160CLT	*60-Sri-6631*	5.62	SE	1082	10.86	ED	12.88	Sri Lanka Transport Board
1161	161CLT		5.62	SE	63	3.85	T	5.85	PVS (breaker), Carlton 5.85 Wigley (breaker), Carlton - scrapped
1162	162CLT		5.62	SE	999	5.91	GM	11.94	PVS (breaker), Carlton 2.95 Wigley (breaker), Carlton - *for scrap*
1163	163CLT		4.62	AR	1389	9.82	BW	6.83	De Dubbeldekkers (dealer), Schilde, Belgium
1164	164CLT	NSG636A	5.62	NB	1108	12.86	AV	5.87	Hampshire Bus (not used) 10.87 Magicbus, Glasgow 4.89 East Midland Motor Services RM1164 10.92 Stagecoach, Perth 603 10.94 Bluebird Buses 603
1165	165CLT	*60-Sri-6640*	5.62	NB	1167	1.88	NX	12.88	Sri Lanka Transport Board
1166	166CLT	GVS498	4.62	FY	825	9.92	AFt	2.93	Zoeftig & Co., Bude
1167	167CLT		5.62	NB	1057	5.88	GM	10.88	PVS (breaker), Carlton - scrapped
1168	168CLT		4.62	NX	1027	10.94	NX	10.94	London Central Buses, London RM1168
1169	169CLT		4.62	NX	1371	9.82	PM	10.82	W.Norths (dealer), Sherburn - scrapped
1170	170CLT	XYJ441	6.62	NX	1221	4.94	NXt	11.94	PVS (breaker), Carlton 5.95 Daly (agent), London 5.95 Exported
1171	171CLT		12.62	AE	1240	10.94	HT	10.94	London Northern Bus Co., London RM1171
1172	172CLT		1.63	W	1381	2.92	TL	7.92	PVS (breaker), Carlton - scrapped
1173	173CLT		1.63	W	1332	9.82	PM	10.82	W.Norths (dealer), Sherburn - scrapped
1174	174CLT		5.62	NB	924	10.94	NX	10.94	London Central Buses, London RM1174
1175	175CLT		12.62	AE	1279	8.82	BN	8.82	PVS (breaker), Carlton - scrapped
1176	176CLT		12.62	AE	1129	10.94	NX	10.94	London Central Buses, London RM1176
1177	177CLT		4.62	NX	1033	10.87	AK	12.87	PVS (breaker), Carlton - scrapped
1178	178CLT		4.62	NX	1044	5.87	PM	10.87	PVS (breaker), Carlton - scrapped
1179	179CLT		12.62	AE	1288	9.82	K	4.83	Berry (bkr), Leicester - scrapped at Aldenham
1180	180CLT		12.62	RL	1243	1.88	NX	11.91	Routemaster Assoc'n (pres'd), Luxemburg
1181	181CLT	*KN-C-989*	5.62	NB	1144	12.91	EWt	6.92	Brandes, Konstanz, Germany
1182	182CLT		12.62	AE	1298	10.82	MH	2.83	Berry (bkr), Leicester - scrapped at Aldenham
1183	183CLT		5.62	NB	1216	7.87	BW	8.88	Southend Transport 109 12.93 London & Country 4109 (RM1183)
1184	184CLT		5.62	NB	1260	9.82	NX	10.82	W.Norths (dealer), Sherburn - scrapped
1185	185CLT	XYJ427	5.62	NB	1199	7.94	HT	10.94	London Northern Bus Co., London RM1185
1186	186CLT	XVS875	5.62	NB	1133	7.93	GM	3.94	PVS (breaker), Carlton - scrapped
1187	187CLT	*2454*	5.62	NB	1185	11.88	HT	1.89	Nissho Iwai Corporation (agent), Japan 1.89 Yagima (Ken-ie Bus Co.), Nagasaki, Japan
1188	188CLT	KGH859A	12.62	RL	1233	7.92	SW	3.93	PVS (breaker), Carlton - scrapped
1189	189CLT		12.62	RL	1359	9.82	B	12.82	Berry (bkr), Leicester - scrapped at Aldenham
1190	190CLT		12.62	RL	1128	9.82	AG	12.82	Berry (bkr), Leicester - scrapped at Aldenham
1191	191CLT		12.62	RL	1256	9.82	NX	7.84	PVS (breaker), Carlton - scrapped
1192	192CLT		12.62	AE	1241	11.88	AD	7.89	Mitsubishi Corporation, Japan
1193	193CLT		12.62	AE	1156	6.84	W	9.84	PVS (breaker), Carlton 9.84 Rollinson (breaker), Carlton - scrapped
1194	194CLT		12.62	RL	1397	9.82	PM	4.83	Berry (bkr), Leicester - scrapped at Aldenham
1195	195CLT		4.62	NX	1099	8.88	AR	11.88	PVS (breaker), Carlton - scrapped
1196	196CLT		4.62	NX	1084	12.86	TH	2.87	PVS (breaker), Carlton - scrapped
1197	197CLT	KGJ29A	5.62	NB	1005	4.91	ONt	11.94	PVS (breaker), Carlton 5.95 Exported
1198	198CLT		5.62	NB	1239	12.86	E	3.87	PVS (breaker), Carlton - scrapped
1199	199CLT		5.62	NB	1373	9.82	SW	10.82	W.Norths (dealer), Sherburn - scrapped
1200	200CLT		5.62	NB	1276	9.82	ED	12.82	Berry (bkr), Leicester - scrapped at Aldenham
1201	201CLT		12.62	RL	1352	9.82	U	3.83	Berry (bkr), Leicester - scrapped at Aldenham
1202	202CLT		5.62	NB	1000	9.82	AL	12.83	Booth (breaker), Rotherham 12.83 Goodwin (breaker), Carlton - scrapped

1203	203CLT		12.62	RL	1274	9.82	B	10.82	W.Norths (dealer), Sherburn - scrapped
1204	204CLT		12.62	RL	1213	12.93	FY	*3.95*	*London Transport Buses reserve fleet*
1205	205CLT	XYJ429	5.62	NB	1077	4.94	AR	*3.95*	*London Transport Buses reserve fleet*
1206	206CLT		5.62	NB	1272	9.82	WH	12.82	Berry (bkr), Leicester - scrapped at Aldenham
1207	207CLT		5.62	NB	1257	9.82	AL	12.82	Berry (bkr), Leicester - scrapped at Aldenham
1208	208CLT		12.62	RL	1619	9.82	BW	4.83	Berry (bkr), Leicester - scrapped at Aldenham
1209	209CLT		5.62	NB	1148	5.93	AF	5.94	PVS (breaker), Carlton - scrapped
1210	210CLT		5.62	NB	1080	3.87	CT	6.87	PVS (breaker), Carlton - scrapped
1211	211CLT		12.62	AF	1271	9.82	PM	5.83	Berry (bkr), Leicester - scrapped at Aldenham
1212	212CLT		5.62	AV	495	2.87	AL	4.87	Harbarth & Shenton, Lipperbruch, Germany
1213	213CLT		12.62	AF	1073	11.86	SF	2.87	PVS (breaker), Carlton - scrapped
1214	214CLT		12.62	AF	1114	5.94	S	*3.95*	*London Transport Buses reserve fleet*
1215	215CLT		12.62	AF	1130	4.91	ONt	6.92	PVS (breaker), Carlton
									6.92 Wigley (breaker), Carlton - scrapped
1216	216CLT		12.62	AF	1304	9.82	B	12.83	Booth (breaker), Rotherham - scrapped
1217	217CLT	KGH887A	12.62	AF	1140	6.91	AKt	12.93	PVS (breaker), Carlton - scrapped
1218	218CLT		12.62	AF	1121	10.94	HT	10.94	London Northern Bus Co., London RM1218
1219	219CLT		12.62	AF	1143	7.93	GM	3.94	PVS (breaker), Carlton - scrapped
1220	220CLT		12.62	AF	1398	10.88	HT	8.90	PVS (breaker), Carlton - scrapped
1221	221CLT	*BD7 871*	12.62	AF	561	3.89	X	1.90	Kent, Missisauga, Ontario, Canada
1222	222CLT		12.62	AF	1698	9.82	TL	3.83	Berry (bkr), Leicester - scrapped at Aldenham
1223	223CLT		12.62	AF	1255	9.82	PM	10.82	W.Norths (dealer), Sherburn - scrapped
1224	224CLT		12.62	AF	1020	11.87	V	1.88	United Counties Omnibus Co. 713
		UYJ654							9.92 Stagecoach, Perth 601
									10.94 Bluebird Buses 601
1225	225CLT		12.62	AF	971	12.86	AL	2.87	PVS (breaker), Carlton - scrapped
1226	226CLT		12.62	AE	1351	11.82	BW	12.83	Booth (breaker), Rotherham - scrapped
1227	227CLT		12.62	AE	995	9.82	B	4.83	Berry (bkr), Leicester - scrapped at Aldenham
1228	228CLT		12.62	AR	552	9.88	Q	10.88	PVS (breaker), Carlton - scrapped
1229	229CLT	GVS448	12.62	AE	1350	3.88	GM	7.92	PVS (breaker), Carlton - scrapped
1230	230CLT		12.62	W	1392	9.82	TL	10.82	W.Norths (dealer), Sherburn - scrapped
1231	231CLT		12.62	W	1266	9.82	WH	7.84	PVS (breaker), Carlton - scrapped
1232	232CLT		12.62	W	1314	12.84	T	1.85	PVS (breaker), Carlton
									1.85 Wigley (breaker), Carlton - scrapped
1233	233CLT		12.62	W	1600	9.82	AR	4.83	Berry (bkr), Leicester - scrapped at Aldenham
1234	234CLT		12.62	W	1341	9.82	X	2.83	Berry (bkr), Leicester - scrapped at Aldenham
1235	235CLT		12.62	W	1679	9.82	T	12.83	Booth (breaker), Rotherham - scrapped
1236	236CLT	MFF579	12.62	AR	867	7.94	St	10.94	PVS (breaker), Carlton - *for scrap*
1237	237CLT		12.62	AR	1395	11.82	AG	12.83	Booth (breaker), Rotherham - scrapped
1238	238CLT		12.62	AR	1065	6.87	X	9.87	PVS (breaker), Carlton
									9.87 Wigley (breaker), Carlton - scrapped
1239	239CLT		2.63	AF	1339	9.82	TL	3.83	Berry (bkr), Leicester - scrapped at Aldenham
1240	240CLT		12.62	AR	1068	12.93	FY	11.94	PVS (breaker), Carlton - *for scrap*
1241	241CLT		12.62	AR	1337	9.82	M	1.83	Berry (bkr), Leicester - scrapped at Aldenham
1242	242CLT	*BC8 553*	12.62	AR	1172	9.83	SW	10.83	Double Deck Tours, Niagara, Canada
1243	243CLT	*60-Sri-6630*	12.62	AR	1209	1.88	NX	12.88	Sri Lanka Transport Board
1244	244CLT		12.62	AR	1126	6.83	PM	1.85	PVS (breaker), Carlton - scrapped
1245	245CLT		12.62	AR	1922	3.87	N	5.87	Hampshire Bus (not used)
		LDS210A							10.87 Magicbus, Glasgow 607
									10.90 Stagecoach, Perth 614
									10.94 Bluebird Buses 614
1246	246CLT		12.62	AE	1291	9.82	PM	3.83	Berry (bkr), Leicester - scrapped at Aldenham
1247	247CLT		12.62	AR	1092	11.87	V	10.88	PVS (breaker), Carlton - scrapped
1248	248CLT		12.62	AE	1312	8.82	AP	10.82	Portman (agent), London
									12.82 Karuizawa Classic Car Museum
									(preserved), Nagano, Japan
1249	249CLT		12,62	AE	1635	8.84	NX	12.84	PVS (breaker), Carlton - scrapped
1250	250CLT		12.62	AE	1053	6.87	PM	11.87	Magicbus, Glasgow
									5.88 Holmes (preservation), Blackburn
									9.89 PVS (breaker), Carlton - scrapped
1251	251CLT		12.62	AE	1245	8.91	AG	7.92	Unknown, Japan
1252	252CLT		12.62	AE	1388	9.82	GM	3.83	Berry (bkr), Leicester - scrapped at Aldenham

1253	253CLT		12.62	AE	1319	9.82	ED	10.82	W.Norths (dealer), Sherburn - scrapped

RMF

1254	254CLT		8.64	BEA	1254	11.66	CS	11.66	Northern General Transport Co. 3129
									3.81 Biddell (preserved), Woodford Bridge

RM

1255	255CLT		12.62	M	1003	9.87	HT	11.87	PVS (breaker), Carlton
									11.87 Wigley (breaker), Carlton - scrapped
1256	256CLT		12.62	AR	863	6.89	X	6.90	PVS (breaker), Carlton - scrapped
1257	257CLT	XYJ442	12.62	W	1105	4.94	NXt	11.94	PVS (breaker), Carlton
									6.95 Daly (agent), London
									6.95 Exported
1258	258CLT		1.63	W	1281	9.82	PM	4.83	Berry (bkr), Leicester - scrapped at Aldenham
1259	259CLT		1.63	W	1568	5.84	AR	11.86	PVS (breaker), Carlton
									11.86 Wigley (breaker), Carlton - scrapped
1260	260CLT		12.62	M	1147	10.94	NX	10.94	London Central Buses, London RM1260
1261	261CLT		12.62	M	1146	5.87	NX	9.87	Clydeside Scottish (for spares)
									5.89 Western Scottish (for spares)
									7.90 Wombwell Diesels (breaker), Wombwell - scrapped
1262	262CLT		12.62	M	1195	9.87	AF	4.88	London Borough of Harrow
		VYJ876							9.93 Dyba (preserved), Upper Norwood
									6.94 Lamming (dealer), Coulsdon
									6.94 Church Group, Norfolk
1263	263CLT		12.62	M	1180	2.87	AG	9.89	PVS (breaker), Carlton - scrapped
1264	264CLT		1.63	W	1295	8.82	NX	10.82	W.Norths (dealer), Sherburn - scrapped
1265	265CLT		1.63	W	1363	9.82	ED	3.83	Berry (bkr), Leicester - scrapped at Aldenham
1266	266CLT		12.62	M	996	4.93	GM	4.94	Unknown
1267	267CLT		12.62	M	1142	5.86	AR	8.86	Clydeside Scottish RM1267
									5.89 Western Scottish C73
									9.90 PVS (breaker), Carlton
									10.90 East Yorkshire Motor Serv's (for spares)
									4.91 W.Norths (dealer), Sherburn
									4.91 Wigley (breaker), Carlton - scrapped
1268	268CLT		1.63	W	1391	4.72	PM	2.74	Scrapped by LTE at Aldenham
1269	269CLT		12.62	M	1081	1.86	AR	6.86	PVS (breaker), Carlton - scrapped
1270	270CLT		12.62	M	1093	2.87	E	4.87	PVS (breaker), Carlton
									6.87 Wigley (breaker), Carlton - scrapped
1271	271CLT	RSK254	12.62	M	997	11.87	BW	4.88	East Yorkshire Motor Services 806
1272	272CLT		4.63	M	1294	10.82	Q	3.83	Berry (bkr), Leicester - scrapped at Aldenham
1273	273CLT		1.63	W	1207	11.85	NB	9.86	PVS (breaker), Carlton
									10.86 Wigley (breaker), Carlton - scrapped
1274	274CLT	LDS67A	12.62	AR	1118	8.87	E	11.87	Magicbus, Glasgow 608
									4.92 Kelvin Central Buses 1922
									9.93 MacTavish, Dalmuir
									11.93 Wright (dealer), Rainham
									3.94 Unknown, Australia
1275	275CLT		1.63	W	1393	9.82	AP	3.83	Berry (bkr), Leicester - scrapped at Aldenham
1276	276CLT		1.63	W	1338	6.82	AG	10.82	W.Norths (dealer), Sherburn - scrapped
1277	277CLT		12.62	AR	994	5.93	S	5.94	PVS (breaker), Carlton - scrapped
1278	278CLT		12.62	M	1261	11.88	HT	6.90	PVS (breaker), Carlton - scrapped
1279	279CLT		12.62	M	1409	9.82	AL	12.82	Berry (bkr), Leicester - scrapped at Aldenham
1280	280CLT		12.62	M	1091	3.89	X	8.90	Burgsport International (dealer), Harrow
									8.92 Burgsport Inter'l (dlr), Hemel Hempstead
									3.94 Miller (preserved), Enfield
1281	281CLT		12.62	M	1086	12.86	AV	6.87	PVS (breaker), Carlton - scrapped
1282	282CLT		12.62	M	1100	11.90	Wt	3.91	Pepsi-Cola, Istanbul, Turkey
1283	283CLT		12.62	M	1151	10.94	HT	10.94	London Northern Bus Co., London RM1283

1284	284CLT		12.62	M	1355	8.92	K	2.83	Berry (bkr), Leicester - scrapped at Aldenham
1285	285CLT		12.62	M	1315	9.82	PM	10.82	W.Norths (dealer), Sherburn - scrapped
1286	286CLT		12.62	AR	1358	9.82	AP	12.82	Berry (bkr), Leicester - scrapped at Aldenham
1287	287CLT		12.62	M	294	10.94	HT	10.94	London Northern Bus Co., London RM1287
1288	288CLT		12.62	AR	866	3.84	SW	9.84	U.T.I., Far East (demonstrator)
		15-0091							4.85 Demonstrated in Guangzhou, China
		HK1931							11.87 Citybus, Hong Kong
1289	289CLT		12.62	AR	1170	2.87	AL	4.87	Hampshire Bus (not used)
									10.87 Magicbus, Glasgow 609
		XSL596A							10.90 Stagecoach, Perth 609
									10.94 Bluebird Buses 609
1290	290CLT		12.62	AR	1163	5.91	GM	5.92	PVS (breaker), Carlton
									6.92 Wigley (breaker), Carlton - scrapped
1291	291CLT		12.62	M	1088	4.87	NX	6.87	PVS (breaker), Carlton - scrapped
1292	292CLT	NVS485	12.62	AR	1175	1.94	AR	*3.95*	*London Transport Buses reserve fleet*
1293	293CLT		12.62	AR	1550	9.82	M	12.83	Booth (breaker), Rotherham - scrapped
1294	294CLT	*60-Sri-6636*	12.62	AR	1136	3.87	WD	12.88	Sri Lanka Transport Board
1295	295CLT		12.62	AR	1408	11.82	CF	12.83	Booth (breaker), Rotherham - scrapped
1296	296CLT		12.62	AR	1563	1.85	AL	10.86	PVS (breaker), Carlton - scrapped
1297	297CLT		12.62	AR	1407	9.82	NX	10.82	W.Norths (dealer), Sherburn - scrapped
1298	298CLT		12.62	AR	1417	9.82	AF	10.82	W.Norths (dealer), Sherburn - scrapped
1299	299CLT		12.62	AR	1085	10.86	AV	4.87	PVS (breaker), Carlton - scrapped
1300	300CLT		12.62	AR	1164	1.88	BW	7.88	Strathtay Scottish (for spares)
									8.89 Cosgrove (breaker), Dundee - scrapped
1301	301CLT		12.62	AR	1343	10.87	BN	1.88	PVS (breaker), Carlton - scrapped
1302	302CLT		12.62	AR	1165	8.82	PM	8.82	Booth (breaker), Rotherham - scrapped
1303	303CLT		12.62	AR	1113	1.88	BW	11.88	PVS (breaker), Carlton - scrapped
1304	304CLT	VYJ809	12.62	M	1106	8.93	RA	3.94	PVS (breaker), Carlton - scrapped
1305	305CLT		12.62	AR	1137	10.94	NX	10.94	London Central Buses, London RM1305
1306	306CLT		12.62	M	1135	5.87	SF	12.87	PVS (breaker), Carlton - scrapped
1307	307CLT		12.62	AR	485	8.85	Q	10.85	PVS (breaker), Carlton - scrapped
1308	308CLT		12.62	AR	1427	5.87	NX	9.87	Clydeside Scottish (for spares)
									6.89 PVS (breaker), Carlton - scrapped
1309	309CLT		12.62	M	1186	4.79	TL	10.82	W.Norths (dealer), Sherburn - scrapped
1310	310CLT		12.62	AR	1238	11.87	GM	12.87	PVS (breaker), Carlton
									12.87 Wigley (breaker), Carlton - scrapped
1311	311CLT		12.62	M	1614	7.84	B	12.84	PVS (breaker), Carlton - scrapped
1312	312CLT	MFF509	12.62	M	1115	2.94	RA	10.94	PVS (breaker), Carlton
									1.95 Haynes (preserved), Old Coulsdon
1313	313CLT		12.62	M	1152	3.87	Q	8.88	British & American Bingo, Alberqueque, USA
1314	314CLT		12.62	M	1237	12.86	V	5.87	Gagg, Bunny
									5.94 Multitrak Services (agent), Peterborough
									6.94 Button Design Contracts, London
1315	315CLT		12.62	AR	1451	10.84	TC	1.85	PVS (breaker), Carlton - scrapped
1316	316CLT		12.62	M	1090	12.86	AV	5.87	Muntaner Mataix, Alicante, Spain
1317	317CLT		12.62	M	1162	11.87	Q	12.87	PVS (breaker), Carlton - scrapped
1318	318CLT		12.62	M	1169	11.88	HT	1.90	PVS (breaker), Carlton - scrapped
1319	319CLT	KGH936A	12.62	AR	1179	7.91	Nt	5.92	PVS (breaker), Carlton - scrapped
1320	320CLT		12.62	AR	1048	3.87	AR	4.87	PVS (breaker), Carlton - scrapped
1321	321CLT		12.62	AR	1200	6.87	CT	10.87	Biddell (preserved), South Woodford
									3.92 Miller (preserved), Enfield
1322	322CLT		12.62	AR	1583	4.84	SW	10.86	PVS (breaker), Carlton
									11.86 Wigley (breaker), Carlton - scrapped
1323	323CLT		12.62	AR	1801	9.87	E	2.89	PVS (breaker), Carlton - scrapped (11.93)
1324	324CLT	VYJ807	12.62	M	1223	12.94	BN	12.84	South London Transport, London RM1324
		324CLT							
1325	325CLT		12.62	M	1282	3.84	V	9.84	PVS (breaker), Carlton - scrapped
1326	326CLT		12.62	M	1426	11.82	Q	12.83	Booth (breaker), Rotherham - scrapped
1327	327CLT		12.62	AR	1119	10.90	AR	11.94	PVS (breaker), Carlton - *for scrap*
1328	328CLT		12.62	AR	1593	6.84	NB	12.84	PVS (breaker), Carlton - scrapped
1329	329CLT		12.62	AR	1198	11.88	HT	5.90	PVS (breaker), Carlton - scrapped
1330	330CLT	KGH975A	12.62	AR	967	5.94	AG	*3.95*	*London Transport Buses reserve fleet*

1331	331CLT		12.62	AR	1218	8.92	X	8.92	PVS (breaker), Carlton - scrapped
1332	332CLT		12.62	AR	1280	9.82	M	3.83	Berry (bkr), Leicester - scrapped at Aldenham
1333	333CLT		12.62	AR	1189	1.88	GM	2.88	PVS (breaker), Carlton - scrapped
1334	334CLT		12.62	AR	1286	4.84	AR	8.84	PVS (breaker), Carlton
									8.84 Wigley (breaker), Carlton - scrapped
1335	335CLT		12.62	W	1585	6.84	AR	8.84	PVS (breaker), Carlton - scrapped
1336	336CLT	*60-Sri-6608*	12.62	W	1305	5.88	AK	12.88	Sri Lanka Transport Board
1337	337CLT		12.62	W	1357	7.82	SW	8.82	T.B.Precision (breaker), West Bromwich - scrapped
1338	338CLT		12.62	W	1284	9.82	M	10.82	W.Norths (dealer), Sherburn - scrapped
1339	339CLT		12.62	W	1249	11.88	WN	8.89	Nomas Co. (agent), Tokyo, Japan
									10.89 Unknown, Osaka, Japan
1340	340CLT		12.62	W	1527	9.82	SW	12.83	Booth (breaker), Rotherham - scrapped
1341	341CLT		12.62	M	1263	5.89	HT	10.89	PVS (breaker), Carlton - scrapped
1342	342CLT		12.62	SW	1202	6.87	AK	8.87	PVS (breaker), Carlton
									8.87 Wigley (breaker), Carlton - scrapped
1343	343CLT		12.62	SW	1236	4.75	WH	11.83	Ensign (dealer), Purfleet - scrapped
1344	344CLT		12.62	SW	1228	1.88	BW	5.88	PVS (breaker), Carlton - scrapped
1345	345CLT		12.62	SW	1356	8.82	NX	10.82	W.Norths (dealer), Sherburn - scrapped
1346	346CLT		12.62	SW	1225	11.86	T	2.87	PVS (breaker), Carlton - scrapped
1347	347CLT		1.63	W	1345	9.82	CT	12.82	Berry (bkr), Leicester - scrapped at Aldenham
1348	348CLT		12.62	SW	2216	10.94	HT	10.94	London Northern Bus Co., London RM1348
1349	349CLT		12.62	SW	476	11.88	AD	8.90	Burgsport International (agent), Harrow
									8.92 Burgsport Int. (agent), Hemel Hempstead
									9.92 Allmey (dealer), Eastcote
1350	350CLT		12.62	SW	1247	8.92	BW	12.93	PVS (breaker), Carlton- scrapped
1351	351CLT		12.62	SW	1676	11.84	Q	1.85	PVS (breaker), Carlton - scrapped
1352	352CLT	SVS616	12.62	SW	1224	7.93	GM	3.94	PVS (breaker), Carlton - scrapped
1353	353CLT		12.62	SW	1222	4.87	PM	7.87	Coombes (preserved), Groes-faen
1354	354CLT		12.62	SW	1283	2.85	Q	8.85	PVS (breaker), Carlton - scrapped
1355	355CLT		12.62	SW	1326	3.85	V	8.85	PVS (breaker), Carlton - scrapped
1356	356CLT		12.62	SW	1289	9.82	W	12.83	Booth (breaker), Rotherham - scrapped
1357	357CLT		12.62	SW	1306	11.87	GM	4.88	Blackpool Transport 528
1358	358CLT		12.62	W	1155	11.83	TL	12.83	Booth (breaker), Rotherham
									12.83 Goodwin (breaker), Carlton - scrapped
1359	359CLT		12.62	SW	1109	7.87	BW	9.87	Brakell (dealer), Cheam
									5.92 Riparo Auto SNC, Palermo, Sicily
1360	360CLT		12.62	SW	1267	9.82	PM	12.82	Berry (bkr), Leicester - scrapped at Aldenham
1361	361CLT	VYJ808	12.62	SW	1110	1.95	BN	1.95	South London Transport, London RM1361
1362	362CLT		12.62	SW	1328	10.82	SW	3.83	Berry (bkr), Leicester - scrapped at Aldenham
1363	363CLT		12.62	SW	1692	8.84	AR	5.87	Southampton Citybus 405
									10.88 Brakell (dealer), Cheam
									7.92 Knight (preserved), Yate
1364	364CLT	*60-Sri-6606*	12.62	SW	1230	11.87	AF	12.88	Sri Lanka Transport Board
1365	365CLT		12.62	SW	1334	12.82	HW	12.83	Booth (breaker), Rotherham
									12.83 Goodwin (breaker), Carlton - scrapped
1366	366CLT	NKH807A	1.63	W	814	11.87	GM	4.88	East Yorkshire Motor Services 807
									4.95 Lister (dealer), Bolton
									4.95 Brakell (dealer), Cheam - *for resale*
1367	367CLT		1.63	W	1297	9.82	H	12.83	Booth (breaker), Rotherham - scrapped
1368	368CLT		12.62	W	1321	12.73	AR	8.90	Burgin (preserved), Hemel Hempstead
1369	369CLT		12.62	W	1336	3.82	Q	10.82	W.Norths (dealer), Sherburn - scrapped
1370	370CLT		1.63	W	1287	9.82	AR	4.83	Berry (bkr), Leicester - scrapped at Aldenham
1371	371CLT	*PVA 046*	12.62	W	1652	9.82	T	3.83	Abegwaet Tours, Charlottetown, Canada
1372	372CLT		12.62	W	1647	3.84	WH	9.84	PVS (breaker), Carlton
									9.84 Rollinson (breaker), Carlton - scrapped
1373	373CLT		1.63	W	1317	9.82	M	12.82	Berry (bkr), Leicester - scrapped at Aldenham
1374	374CLT		1.63	RL	1316	9.82	AR	4.83	Berry (bkr), Leicester - scrapped at Aldenham
1375	375CLT		1.63	W	1318	9.82	M	1.83	Berry (bkr), Leicester - scrapped at Aldenham
1376	376CLT		1.63	W	1327	12.83	AK	6.84	Way (breaker), Cardiff - scrapped
1377	377CLT		1.63	W	1412	12.82	HW	12.83	Booth (breaker), Rotherham - scrapped

1378	378CLT		1.63	RL	1313	6.87	HT	2.89	PVS (breaker), Carlton
									2.89 Wigley (breaker), Carlton - scrapped
1379	379CLT		1.63	RL	1277	8.82	AL	12.82	Berry (bkr), Leicester - scrapped at Aldenham
1380	380CLT		1.63	RL	1244	10.94	NX	10.94	London Central Buses, London RM1380
1381	381CLT		1.63	RL	1054	11.87	GM	10.88	PVS (breaker), Carlton - scrapped
1382	382CLT		1.63	RL	1159	10.87	AK	12.87	PVS (breaker), Carlton - scrapped
1383	383CLT		1.63	RL	1290	8.82	AG	12.83	Booth (breaker), Rotherham
									12.83 Goodwin (breaker), Carlton - scrapped
1384	384CLT		1.63	RL	1012	10.87	SF	9.88	Nissho Iwai Corporation (agent), Japan
1385	385CLT		1.63	RL	1201	9.89	AR	9.89	PVS (breaker), Carlton
									9.89 Wigley (breaker), Carlton - scrapped
1386	386CLT		1.63	RL	1374	3.84	NX	8.84	PVS (breaker), Carlton - scrapped
1387	387CLT		1.63	RL	1212	11.87	AG	11.88	PVS (breaker), Carlton - scrapped
1388	388CLT		1.63	RL	1303	9.82	AR	3.83	Berry (bkr), Leicester - scrapped at Aldenham
1389	389CLT		1.63	RL	1598	9.82	CT	1.83	Berry (bkr), Leicester - scrapped at Aldenham
1390	390CLT		1.63	RL	1353	8.82	NX	8.82	Way & Williams, Cardiff - scrapped
1391	391CLT		1.63	RL	1383	8.83	V	12.83	Booth (breaker), Rotherham
									12.83 Goodwin (breaker), Carlton - scrapped
1392	392CLT		1.63	RL	1194	8.91	X	12.93	PVS (breaker), Carlton - scrapped
1393	393CLT		1.63	RL	1182	2.87	TH	4.87	PVS (breaker), Carlton
									4.87 Wigley (breaker), Carlton - scrapped
1394	394CLT		1.63	RL	1311	9.82	AR	11.84	Brakell (dealer), Cheam
									7.92 Stafford County Fruit Farm, Stafford
1395	395CLT		1.63	RL	1372	9.82	PM	10.82	W.Norths (dealer), Sherburn - scrapped
1396	396CLT		1.63	RL	1380	11.82	Q	12.82	Booth (breaker), Rotherham - scrapped
1397	397CLT		1.63	RL	1139	6.87	AK	11.87	Magicbus, Glasgow 610
		OWJ871A							2.90 East Midland Motor Services RM1397
									9.92 Fisher (Remar Association), Nottingham
		71AWN							2.93 Naish (preserved), Loughborough
1398	398CLT	KGJ118A	1.63	RL	1757	1.95	BN	1.95	South London Transport, London RM1398
1399	399CLT		1.63	RL	1203	9.82	AL	4.83	Berry (bkr), Leicester - scrapped at Aldenham
1400	400CLT		1.63	RL	1368	10.94	Q	10.94	London Central Buses, London RM1400
1401	401CLT	*60-Sri-6638*	1.63	RL	1192	5.88	AR	12.88	Sri Lanka Transport Board
1402	402CLT		1.63	RL	1329	9.82	AG	10.82	W.Norths (dealer), Sherburn - scrapped
1403	403CLT		2.63	RL	1324	3.84	V	5.84	Ind Coope Ltd. (Benskins), Watford
									4.92 Sapte & Stirling (prerserved), Watford
1404	404CLT		1.63	RL	1309	10.84	V	10.87	Southampton Citybus (not used)
									7.89 Unknown, Japan
1405	405CLT		1.63	RL	1268	9.82	SW	10.82	W.Norths (dealer), Sherburn - scrapped
1406	406CLT		2.63	RL	1362	5.83	AL	10.83	W.Norths (dealer), Sherburn - scrapped
1407	407CLT		2.63	RL	1190	6.87	PM	11.87	Clydeside Scottish (for spares)
									1.89 Kelvin Scottish (for spares)
									3.89 Dunsmore (breaker), Larkhall - scrapped
1408	408CLT		2.63	RL	1364	9.82	BN	3.83	Berry (bkr), Leicester - scrapped at Aldenham
1409	409CLT		2.63	RL	1386	9.82	AR	10.83	Berry (bkr), Leicester - scrapped at Aldenham
1410	410CLT		2.63	RL	1299	9.82	PM	10.82	W.Norths (dealer), Sherburn - scrapped
1411	411CLT		2.63	RL	1285	10.82	CT	12.83	Booth (breaker), Rotherham - scrapped
1412	412CLT		2.63	RL	1292	9.82	CT	10.82	W.Norths (dealer), Sherburn - scrapped
1413	413CLT	*60-Sri-6629*	2.63	RL	1016	11.87	BW	12.88	Sri Lanka Transport Board
1414	414CLT		2.63	RL	1331	9.82	CF	11.82	Gtr Manchester Transport Museum (pres'd)
1415	415CLT	*AP6 119*	2.63	RL	1007	10.86	AC	7.88	Camp Edphy, Valmorin, Quebec, Canada
1416	416CLT		2.63	RL	1323	9.82	AR	1.83	Berry (bkr), Leicester - scrapped at Aldenham
1417	417CLT		2.63	RL	1532	5.84	AP	12.84	Dolphin International, St.Albans
									2.85 Artas Promotions, Hungary
1418	418CLT		2.63	RL	1273	9.82	AL	1.83	Berry (bkr), Leicester - scrapped at Aldenham
1419	419CLT		2.63	RL	1335	9.82	GM	5.83	Berry (bkr), Leicester - scrapped at Aldenham
1420	420CLT		2.63	RL	1542	1.85	NB	3.85	PVS (breaker), Carlton
									3.85 Rollinson (breaker), Carlton - scrapped
1421	421CLT	AEW440A	2.63	RL	1204	12.88	FW	9.89	Arena Complex Ltd., Peterborough
									6.90 London Bus Export Co. (dlr), Chepstow
									10.91 Unknown, London

1422	422CLT		2.63	RL	1670	6.84	ED	8.84	PVS (breaker), Carlton
									8.84 Wigley (breaker), Carlton - scrapped
1423	423CLT		2.63	RL	1878	6.84	AL	12.84	PVS (breaker), Carlton - scrapped
1424	424CLT	*BB4 289*	2.63	RL	1625	9.82	AR	5.84	Piccadilly Bus Tours, Ottowa, Canada
		BC9 998							3.92 Unknown, Ontario, Canada
1425	425CLT		2.63	RL	1739	11.87	X	8.88	Slug & Lettuce, London
									4.89 Slug & Lettuce, Gloucester
									5.91 Allmey (dealer), Eastcote
									8.91 West London Bus Preserv'ists, London
									8.91 Fiarce, St.Egreve, France
1426	426CLT		2.63	RL	1423	9.82	SW	10.82	W.Norths (dealer), Sherburn - scrapped
1427	427CLT		2.63	RL	1365	9.82	BN	12.82	Berry (bkr), Leicester - scrapped at Aldenham
1428	428CLT		2.63	RL	1227	2.94	HT	*3.95*	*London Transport Buses reserve fleet*
1429	429CLT		2.63	RL	1265	9.82	TL	10.82	W.Norths (dealer), Sherburn - scrapped
1430	430CLT		2.63	RL	1344	9.82	AR	3.83	Berry (bkr), Leicester - scrapped at Aldenham
1431	431CLT		2.63	RL	1348	5.85	ED	5.85	PVS (breaker), Carlton - scrapped
1432	432CLT		2.63	RL	1410	8.84	AR	12.84	PVS (breaker), Carlton
									12.84 Rollinson (breaker), Carlton - scrapped
1433	433CLT		2.63	PM	865	7.87	N	10.88	Maniglia, Minerbio, Italy
1434	434CLT		2.63	PM	1537	10.87	AF	12.87	PVS (breaker), Carlton - scrapped
1435	435CLT	KGJ184A	2.63	PM	1231	7.93	GM	3.94	PVS (breaker), Carlton - scrapped
1436	436CLT		2.63	PM	1308	8.82	NX	10.83	Berry (bkr), Leicester - scrapped at Aldenham
1437	437CLT		2.63	PM	1586	9.84	AR	12.84	PVS (breaker), Carlton - scrapped
1438	438CLT		3.63	W	1325	2.85	V	11.86	PVS (breaker), Carlton - scrapped
1439	439CLT		2.63	PM	1278	4.84	V	9.84	PVS (breaker), Carlton - scrapped
1440	440CLT		2.63	PM	712	8.86	NX	10.86	PVS (breaker), Carlton - scrapped
1441	441CLT		2.63	PM	1632	11.83	AK	12.83	Booth (breaker), Rotherham - scrapped
1442	442CLT		4.63	PM	1396	8.82	SW	8.82	P.Sykes (dealer), Barnsley
									8.82 Wigley (breaker), Carlton - scrapped
1443	443CLT		4.63	PM	1385	8.82	HT	8.82	Bird (breaker), Stratford-on-Avon - scrapped
1444	444CLT		4.63	PM	1403	9.82	A	10.82	W.Norths (dealer), Sherburn - scrapped
1445	445CLT		4.63	PM	1173	9.82	AP	10.82	W.Norths (dealer), Sherburn - scrapped
1446	446CLT		4.63	PM	1620	11.87	GM	1.89	PVS (breaker), Carlton
									2.89 Wigley (breaker), Carlton - scrapped
1447	447CLT		4.63	PM	1596	4.72	PM	2.74	Scrapped by LTE at Aldenham
1448	448CLT	*BC9 997*	4.63	PM	1434	9.82	SW	5.84	Piccadilly Bus Tours, Ottowa, Canada
									3.92 Mulligan, Carp, Ontario, Canada
1449	449CLT		4.63	PM	1252	5.87	NX	6.87	Hampshire Bus (not used)
		LDS190A							11.87 Magicbus, Glasgow 611
									4.92 Kelvin Central Buses 1923
		449CLT							7.93 Forrest (Blue Triangle), Bootle
									5.94 Forrest (preserved), Bootle
1450	450CLT		4.63	H	1401	9.82	SW	10.82	W.Norths (dealer), Sherburn - scrapped
1451	451CLT		4.63	PM	1447	1.82	WL	10.83	W.Norths (dealer), Sherburn - scrapped
1452	452CLT		4.63	AR	1259	9.82	W	3.83	Berry (bkr), Leicester - scrapped at Aldenham

RMC

1453	453CLT		8.62	HG	1455	12.69	HG	1.70	London Country Bus Services RMC1453
									1.80 London Transport RMC1453
			6.81	Kt		9.94	SF	9.94	Leaside Bus Co., London RMC1453
1454	454CLT		8.62	HG	1496	12.69	HG	1.70	London Country Bus Services RMC1454
									8.79 London Transport (not used)
									7.81 Wombwell Diesels (breaker) - scrapped
1455	455CLT		8.62	HG	1515	12.69	WR	1.70	London Country Bus Services RMC1455
									10.79 London Transport (not used)
									7.81 Wombwell Diesels (breaker) - scrapped
1456	456CLT		8.62	GF	1513	12.69	WR	1.70	London Country Bus Services RMC1456
									6.79 London Transport RMC1456
		LFF875	9.79	WWt		9.94	Ut	9.94	Stagecoach East London, London RMC1456
1457	457CLT		8.62	HG	1477	12.69	GF	1.70	London Country Bus Services RMC1457
									7.79 London Transport RMC1457
			7.81	FYt		5.90	PBt	5.92	PVS (breaker), Carlton
									6.92 Wigley (breaker), Carlton - scrapped

1458	458CLT	8.62	HG	1490	12.69	GF	1.70	London Country Bus Services RMC1458
								6.79 London Transport RMC1458
		8.81	Tt		9.93	W	3.94	Unknown, France
1459	459CLT	8.62	HG	1458	12.69	HG	1.70	London Country Bus Services RMC1459
								12.77 London Transport RMC1459
		1.78	CTt		11.90	AFt	1.91	Almeroth (preserved), Romford
1460	460CLT	8.62	GF	1484	12.69	HG	1.70	London Country Bus Services RMC1460
								3.79 Wombwell Diesels (breaker), Wombwell
								7.79 London Transport (not used)
								7.81 Wombwell Diesels (breaker) - scrapped
1461	461CLT	8.62	GF	1453	12.69	HG	1.70	London Country Bus Services RMC1461
								6.79 London Transport RMC1461
		11.79	Rt		9.94	Ut	9.94	Stagecoach East London, London RMC1461
1462	462CLT	8.62	GF	1499	12.69	GY	1.70	London Country Bus Services RMC1462
								12.77 London Transport RMC1462
		1.78	CTt		6.87	WDt	3.88	Liston (preserved), Addiscombe
								12.88 Brakell (dealer), Cheam
								1.89 Macnamara (preserved), London
								10.91 Nostalgiabus, Mitcham
1463	463CLT	8.62	GF	1517	12.69	GY	1.70	London Country Bus Services RMC1463
								7.79 London Transport (not used)
								10.81 Wombwell Diesels (breaker) - scrapped
1464	464CLT	8.62	GF	1460	12.69	R	1.70	London Country Bus Services RMC1464
								6.79 London Transport RMC1464
		4.80	At		12.94	N	12.94	South London Transport, London RMC1464
1465	465CLT	8.62	GF	1461	12.69	GF	1.70	London Country Bus Services RMC1465
								7.79 London Transport (not used)
								7.81 Wombwell Diesels (breaker) - scrapped
1466	466CLT	8.62	HG	1457	12.69	GY	1.70	London Country Bus Services RMC1466
								6.79 London Transport RMC1466
		9.80	Vt		8.89	CSt	8.89	Scrapped by LT at Wandsworth garage

Purchased for spares by Kelvin Scottish from Clydeside Scottish who never placed it in service is RM878. Still in London red livery, it stands in Old Kilpatrick depot in March 1988 alongside Kelvin's withdrawn RM293 which was also being cannibalised. *(K.A.Jenkinson)*

1467	467CLT		8.62	HG	1454	12.69	HG	1.70	London Country Bus Services RMC1467
									12.77 London Transport RMC1467
			5.78	HTt		12.89	WD	3.90	Lamming (dealer), Coulsdon
									5.90 PVS (breaker), Carlton - scrapped
1468	468CLT		8.62	HG	1511	12.69	GY	1.70	London Country Bus Services RMC1468
									6.79 London Transport RMC1468
			5.80	ONt		2.88	ACt	4.88	PVS (breaker), Carlton - scrapped
1469	469CLT		8.62	HG	1491	12.69	HF	1.70	London Country Bus Services RMC1469
									3.80 London Transport RMC1469
			7,81	TCt		11.94	St	11.94	London United Busways, London RMC1469
1470	470CLT		8.62	HG	1485	12.69	HG	1.70	London Country Bus Services RMC1470
									12.77 London Transport RMC1470
			4.78	Rt		8.83	Vt	7.84	PVS (breaker), Carlton - scrapped
1471	471CLT		8.62	HG	1493	12.69	WY	1.70	London Country Bus Services RMC1471
									2.80 London Transport RMC1471
			11.81	PMt		10.90	SWt	6.91	PVS (breaker), Carlton - scrapped
1472	472CLT		8.62	GF	1462	12.69	HA	1.70	London Country Bus Services RMC1472
									3.79 Wombwell Diesels (breaker), Wombwell
									7.79 London Transport (not used)
									10.81 Wombwell Diesels (breaker) - scrapped
1473	473CLT		10.62	HG	1464	12.69	WY	1.70	London Country Bus Services RMC1473
									12.77 London Transport RMC1473
			5.78	Qt		8.90	WDt	8.90	Lamming (preserved), Coulsdon
1474	474CLT		9.62	HG	1459	12.69	HG	1.70	London Country Bus Services RMC1474
									6.79 London Transport RMC1474
			1.81	St		6.90	Wt	8.90	Lamming (preserved), Coulsdon
									10.91 Wright, Rainham
1475	475CLT		10.62	HG	1472	12.69	GY	1.70	London Country Bus Services RMC1475
									10.79 London Transport RMC1475
			11.80	Kt		8.90	Ut	5.92	PVS (breaker), Carlton
									6.92 Wigley (breaker), Carlton - scrapped
1476	476CLT		10.62	GF	1467	12.69	GY	1.70	London Country Bus Services RMC1476
									7.79 London Transport RMC1476
			2.81	PMt		5.92	WD	5.92	London Coaches, London RMC1476
									3.93 Knorn (preserved), St.Albans
									5.94 Knorn (preserved), Wiltshire
1477	477CLT		10.62	GF	1456	12.69	HA	1.70	London Country Bus Services RMC1477
									7.79 London Transport RMC1477
			2.80	GMt		11.90	ALt	4.91	Greenpeace, London
									2.93 Wacton Trading (dealer), Bromyard
									5.93 Brown, Shaftesbury
									9.94 Wright & Biddell, Rainham
1478	478CLT		10.62	EP	1465	12.69	GF	1.70	London Country Bus Services RMC1478
									7.79 London Transport (not used)
									7.81 Wombwell Diesels (breaker) - scrapped
1479	479CLT		10.62	WR	1466	12.69	HA	1.70	London Country Bus Services RMC1479
									6.79 London Transport (not used)
									2.82 Wombwell Diesels (breaker) - scrapped
1480	480CLT		10.62	EP	1474	12.69	HA	1.70	London Country Bus Services RMC1480
									7.79 London Transport RMC1480
		KGJ52A	4.80	At		7.90	AKt	4.92	Jan-Ake-Haggren, Vasta Froluna, Sweden
1481	481CLT		10.62	EP	1479	12.69	WR	1.70	London Country Bus Services RMC1481
									7.79 London Transport RMC1481
			6.82	Mt		6.86	Wt	6.87	Venhofen, Bremerhaven, Germany
1482	482CLT		10.62	EP	1486	12.69	HF	1.70	London Country Bus Services RMC1482
									8.79 London Transport (not used)
									10.81 Wombwell Diesels (breaker) - scrapped
1483	483CLT		10.62	EP	1489	12.69	HA	1.70	London Country Bus Services RMC1483
									2.80 London Transport RMCl483
			3.81	Rt		8.89	CSt	8.89	Scrapped by LT at Wandsworth garage
1484	484CLT		10.62	EP	1463	12.69	GF	1.70	London Country Bus Services RMC1484
									7.79 London Transport RMC1484
			3.80	AKt		6.91	FWt	5.92	PVS (breaker), Carlton
									6.92 Wigley (breaker), Carlton - scrapped

1485	485CLT		10.62	WR	1520	12.69	WR	1.70	London Country Bus Services RMC1485
									2.80 London Transport RMC1485
			2.81	ACt		9.94	U	9.94	Stagecoach East London, London RMC1485
1486	486CLT		10.62	WR	1473	12.69	WR	1.70	London Country Bus Services RMC1486
									6.79 London Transport RMC1486
		276KVS	4.81	FYt		2.93	Tt	12.93	Unknown, Germany
1487	487CLT		10.62	EP	1478	12.69	HF	1.70	London Country Bus Services RMC1487
									10.79 London Transport (not used)
									5.82 Crispin (preserved), London
									12.84 London RM Pres'n Group, London
									8.88 Sullivan (preserved), Leytonstone
									4.92 Sullivan (preserved), Harrow
1488	488CLT		10.62	WR	1475	12.69	GF	1.70	London Country Bus Services RMC1488
									12.77 London Transport RMC1488
			3.78	ADt		3.90	AVt	4.91	Octobus SARL, Paris, France
1489	489CLT		10.62	WR	1476	12.69	WY	1.70	London Country Bus Services RMC1489
									12.77 London Transport RMC1489
			1.78	Qt		6.87	PMt	4.88	PVS (breaker), Carlton - scrapped
1490	490CLT		10.62	EP	1516	1516	GF	1.70	London Country Bus Services RMC1490
									6.79 London Transport RMC1490
			12.80	St		9.94	PD	9.94	Stagecoach Selkent, London RMC1490
									10.94 Bluebird Buses, Scotland 608
1491	491CLT		10.62	EP	1480	12.69	WY	1.70	London Country Bus Services RMC1491
									12.77 London Transport RMC1491
			1.78	WLt		4.91	WDt	4.91	Lamming (dealer), Coulsdon
									4.91 PVS (breaker), Carlton - scrapped
1492	492CLT		10.62	EP	1488	12.69	GY	1.70	London Country Bus Services RMC1492
									1.80 London Transport RMC1492
			11.81	Rt		9.94	X	9.94	CentreWest, London RMC1492
1493	493CLT		10.62	WR	1487	12.69	WR	1.70	London Country Bus Services RMC1493
									10.79 London Transport (not used)
									7.81 Wombwell Diesels (breaker) - scrapped
1494	494CLT		10.62	EP	1508	12.69	WY	1.70	London Country Bus Services RMC1494
									12.77 London Transport RMC1494
			1.78	TLt		4.90	PBt	6.91	PVS (breaker), Carlton - scrapped
1495	495CLT		10.62	WR	1481	12.69	HF	1.70	London Country Bus Services RMC1495
									1.79 London Transport RMC1495
			1.79	BXt		12.87	NXt	9.89	Sears, Addlestone
1496	496CLT		10.62	EP	1470	12.69	GY	1.70	London Country Bus Services RMC1496
									6.79 London Transport RMC1496
			7.81	AV		9.93	NS	3.94	Sexton (preserved), London
1497	497CLT		11.62	GF	1482	12.69	GY	1.70	London Country Bus Services RMC1497
									12.77 London Transport RMC1497
			1.78	BN		9.86	AVt	12.86	Gale (preserved), Diptford
1498	498CLT		1.63	WY	1495	12.69	HF	1.70	London Country Bus Services RMC1498
									12.77 London Transport RMC1498
			1.78	WLt		8.79	WLt	10.83	W.Norths (dealer), Sherburn - scrapped
1499	499CLT		11.62	GR	1468	12.69	GF	1.70	London Country Bus Services RMC1499
									12.77 London Transport RMC1499
			7.78	Rs		5.91	St	6.91	Kane, Birmingham
									6.91 Kane, Perpignon, France
1500	500CLT		11.62	GR	1492	12.69	HF	1.70	London Country Bus Services RMC1500
									2.80 London Transport RMC1500
		ALC368A	8.81	HDt		6.91	AVt	3.92	North Mimms Coaches, Potters Bar
									8.92 Hemmings & Saltmarsh, Radlett
									11.92 Time, Thornton Heath
1501	501CLT		11.62	GR	1483	12.69	SV	1.70	London Country Bus Services RMC1501
									2.80 London Transport RMC1501
			4.82	AGt		3.85	AGt	2.86	PVS (breaker), Carlton - scrapped
1502	502CLT		11.62	GR	1469	12.69	GY	1.70	London Country Bus Services RMC1502
									2.79 London Transport RMC1502
			2.79	CTt		12.87	NXt	4.88	PVS (breaker), Carlton
									6.88 Wigley (breaker), Carlton - scrapped

1503	503CLT		11.62	GR	1498	12.69	HG	1.70	London Country Bus Services RMC1503
									7.79 London Transport RMC1503
			9.80	CTt		7.91	St	12.91	Parkes, Vannes, France
1504	504CLT		11.62	GR	1501	12.69	WY	1.70	London Country Bus Services RMC1504
									2.80 London Transport RMC1504
			9.81	PMt		8.90	WDt	8.90	Lamming (dealer), Coulsdon
									9.91 PVS (breaker), Carlton - scrapped
1505	505CLT		11.62	GR	1510	12.69	HF	1.70	London Country Bus Services RMC1505
									12.77 London Transport (not used)
									1.78 Wombwell Diesels (breaker) - scrapped
1506	506CLT		11.62	GR	1503	12.69	HF	1.70	London Country Bus Services RMC1506
									12.77 London Transport RMC1506
			1.78	SWt		8.90	WDt	8.90	Lamming (dealer), Coulsdon
									3.91 PVS (breaker), Carlton - scrapped
1507	507CLT		1.63	SV	1514	12.69	SV	1.70	London Country Bus Services RMC1507
									12.77 London Transport RMC1507
			1.78	ACt		8.79	SEt	9.81	Wright & Humphries (preserved), Dagenham
									10.90 Humphries (preserved), Dagenham
1508	508CLT		1.63	WY	1500	12.69	HF	1.70	London Country Bus Services RMC1508
									12.77 London Transport RMC1508
			1.78	SWt		10.90	GMt	11.92	PVS (breaker), Carlton - scrapped
1509	509CLT		1.63	SV	1497	12.69	HF	1.70	London Country Bus Services RMC1509
									12.77 London Transport (not used)
									1.78 Wombwell Diesels (breaker) - scrapped
1510	510CLT		1.63	SV	1471	12.69	HF	1.70	London Country Bus Services RMC1510
									12.77 London Transport RMC1510
			1.78	HTt		9.94	X	9.94	CentreWest, London RMC1510
1511	511CLT		1.63	SV	1505	12.69	SV	1.70	London Country Bus Services RMC1511
									2.80 London Transport RMC1511
			1.81	AFt		4.85	WDt	8.85	PVS (breaker), Carlton
									8.85 Wigley (breaker), Carlton - scrapped
1512	512CLT		1.63	WY	1502	12.69	HF	1.70	London Country Bus Services RMC1512
									3.80 London Transport RMC1512
			12.80	FWt		7.91	St	10.92	PVS (breaker), Carlton - scrapped
1513	513CLT		1.63	SV	1494	12.69	WY	1.70	London Country Bus Services RMC1513
									7.79 London Transport RMC1513
			5.81	NSt		10.94	AC	10.94	Metroline Travel, London RMC1513
1514	514CLT		1.63	WR	1509	12.69	SV	1.70	London Country Bus Services RMC1514
									7.79 London Transport (not used)
									10.81 Wombwell Diesels (breaker) - scrapped
1515	515CLT		1.63	WY	1507	12.69	GY	1.70	London Country Bus Services RMC1515
									3.80 London Transport RMC1515
			3.81	NSt		9.94	PD	9.94	Stagecoach Selkent, London RMC1515
1516	516CLT		1.63	WY	1519	12.69	HF	1.70	London Country Bus Services RMC1516
									12.77 London Transport RMC1516
			1.78	SEt		8.90	BKt	6.92	Almeroth (preserved), Romford
1517	517CLT		1.63	WY	1506	12.69	SV	1.70	London Country Bus Services RMC1517
									10.79 London Transport RMC1517
			6.81	CFt		4.87	GMt	7.87	PVS (breaker), Carlton - scrapped at LT Battersea garage
1518	518CLT		1.63	WY	1512	12.69	WY	1.70	London Country Bus Services RMC1518
									12.77 London Transport RMC1518
			1.78	SEt		10.85	CS-	2.86	PVS (breaker), Carlton - scrapped
1519	519CLT		1.63	WY	1504	12.69	WY	1.70	London Country Bus Services RMC1519
									10.79 London Transport RMC1519
		KGH991A	10.81	At		12.91	EWt	7.92	Unknown, Germany
1520	520CLT		1.63	WY	1518	12.69	HF	1.70	London Country Bus Services RMC1520
									3.79 Wombwell Diesels (breaker), Wombwell
									7.79 London Transport (not used)
									7.81 Wombwell Diesels (breaker) - scrapped

1521	521CLT		2.63	PM	500	3.84	Q	7.84	PVS (breaker), Carlton
									7.84 Rollinson (breaker), Carlton - scrapped
1522	522CLT		2.63	PM	1711	7.84	B	6.86	Kompas Touriftik International, Frankfurt, Germany
									8.86 Top, Portoroz, Yugoslavia
1523	523CLT		3.63	RL	1533	6.84	AL	8.84	PVS (breaker), Carlton - scrapped
1524	524CLT		3.63	NX	1188	4.89	HT	1.90	PVS (breaker), Carlton
									1.90 Wigley (breaker), Carlton - scrapped
1525	525CLT		3.63	PM	1394	9.82	NX	2.83	Berry (bkr), Leicester - scrapped at Aldenham
1526	526CLT		3.63	RL	1349	9.82	T	7.83	McGinley (agent), Coventry
									9.83 Unknown, Spain
1527	527CLT		3.63	SW	1732	9.94	U%	9.94	Stagecoach East London, London RM1527
1528	528CLT	KGJ117A	3.63	WN	1991	7.93	GM	9.94	PVS (breaker), Carlton
									10.94 Benson, Greasby
1529	529CLT		3.63	AR	1333	11.86	SF	6.87	PVS (breaker), Carlton
									7.87 Wigley (breaker), Carlton - scrapped
1530	530CLT	*60-Sri-6607*	3.63	WN	1250	1.88	BW	12.88	Sri Lanka Transport Board
1531	531CLT		3.63	EM	877	6.87	SW	9.87	Brakell (dealer), Cheam
									8.90 Octobus SARL, Paris, France
									10.90 Unknown, Spain
1532	532CLT		3.63	PM	1235	8.82	B	10.82	W.Norths (dealer), Sherburn - scrapped
1533	533CLT		3.63	NX	1711	12.82	HW	12.83	Booth (breaker), Rotherham - scrapped
1534	534CLT		3.63	PM	1404	9.82	B	3.83	Berry (bkr), Leicester - scrapped at Aldenham
1535	535CLT		3.63	PM	1382	8.83	AP	12.83	Booth (breaker), Rotherham - scrapped
1536	536CLT		3.63	PM	1275	11.83	TL	1.84	9-9 Cars, Elstree
									1.84 Scrapped in Kent
1537	537CLT		3.63	PM	1547	10.82	Q	3.83	Berry (bkr), Leicester - scrapped at Aldenham
1538	538CLT		4.63	M	1411	8.82	NX	10.82	W.Norths (dealer), Sherburn - scrapped
1539	539CLT		4.63	M	1406	10.84	SW	6.87	Southampton Citybus 410
									10.89 Amex Trading (dealer), Buxton
									12.89 Unknown, Belgium
									2.90 Amex Trading (dealer), Buxton
									4.90 Unknown, Japan
1540	540CLT		3.63	PM	1145	7.82	BW	7.83	Wombwell Diesels (breaker), Wombwell - scrapped
1541	541CLT		3.63	PM	1157	9.82	K	10.82	W.Norths (dealer), Sherburn - scrapped
1542	542CLT	KGJ164A	4.63	PM	1062	12.91	GM	5.92	PVS (breaker), Carlton
									6.92 Wigley (breaker), Carlton - scrapped
1543	543CLT		4.63	M	1536	8.84	AG	6.87	Southampton Citybus 411
									1.91 Southend Transport 116
									2.94 Routemaster Heritage Trust (preserved), Twickenham
1544	544CLT		4.63	PM	1034	2.87	X	5.87	PVS (breaker), Carlton
									5.87 Wigley (breaker), Carlton - scrapped
1545	545CLT	KGJ37A	4.63	PM	573	1.92	WKt	7.93	Chamberlain et al (pres'd), Hounslow Heath
1546	546CLT		4.63	PM	1592	7.84	CT	6.87	Southampton Citybus (for spares)
									9.87 London Transport, London (not used)
									1.88 Southampton Citybus 415
									10.89 Amex Trading (dealer), Buxton
									11.89 Unknown, Japan
1547	547CLT		4.63	PM	1196	1.85	Q	5.85	PVS (breaker), Carlton
									5.85 Rollinson (breaker), Carlton - scrapped
1548	548CLT	*BC8 554*	4.63	PM	1529	9.82	K	10.83	Double Deck Tours, Niagara, Canada
1549	549CLT		4.63	M	1553	5.84	SW	10.86	Kent County Council, Aylesford
									2.90 Ensign (dealer), Purfleet
									4.90 Ensign, Purfleet 149
									10.90 Nissho Iwai Corporation (agent), Japan
1550	550CLT		4.63	M	1310	9.82	BW	12.82	Berry (bkr), Leicester - scrapped at Aldenham
1551	551CLT		4.63	M	1713	9.82	T	10.82	W.Norths (dealer), Sherburn - scrapped
1552	552CLT		4.63	M	1390	9.82	W	7.84	PVS (breaker), Carlton - scrapped

1553	553CLT		4.63	M	1809	8.85	B	8.85	PVS (breaker), Carlton
									8.85 Wigley (breaker), Carlton - scrapped
1554	554CLT		4.63	M	1439	8.82	NX	10.82	W.Norths (dealer), Sherburn - scrapped
1555	555CLT	EBY315B	4.63	AR	1258	7.92	EW	8.92	Domino Steak House, Eupen, Belgium
1556	556CLT		4.63	D	1722	11.89	GM	4.90	PVS (breaker), Carlton - scrapped at LBL GM garage
1557	557CLT		4.63	D	1590	2.85	AC	3.85	PVS (breaker), Carlton
									3.85 Wigley (breaker), Carlton - scrapped
1558	558CLT		4.63	M	1405	12.82	U	12.83	Booth (breaker), Rotherham - scrapped
1559	559CLT		4.63	M	993	11.82	AG	12.83	Booth (breaker), Rotherham - scrapped
1560	560CLT		4.63	M	1438	11.87	GM	6.90	PVS (breaker), Carlton
									6.90 Wigley (breaker), Carlton - scrapped
1561	561CLT		4.63	M	1820	11.84	AG	2.85	PVS (breaker), Carlton
									2.85 Rollinson (breaker), Carlton - scrapped
1562	562CLT		4.63	M	1031	3.94	AR	*3.95*	*London Transport Buses reserve fleet*
1563	563CLT		4.63	NX	1552	5.84	V	3.87	Townsend (preserved), Chiswick
1564	564CLT		4.63	M	1375	9.82	AP	12.82	Berry (bkr), Leicester - scrapped at Aldenham
1565	565CLT		4.63	AR	1399	6.87	AK	9.87	Clydeside Scottish (for spares)
									5.89 Western Scottish (for spares)
									8.89 Kelvin Scottish (for spares) - scrapped
1566	566CLT		5.63	AR	1400	9.82	SW	12.83	Booth (breaker), Rotherham - scrapped
1567	567CLT		5.63	RL	1523	8.84	AR	11.84	PVS (breaker), Carlton - scrapped
1568	568CLT		4.63	AR	1234	10.94	HT	10.94	London Northern Bus Co., London RM1568
1569	569CLT		5.63	AR	1379	9.82	GM	1.83	Berry (bkr), Leicester - scrapped at Aldenham
1570	570CLT		5.63	AR	1435	9.82	B	10.82	W.Norths (dealer), Sherburn - scrapped
1571	571CLT		5.63	RL	1576	10.84	WH	7.86	Stagecoach, Perth (not used)
									8.86 Taffell (preserved), Ruislip
									4.92 Humphries, Willesden
									9.93 Routemaster, Watford
1572	572CLT		5.63	AR	1433	9.82	CT	3.83	Berry (bkr), Leicester - scrapped at Aldenham
1573	573CLT		5.63	AR	1525	7.84	Q	8.84	PVS (breaker), Carlton
									8.84 Wigley (breaker), Carlton - scrapped
1574	574CLT		5.63	RL	1369	9.82	TL	12.82	Berry (bkr), Leicester - scrapped at Aldenham
1575	575CLT		5.63	RL	1419	8.86	NX	9.86	PVS (breaker), Carlton
									10.86 Wigley (breaker), Carlton - scrapped
1576	576CLT		5.63	RL	1402	11.84	AR	12.84	PVS (breaker), Carlton
									12.84 Wigley (breaker), Carlton - scrapped
1577	577CLT		6.63	AF	1833	3.84	SW	9.84	PVS (breaker), Carlton - scrapped
1578	578CLT		5.63	M	1413	9.82	AG	4.83	Berry (bkr), Leicester - scrapped at Aldenham
1579	579CLT		5.63	RL	1414	2.84	TL	8.84	PVS (breaker), Carlton
									8.84 Wigley (breaker), Carlton - scrapped
1580	580CLT		5.63	RL	1437	2.85	AR	6.85	PVS (breaker), Carlton - scrapped
1581	581CLT	*60-Sri-6634*	5.63	M	1116	5.88	AK	12.88	Sri Lanka Transport Board
1582	582CLT		5.63	RL	1232	7.90	Wt	8.90	PVS (breaker), Carlton
									8.90 Wigley (breaker), Carlton - scrapped
1583	583CLT		5.63	M	1354	7.84	TC	4.86	Blackpool Transport 521
1584	584CLT		5.63	RL	1376	9.82	NX	3.83	Berry (bkr), Leicester - scrapped at Aldenham
1585	585CLT	ALC459A	5.63	M	1727	6.94	AC	11.94	PVS (breaker), Carlton
									2.95 Unknown, France
1586	586CLT		5.63	M	466	4.85	X	5.85	PVS (breaker), Carlton
									6.85 Wigley (breaker), Carlton - scrapped
1587	587CLT		5.63	M	1058	2.87	HT	5.87	Clydeside Scottish (for spares)
									2.89 PVS (breaker), Carlton - scrapped
1588	588CLT		5.63	M	1549	9.82	M	4.83	Berry (bkr), Leicester - scrapped at Aldenham
1589	589CLT		5.63	D	1579	10.82	U	12.82	Berry (bkr), Leicester - scrapped at Aldenham
1590	590CLT		5.63	D	1761	4.94	RA	10.94	PVS (breaker), Carlton
									11.94 Unknown, Middlesex
1591	591CLT		5.63	D	1646	3.84	AR	6.84	Booth (breaker), Rotherham - scrapped
1592	592CLT		5.63	D	1606	4.84	NX	8.84	PVS (breaker), Carlton - scrapped
1593	593CLT		5.63	D	1193	1.95	BN	1.95	South London Transport, London RM1593
1594	594CLT		5.63	D	1581	9.82	NX	3.83	Berry (bkr), Leicester - scrapped at Aldenham
1595	595CLT		6.63	D	1584	9.82	BW	12.83	Booth (breaker), Rotherham - scrapped

1596	596CLT		6.63	D	1429	11.84	AL	5.85	Stagecoach, Perth
		EDS146A							10.86 Magicbus, Glasgow
									7.89 PVS (breaker), Carlton - scrapped
1597	597CLT		7.63	M	1667	11.84	PM	12.84	PVS (breaker), Carlton - scrapped
1598	598CLT		6.63	D	1629	10.84	NX	2.85	PVS (breaker), Carlton
									2.85 Wigley (breaker), Carlton - scrapped
1599	599CLT		6.63	D	1573	11.84	NX	5.85	Stagecoach, Perth
		YTS820A							10.86 Magicbus, Glasgow 612
									2.90 East Midland Motor Services RM1599
									10.92 Stagecoach, Perth 604
									10.94 Bluebird Buses 604
1600	600CLT		6.63	D	1763	11.86	SF	1.87	PVS (breaker), Carlton - scrapped
1601	601DYE		6.63	D	1686	6.84	HT	1.85	Stagecoach, Perth
		EDS379A							10.86 Magicbus, Glasgow 613
									5.90 East Midland Motor Services (for spares)
									1.91 PVS (breaker), Carlton - scrapped
1602	602DYE		6.63	D	1634	4.84	Q	1.85	Stagecoach, Perth
									10.86 Magicbus, Glasgow
									7.89 PVS (breaker), Carlton - scrapped
1603	603DYE		6.63	RL	1522	3.85	AL	10.86	PVS (breaker), Carlton - scrapped
1604	604DYE		6.63	D	1545	3.87	Q	8.88	Gtr Manchester Buses, Manchester 2203
									7.90 Pegg (Rotherham & Dist.), Rotherham
									12.90 J.Sykes (breaker), Carlton
									6.92 Merriott Bros., Sheffield
									6.92 Lister (dealer), Bolton
									6.92 Brakell (dealer), Cheam
									2.94 Beach Bus Co., Kittyhawk, USA
1605	605DYE		6.63	RL	1837	10.84	Q	12.84	PVS (breaker), Carlton - scrapped
1606	606DYE		6.63	D	963	10.86	H	4.87	PVS (breaker), Carlton - scrapped
1607	607DYE		6.63	RL	1910	10.84	WH	5.86	Stagecoach, Perth
		LDS201A							10.86 Magicbus, Glasgow 614
									10.90 Stagecoach, Perth 607
									10.94 Bluebird Buses 607
1608	608DYE		6.63	W	1841	3.85	AL	7.85	PVS (breaker), Carlton - scrapped
1609	609DYE		8.65	MH	438	2.94	NX	11.94	PVS (breaker), Carlton
									1.95 Unknown, France
1610	610DYE		6.63	W	1607	8.84	AF	2.85	PVS (breaker), Carlton
									2.85 Wigley (breaker), Carlton - scrapped
1611	611DYE		6.63	MH	1857	7.84	WH	1.85	Stagecoach, Perth
		EDS129A							10.86 Magicbus, Glasgow
									5.89 Lamming, Coulsdon (for spares)
									3.90 Scrapped by Lamming
1612	612DYE		6.63	SW	1010	7.85	AR	8.85	PVS (breaker), Carlton
									8.85 Wigley (breaker), Carlton - scrapped
1613	613DYE		6.63	MH	953	5.87	WD	9.87	PVS (breaker), Carlton - scrapped
1614	614DYE	GVS481	6.63	MH	1657	7.92	SW	9.92	PVS (breaker), Carlton - scrapped
1615	615DYE		6.63	MH	1839	12.84	Q	11.86	PVS (breaker), Carlton
									11.86 Wigley (breaker), Carlton - scrapped
1616	616DYE		6.63	MH	311	3.89	HT	5.90	PVS (breaker), Carlton - scrapped
1617	617DYE		6.63	MH	1428	7.84	AL	1.85	PVS (breaker), Carlton - scrapped
1618	618DYE		6.63	MH	1799	3.87	Q	8.88	Gtr Manchester Buses, Manchester 2205
									7.90 Pegg (Rotherham & Dist.), Rotherham
									12.90 J.Sykes (breaker), Carlton
		OKU105A							3.91 Wombwell Diesels (breaker), Wombwell
		BA4 802							1.93 Double Deck Tours, Niagara, Canada
1619	619DYE	KGJ188A	6.63	MH	1572	3.93	GM	11.94	PVS (breaker), Carlton
									2.95 Daly (agent), London
									2.95 Exported
1620	620DYE	*PVA 079*	6.63	MH	1019	9.82	AL	3.83	Abegweit Tours, Charlottetown, Canada
1621	621DYE	KGJ187A	6.63	MH	1725	10.94	NX	10.94	London Central Buses, London RM1621
1622	622DYE		6.63	MH	1422	9.82	TL	12.82	Berry (bkr), Leicester - scrapped at Aldenham
1623	623DYE		6.63	MH	1543	11.84	NB	2.85	PVS (breaker), Carlton
									2.85 Rollinson (breaker), Carlton - scrapped

1624	624DYE		7.63	W	1436	8.84	AK	1.85	PVS (breaker), Carlton
									1.85 Wigley (breaker), Carlton - scrapped
1625	625DYE		6.63	MH	1735	6.87	WD	11.87	Clydeside Scottish (for spares)
									5.89 Western Scottish (for spares)
									3.90 PVS (breaker), Carlton - scrapped
1626	626DYE		7.63	W	1860	6.84	AL	8.84	PVS (breaker), Carlton
									8.84 Wigley (breaker), Carlton - scrapped
1627	627DYE		11.63	SW	1849	6.84	SW	4.86	Blackpool Transport 523
1628	628DYE		6.63	W	1892	9.84	AG	7.86	Stagecoach, Perth
									10.86 Magicbus, Glasgow
									5.90 PVS (breaker), Carlton
									5.90 Wigley (breaker), Carlton - scrapped
1629	629DYE		7.63	MH	1715	9.82	AL	10.82	W.Norths (dealer), Sherburn - scrapped
1630	630DYE	EDS537B	4.64	U	425	8.85	HT	5.86	Kelvin Scottish RM630 (1937)
									4.89 Kelvin Central Buses 1937
									11.92 Regal (dealer), Kirkintilloch
									11.93 Pegg (Rotherham & Dist.), Rotherham
									4.94 Wigley (breaker), Carlton
									8.94 PVS (breaker), Carlton
									11.94 J.Sykes (breaker), Carlton
									11.94 Hunter, Garston V26
1631	631DYE		7.63	MH	1538	1.85	Q	11.86	PVS (breaker), Carlton - scrapped
1632	632DYE		7.63	W	1603	7.84	ED	11.84	PVS (breaker), Carlton - scrapped
1633	633DYE		7.63	W	1229	2.87	CT	3.87	PVS (breaker), Carlton
									3.87 Wigley (breaker), Carlton - scrapped
1634	634DYE		7.63	MH	1643	2.84	PM	9.84	PVS (breaker), Carlton - scrapped
1635	635DYE		7.63	MH	1677	9.82	SW	12.82	Berry (bkr), Leicester - scrapped at Aldenham
1636	636DYE		7.63	MH	1441	6.82	NS	12.82	Berry (bkr), Leicester - scrapped at Aldenham
1637	637DYE		7.63	MH	1422	11.84	WH	1.85	PVS (breaker), Carlton - scrapped
1638	638DYE		7.63	MH	1444	10.84	PM	10.86	PVS (breaker), Carlton - scrapped
1639	639DYE		7.63	MH	1361	9.82	AG	3.83	Berry (bkr), Leicester - scrapped at Aldenham
1640	640DYE		7.63	MH	1556	1.85	NX	5.86	Blackpool Transport 524
1641	641DYE		7.63	MH	1530	1.85	CT	2.86	Penta, Reading
									6.91 Victoria Motor Co. (dealer), Brimsdown
									7.91 Springtime Nurseries, Crews Hill
									9.91 Roberts (preserved), Brimsdown
									3.92 Wright & Biddell, Rainham
1642	642DYE		7.63	MH	1450	1.85	AR	3.85	PVS (breaker), Carlton - scrapped
1643	643DYE		7.63	MH	1644	9.82	HW	4.84	Queen Elizabeth Hospital, Edgbaston
1644	644DYE		7.63	MH	1560	2.85	SW	3.85	PVS (breaker), Carlton - scrapped
1645	645DYE		7.63	W	1534	2.87	X	6.87	PVS (breaker), Carlton
									6.87 Wigley (breaker), Carlton - scrapped
1646	646DYE		7.63	MH	1561	10.84	V	6.85	PVS (breaker), Carlton
									7.85 Wigley (breaker), Carlton - scrapped
1647	647DYE	BNK32A	7.63	W	1445	11.87	X	1.88	United Counties Omnibus Co. 706
1648	648DYE		7.63	MH	1906	5.84	AR	9.84	PVS (breaker), Carlton
									9.84 Rollinson (breaker), Carlton - scrapped
1649	649DYE		7.63	MH	1424	12.82	U	8.83	TT (UK) Ltd., Bedford
									1.90 London Bus Export Co. (dlr), Chepstow
									6.92 Kerpen Special Cables, Wellesbourne
1650	650DYE		7.63	W	1608	2.85	BW	4.86	Blackpool Transport 525
1651	651DYE	BA4 805	7.63	PM	1651	8.83	BN	10.83	Double Deck Tours, Niagara, Canada
1652	652DYE		7.63	MH	1416	6.84	SW	12.84	PVS (breaker), Carlton - scrapped
1653	653DYE		7.63	PM	1425	9.82	AR	12.83	Gallaghers International
									7.86 Dolphin Internat'l Displays, Harpenden
									4.91 Chelmsford Car Auctions
									4.91 Parkway Commercials (dlr), Chelmsford
									5.91 Allmey (dealer), Eascote - scrapped
1654	654DYE		7.63	PM	1270	1.85	V	11.87	Southampton Citybus 418
									10.90 Forrest (preserved), Southampton
1655	655DYE		7.63	PM	1655	11.84	SW	10.86	PVS (breaker), Carlton - scrapped
1656	656DYE	KGH932A	7.63	PM	1748	7.91	Nt	12.93	PVS (breaker), Carlton - scrapped
1657	657DYE		7.63	PM	1546	9.82	K	5.83	Berry (bkr), Leicester - scrapped at Aldenham

1658	658DYE		7.63	PM	1440	9.82	AG	10.82	W.Norths (dealer), Sherburn - scrapped
1659	659DYE		7.63	PM	1639	4.72	PM	2.74	Scrapped by LTE at Aldenham
1660	660DYE	*NC7416*	7.63	PM	1660	8.86	GM	12.86	Bradshaw Hawkins, Auckland, New Zealand
									2.88 Taylor, Rotoria, New Zealand
									8.89 Ferner, Queenstown, New Zealand
1661	661DYE		8.63	PM	1526	9.82	A	12.82	Berry (bkr), Leicester - scrapped at Aldenham
1662	662DYE		8.63	PM	1548	5.84	NX	6.84	Paul Sykes (dealer), Barnsley - scrapped
1663	663DYE		8.63	PM	1699	9.82	NX	4.83	Berry (bkr), Leicester - scrapped at Aldenham
1664	664DYE		8.63	PM	1443	11.88	AD	7.90	PVS (breaker), Carlton - scrapped
1665	665DYE		10.63	AF	1528	9.82	AR	12.82	Berry (bkr), Leicester - scrapped at Aldenham
1666	666DYE		8.63	PM	1747	10.94	Q	10.94	London Central Buses, London RM1666
1667	667DYE		9.63	PM	1729	2.87	CT	5.87	Clydeside Scottish (for spares)
									5.89 PVS (breaker), Carlton - scrapped
1668	668DYE		8.63	NX	1900	12.84	AF	10.86	PVS (breaker), Carlton
									11.86 Wigley (breaker), Carlton - scrapped
1669	669DYE		8.63	PM	1050	10.82	SW	2.83	Berry (bkr), Leicester - scrapped at Aldenham
1670	670DYE	*QA8416*	9.63	PM	1559	9.82	M	4.84	International Distillers, New Zealand
									7.84 Museum of Transport, Auckland, New Zealand
		4 HIRE 2							5.90 Gibson, Mount Albert, Auckland, New Zealand
1671	671DYE		9.63	PM	1706	9.82	TC	12.82	Berry (bkr), Leicester - scrapped at Aldenham
1672	672DYE		9.63	PM	1541	2.87	GM	6.87	PVS (breaker), Carlton
									7.87 Wigley (breaker), Carlton - scrapped
1673	673DYE		9.63	PM	1682	10.84	W	12.84	PVS (breaker), Carlton - scrapped
1674	674DYE		9.63	AF	1567	9.82	T	2.83	Berry (bkr), Leicester - scrapped at Aldenham
1675	675DYE		9.63	PM	1716	9.82	B	10.82	W.Norths (dealer), Sherburn - scrapped
1676	676DYE		9.63	PM	1771	4.94	AR	*3.95*	*London Transport Buses reserve fleet*
1677	677DYE		9.63	PM	1697	11.84	ED	1.85	Brakell (dealer), Cheam
									5.85 Hunt (preserved), LTE Battersea garage
									12.85 Brakell (dealer), Cheam
									1.86 Brewis (preserved), Borley
									5.89 Morgan (Bygone Tours), Sutton Vallance
									.91 Morgan (Bygone Buses), Biddenden
									.93 Morgan (Bygone Buses), Staplehurst
1678	678DYE		9.63	PM	1558	6.84	V	9.84	PVS (breaker), Carlton - scrapped
1679	679DYE		10.63	AF	1575	11.82	BW	12.83	Booth (breaker), Rotherham
									12.83 Goodwin (breaker), Carlton - scrapped
1680	680DYE		9.63	PM	1557	9.82	T	12.83	Booth (breaker), Rotherham - scrapped
1681	681DYE		9.63	PM	1591	9.92	WKt	7.93	Chamberlain et al. (pres'd), Hounslow Heath
1682	682DYE		9.63	PM	1452	3.84	AR	11.87	Southampton Citybus 405
									1.91 Southend Transport 117
									1.94 Lister (dealer), Bolton
									1.94 Brakell (dealer), Cheam
									.94 Unknown, Germany
1683	683DYE		10.63	AF	1246	10.88	HT	2.89	PVS (breaker), Carlton - scrapped
1684	684DYE		10.63	AF	1566	9.82	BW	6.83	De Dubbeldekkers (dealer), Schilde, Belgium

---

Next page

South London's RM1593 is one of several Routemasters which have been given a special red & cream livery for use on route 159.

Maintained in London red livery is former RM1677, now owned by Bygone Tours of Staplehurst with whom it is seen here in Maidstone operating a local service to Park Wood. (G.M.Dinnage)

Still wearing the livery of its previous owner Verwood Transport of Poole, Dorset, former British Airways NMY648E is seen here in 1990 after its purchase by Legg of Aylesbury (Routemaster Travel). (P.T.Stokes)

Having spent several years in service with United Counties, Stagecoach corporate liveried RM2192 is seen at Box Hill, Dorking on 16 July 1995 adorned with Stagecoach Selkent fleet names. (J.A.Godwin)

ROUTE 159
159
STREATHAM STN
159
593 CLT

AMAZING
82
PARK WOOD
AMAZING
BYGONE TOURS
677 DYE

FLASH GORDON
92
VERWOOD
FLASH GORDON
VER 826724
NMY 648 E

Stagecoach
53
OXFORD CIRCUS
Stagecoach
53
CUV 192C

Sporting large Southampton CityBus fleet names and dedicated route 16 advertisements, 406 (WLT564) appears to lack a destination blind in its three-aperture box. (F.W.York)

On long term loan to Delaine of Bourne from a preservationist and repainted into that operator's livery is RM2059 (ALM59B). (C.Morrison)

1685	685DYE	BNK31A	10.63	W	1181	12.87	AG	1.88	United Counties Omnibus Co. 714
									12.93 Stageoach, Perth (for spares)
									9.94 Dunsmore (breaker), Larkhall - scrapped
1686	686DYE		10.63	AF	1580	10.82	NS	12.82	Berry (bkr), Leicester - scrapped at Aldenham
1687	687DYE		10.63	W	1597	9.82	CT	12.82	Berry (bkr), Leicester - scrapped at Aldenham
1688	688DYE		10.63	W	1601	8.83	CT	12.83	Booth (breaker), Rotherham - scrapped
1689	689DYE		10.63	W	1624	10.82	NS	12.82	Berry (bkr), Leicester - scrapped at Aldenham
1690	690DYE		10.63	W	1555	8.84	PM	1.85	PVS (breaker), Carlton - scrapped
1691	691DYE	WTS87A	10.63	W	948	5.86	NX	9.86	Strathtay Scottish SR7
									4.90 Kelbie (dealer), Turriff
									5.90 Ripley (breaker), Carlton
									7.90 Lonsdale (dealer), Heysham
		691DYE							7.90 Fozzard (preserved), Baildon
1692	692DYE		10.63	W	1098	8.87	E	9.87	PVS (breaker), Carlton
									9.87 Wigley (breaker), Carlton - scrapped
1693	693DYE		10.63	W	1168	9.82	BN	10.82	W.Norths (dealer), Sherburn - scrapped
1694	694DYE		10.63	W	1753	3.87	Q	4.88	Ciclo Tours, Santander, Spain
1695	695DYE		10.63	W	1690	8.82	AL	12.82	Berry (bkr), Leicester - scrapped at Aldenham
1696	696DYE		10.63	W	1685	8.82	NX	10.82	W.Norths (dealer), Sherburn - scrapped
1697	697DYE		10.63	W	1079	7.87	E	11.87	PVS (breaker), Carlton
									11.87 Wigley (breaker), Carlton - scrapped
1698	698DYE	KGJ173A	10.63	W	1578	8.92	GM	7.93	PVS (breaker), Carlton - scrapped
1699	699DYE		10.63	W	1043	9.87	E	11.87	Magicbus, Glasgow
									5.89 Watson (dealer), Chesterfield
									8.90 Lowings (preserved), Amersham
									1.94 Begre & Richardson (preserved), Sidcup
1700	700DYE	KGJ167A	10.63	W	1569	10.94	HT	10.94	London Northern Bus Co., London RM1700
1701	701DYE	*PAH502*	10.63	W	1783	11.88	AD	10.89	Hogber, Sweden
1702	702DYE		10.63	W	1570	9.82	Q	12.82	Berry (bkr), Leicester - scrapped at Aldenham
1703	703DYE		10.63	W	1023	3.87	Q	9.87	Clydeside Scottish RM1703
		LDS286A							5.89 Western Scottish C74
									8.90 PVS (breaker), Carlton
									2.91 Ensign (dealer), Purfleet
		EZ8347							6.91 Citybus, Kowloon, Hong Kong 3
1704	704DYE		10.63	J	1616	11.82	X	12.83	Booth (breaker), Rotherham - scrapped
1705	705DYE		10.63	J	1035	3.87	AK	6.87	Clydeside Scottish (for spares)
									7.88 PVS (breaker), Carlton - scrapped
1706	706DYE		10.63	J	1622	9.82	NX	10.82	W.Norths (dealer), Sherburn - scrapped
1707	707DYE		10.63	J	1696	9.82	AR	12.83	Booth (breaker), Rotherham - scrapped
1708	708DYE	*TC2323*	10.63	J	1141	2.88	PM	8.88	Collins, Perth, Australia
		7NO-115							
1709	709DYE		10.63	J	1618	5.84	MH	8.84	PVS (breaker), Carlton
									8.84 Wigley (breaker), Carlton - scrapped
1710	710DYE		10.63	J	1623	4.84	AR	8.84	PVS (breaker), Carlton - scrapped
1711	711DYE		10.63	J	1540	9.82	BW	9.83	De Dubbeldekkers (dealer), Schilde, Belgium
1712	712DYE		10.63	J	1431	6.84	AL	9.84	PVS (breaker), Carlton - scrapped
1713	713DYE		10.63	J	1714	8.84	Q	6.87	Southampton Citybus 408
									10.89 Amex Trading (dealer), Buxton
									11.89 Unknown, Japan
1714	714DYE		10.63	J	1621	1.85	B	11.86	PVS (breaker), Carlton - scrapped
1715	715DYE		10.63	J	1653	9.83	Q	8.84	PVS (breaker), Carlton - scrapped
1716	716DYE		10.63	J	1859	4.84	AK	8.84	PVS (breaker), Carlton
									8.84 Rollinson (breaker), Carlton - scrapped
1717	717DYE		10.63	J	1602	7.86	CFs	5.88	PVS (breaker), Carlton - scrapped
1718	718DYE		10.63	J	1582	9.82	NX	1.83	Berry (bkr), Leicester - scrapped at Aldenham
1719	719DYE		10.63	J	1645	2.85	B	4.85	PVS (breaker), Carlton - scrapped
1720	720DYE	*KP.109.650*	11.63	W	1640	5.84	AR	6.84	Phoenix Holidays, Yugoslavia
									5.85 Kompas, Portoroz, Yugoslavia
1721	721DYE		11.63	CF	1709	8.84	AL	2.89	PVS (breaker), Carlton - scrapped
1722	722DYE		11.63	AF	1721	2.87	GM	6.87	PVS (breaker), Carlton - scrapped
1723	723DYE		11.63	AF	1617	12.84	NX	4.85	PVS (breaker), Carlton - scrapped
1724	724DYE		11.63	AF	1638	9.82	AR	12.83	Booth (breaker), Rotherham
									12.83 Goodwin (breaker), Carlton - scrapped

1725	725DYE		11.63	W	1726	1.95	BN	1.95	South London Transport, London RM1725
1726	726DYE		11.63	AF	1631	9.82	CT	12.83	Booth (breaker), Rotherham
									12.83 Goodwin (breaker), Carlton - scrapped
1727	727DYE		11.63	AF	1708	9.93	BW	3.94	Unknown
1728	728DYE		11.63	CF	1588	10.84	AR	1.85	PVS (breaker), Carlton
									9.86 Rollinson (breaker), Carlton - scrapped
1729	729DYE		11.63	CF	1731	10.88	WN	2.89	PVS (breaker), Carlton
									2.89 Wigley (breaker), Carlton - scrapped
1730	730DYE		11.63	CF	1718	8.82	TC	10.82	Portman (agent), London
									2.83 Karuizawa Clas. Car Museum, (preserved), Nagano, Japan
1731	731DYE		11.63	CF	1730	3.87	HT	9.87	Clydeside Scottish RM1731
									5.81 Western Scottish C75
									8.90 PVS (breaker), Carlton
									8.90 Wright (dealer), Rainham
									9.90 Lane (preserved), Canterbury
									9.93 Brakell (dealer), Cheam *- for resale*
1732	732DYE	*ESU332*	11.63	CF	1421	11.82	HT	11.83	Bureau Technique Internat'l, Ostend, Belgium
		B4383							8.91 Roisin, Chatalet, Belgium
1733	733DYE		11.63	CF	1691	3.85	HT	5.85	PVS (breaker), Carlton
									5.85 Rollinson (breaker), Carlton - scrapped
1734	734DYE		11.63	CF	1733	1.95	BN	1.95	South London Transport, London RM1734
1735	735DYE		11.63	AF	1821	12.84	WH	5.86	Blackpool Transport 526
1736	736DYE		11.63	CF	1599	1.85	SW	3.85	PVS (breaker), Carlton
									3.85 Wigley (breaker), Carlton - scrapped
1737	737DYE		11.63	W	1772	4.85	AG	1.86	London Transport Museum (pres'd), London
1738	738DYE		11.63	W	1695	3.84	AG	2.85	PVS (breaker), Carlton
									8.85 Rollinson (breaker), Carlton - scrapped
1739	739DYE		11.63	W	1636	9.82	CF	3.83	Berry (bkr), Leicester - scrapped at Aldenham
1740	740DYE		11.63	W	1346	7.90	Vt	10.91	Parasel Society Anatomy, Montevideo, Uruguay
									2.92 94.7FM Concerto, Montevideo, Uruguay
1741	741DYE		11.63	CF	1684	7.84	AR	1.85	Stagecoach, Perth
									1.87 Magicbus, Glasgow
									4.88 Coster, Hull
									3.89 Kingston-upon-Hull City Trans. (not used)
		PAG809A							7.89 East Yorkshire Motor Services 809
1742	742DYE		11.63	CF	1689	5.85	CT	8.85	PVS (breaker), Carlton
									8.85 Wigley (breaker), Carlton - scrapped
1743	743DYE		11.63	CF	1700	9.82	PM	1.83	Berry (bkr), Leicester - scrapped at Aldenham
1744	744DYE		11.63	CF	1666	5.84	NX	11.84	PVS (breaker), Carlton - scrapped
1745	745DYE		11.63	CF	1738	11.87	AK	6.90	PVS (breaker), Carlton - scrapped
1746	746DYE		11.63	CF	1672	8.83	AF	7.84	PVS (breaker), Carlton - scrapped
1747	747DYE		11.63	CF	1915	10.84	Q	10.85	Allmey (dealer), Eastcote
									10.86 London Borough of Wandsworth
1748	748DYE		11.63	CF	1688	3.85	SW	5.85	PVS (breaker), Carlton - scrapped
1749	749DYE		11.63	CF	1661	6.84	Q	8.84	PVS (breaker), Carlton
									8.84 Rollinson (breaker), Carlton - scrapped
1750	750DYE		11.63	CF	1678	8.92	UXt	11.94	PVS (breaker), Carlton *- for scrap*
1751	751DYE		11.63	CF	1683	9.82	T	12.82	Berry (bkr), Leicester - scrapped at Aldenham
1752	752DYE	*BC9 998*	11.63	CF	1539	9.82	X	5.84	Piccadilly Bus Tours, Ottawa, Canada
		BB4 289							3.92 Mulligan Corporation, Ontario, Canada
1753	753DYE		11.63	CF	1741	5.87	NX	10.87	PVS (breaker), Carlton - scrapped
1754	754DYE		11.63	CF	1669	6.84	SW	7.84	W.Norths (dealer), Sherburn
									7.84 Top Deck (agent), Edgware
									8.84 LA Motor Coach Co., Los Angeles, USA
1755	755DYE		11.63	CF	1531	1.85	W	11.86	PVS (breaker), Carlton - scrapped
1756	756DYE	*U31 275*	12.63	CF	1595	8.84	AL	12.85	Brandon, Irvine, Texas, USA
									5.87 Bright Horizons School, Carrolton, Texas, USA
1757	757DYE		12.63	CF	1420	5.84	NB	8.84	PVS (breaker), Carlton
									8.84 Rollinson (breaker), Carlton - scrapped
1758	758DYE		12.63	CF	1758	10.94	HT	10.94	London Northern Bus Co., London RM1758

After serving London Transport, Stagecoach Perth, Magicbus of Glasgow and Coster of Hull, 741DYE eventually found its way to the East Yorkshire Group who initially placed it in its Scarborough & District flee whose red livery it adopted. Seen here in this Yorkshire coastal resort in 1989, it was later transferred to Eas Yorkshire's Hull operations where it gained the traditional blue & cream colour scheme employed on the company's other buses of this type. (P.Shipp)

Nottinghamshire independent Gagg of Bunny at one time operated two former London Routemasters, 314CLT and WLT790 which are seen in 1989 at their owner's depot still wearing London-style red livery. The former was later repainted into Gagg's standard blue & cream and was eventually sold in 1994, some five years afte its sister left the fleet. (P.T.Stokes)

410
Nutfield
Bletchingley
Godstone Oxted
WESTERHAM
RMC1462
NOSTALGIABUS
462 CLT

7A
Asda Bournes Grn.
Woodgrange Drive
Southend Rochford
SHOEBURYNESS EAST BEACH
CARLTON. Television for Essex.
116
Southend Transport
543 CLT
ERTHSHIRE
DVERTISER
Brighton &
RINGMER
C.COLLEG
RESTON CIRCUS

1759	759DYE		12.63	X	1589	2.85	CT	10.86	PVS (breaker), Carlton
									11.86 Wigley (breaker), Carlton - scrapped
1760	760DYE		12.63	CF	1658	9.82	TL	10.82	W.Norths (dealer), Sherburn - scrapped
1761	761DYE		12.63	CF	1446	6.84	SW	11.84	PVS (breaker), Carlton
									12.84 Wigley (breaker), Carlton - scrapped
1762	762DYE		12.63	CF	1656	9.82	BW	12.82	Berry (bkr), Leicester - scrapped at Aldenham
1763	763DYE		12.63	X	1762	6.83	CT	12.83	Booth (breaker), Rotherham - scrapped
1764	764DYE		12.63	X	1780	7.90	ARt	3.91	PVS (breaker), Carlton - scrapped
1765	765DYE		12.63	X	1845	1.85	AL	10.85	PVS (breaker), Carlton - scrapped
1766	766DYE		12.63	X	571	8.85	SP	7.86	PVS (breaker), Carlton - scrapped
1767	767DYE		12.63	X	1637	2.85	AL	10.85	Winged Fellowship Trust, London
									11.85 Winged Fellowship Trust, Nottingham
									5.86 Winged Fellowship Trust, Southport
1768	768DYE		12.63	X	946	11.87	AF	2.88	Clydeside Scottish (for spares)
		EDS567B							5.89 Western Scottish (for spares)
									8.90 Kelvin Central Buses (for spares)
									1.92 Dunsmore (breaker), Larkhall - *for scrap*
1769	769DYE		12.63	X	1432	11.82	HT	8.84	PVS (breaker), Carlton - scrapped
1770	770DYE		12.63	X	1740	12.93	FY	5.94	PVS (breaker), Carlton - scrapped
1771	771DYE		12.63	X	1680	9.82	PM	10.82	W.Norths (dealer), Sherburn
									4.89 Radio Humberside, Hull
									11.89 Warehouse Nightclub, Doncaster
1772	772DYE	KGJ116A	12.63	X	1707	7.93	GM	3.94	PVS (breaker), Carlton - scrapped
1773	773DYE	*BB4 292*	12.63	X	1687	9.82	AL	5.84	Piccadilly Bus Tours, Ottawa, Canada
1774	774DYE		12.63	X	1720	4.86	X	5.86	PVS (breaker), Carlton
									7.86 Wigley (breaker), Carlton - scrapped
1775	775DYE		12.63	X	1817	6.84	TL	9.84	PVS (breaker), Carlton - scrapped
1776	776DYE		12.63	X	1775	11.87	AF	8.88	Gtr Manchester Buses, Manchester 2202
									10.90 Lister (dealer), Bolton
									10.90 Liverline, Liverpool 01 (776)
1777	777DYE		12.63	X	1779	11.88	GM	3.89	PVS (breaker), Carlton - scrapped
1778	778DYE		12.63	X	846	3.85	TH	5.85	PVS (breaker), Carlton
									5.85 Wigley (breaker), Carlton - scrapped
1779	779DYE		1.64	W	1673	6.84	AR	8.84	PVS (breaker), Carlton - scrapped
1780	780DYE		12.63	X	1613	6.84	AR	6.85	PVS (breaker), Carlton
									6.85 Rollinson (breaker), Carlton - scrapped
1781	781DYE		12.63	X	1663	8.82	AK	8.82	W.Norths (dealer), Sherburn - scrapped
1782	782DYE		1.64	W	1655	4.94	NXt	10.94	PVS (breaker), Carlton - *for scrap*
1783	783DYE		1.64	X	1671	7.84	WH	5.86	Rees Industries, Liverpool
									6.87 London Buses, London RM1783
						5.92	WD	5.92	London Coaches, London RM1783
1784	784DYE		1.64	X	1630	6.84	NX	8.84	PVS (breaker), Carlton - scrapped
1785	785DYE		1.64	W	1587	12.84	CT	2.85	PVS (breaker), Carlton
									7.85 Rollinson (breaker), Carlton - scrapped
1786	786DYE		1.64	X	1785	1.88	PD	11.88	PVS (breaker), Carlton - scrapped
1787	787DYE		1.64	W	565	2.87	AR	6.87	PVS (breaker), Carlton - scrapped
1788	788DYE	*BB4 954*	1.64	W	1633	9.84	SW	5.86	Piccadilly Bus Tours, Ottawa, Canada
1789	789DYE		1.64	W	1544	5.84	AR	9.84	PVS (breaker), Carlton - scrapped
1790	790DYE		1.64	X	1704	6.84	AL	3.85	London Borough of Lewisham Poverty Action Group.
1791	791DYE		1.64	X	1701	11.82	AD	9.83	De Dubbeldekkers, Schilde, Belgium (for spares)

Next page

Restored to Green Line livery, Nostalgiabus RMC1462 is seen here at Outwood Windmill whilst operating the Sunday 410 service on hire to London & Country on 16 July 1995. (J.A.Godwin)

Now preserved in the livery of its final operator Southend Transport, former RM1543 poses for the photographer at the Cobham bus rally in April 1994. (P.T.Stokes)

1792	792DYE		1.64	X	1807	2.92	TL	7.92	PVS (breaker), Carlton
									7.92 Wigley (breaker), Carlton - scrapped
1793	793DYE		1.64	W	1826	4.84	AL	5.87	Southampton Citybus 402
									9.89 Amex Trading (dealer), Buxton
									10.89 Unknown, Japan
1794	794DYE		1.64	X	413	8.85	S	8.85	PVS (breaker), Carlton
									9.85 Wigley (breaker), Carlton - scrapped
1795	795DYE		1.64	WH	1664	8.85	CA	11.85	PVS (breaker), Carlton - scrapped
1796	796DYE		1.64	WH	1784	11.88	AD	4.89	Nissho Iwai Corporation (agent), Japan
1797	797DYE		2.64	AR	1808	10.94	NX	10.94	London Central Buses, London RM1797
1798	798DYE		1.64	X	1830	2.84	Q	8.84	PVS (breaker), Carlton - scrapped
1799	799DYE		1.64	X	1789	10.94	HT	10.94	London Northern Bus Co., London RM1799
1800	800DYE		2.64	AR	1804	2.88	AD	3.88	PVS (breaker), Carlton - scrapped
1801	801DYE		1.64	X	1827	1.95	BN	1.95	South London Transport, London RM1801
1802	802DYE		1.64	X	1694	10.84	SW	12.84	PVS (breaker), Carlton
									12.84 Wigley (breaker), Carlton - scrapped
1803	803DYE		1.64	X	528	10.86	WD	2.87	SBG Engineering, Kilmarnock
									2.87 Clydeside Scottish RM1803
		EDS568B							5.89 Western Scottish C76
									9.90 PVS (breaker), Carlton
									3.92 Pinewood Studios, Iver Heath
									4.92 PVS (breaker), Carlton - scrapped
1804	804DYE	EYY327B	2.64	AR	1723	10.94	HT	10.94	London Northern Bus Co., London RM1804
1805	805DYE		2.64	AR	1744	12.87	Q	1.88	PVS (breaker), Carlton
									1.88 Wigley (breaker), Carlton - scrapped
1806	806DYE		2.64	AR	1895	7.84	AK	1.85	PVS (breaker), Carlton - scrapped
1807	807DYE		2.64	AR	1770	10.87	AF	8.88	Gtr Manchester Buses, Manchester 2209
									7.90 Pegg (Rotherham & Dist.), Rotherham
									11.90 J.Sykes (breaker), Carlton
		EVM132B							4.92 McDonalds Restaurants, Manchester
1808	808DYE		2.64	AR	1649	8.84	SW	1.85	PVS (breaker), Carlton - scrapped
1809	809DYE	EBY257B	2.64	AR	1736	8.92	GM	6.93	PVS (breaker), Carlton - scrapped
1810	810DYE	EBY247B	2.64	AR	1760	11.88	HT	5.90	Burgsport International (dealer), Harrow
									5.90 Martin Dawes Communications, Paris, France
1811	811DYE	EGF220B	2.64	AR	1759	12.95	BN	1.95	South London Transport, London RM1811
1812	812DYE		2.64	AR	566	12.86	AV	4.87	PVS (breaker), Carlton - scrapped
1813	813DYE		2.64	AR	1777	1.87	AL	5.87	PVS (breaker), Carlton - scrapped
1814	814DYE		2.64	AR	1642	11.84	AR	11.86	PVS (breaker), Carlton - scrapped
1815	815DYE	EGF286B	2.64	AR	1743	8.91	BN	8.93	Unknown, Germany
1816	816DYE		2.64	AR	1724	4.85	X	8.85	PVS (breaker), Carlton
									9.85 Wigley (breaker), Carlton - scrapped
1817	817DYE		2.64	AR	1693	11.87	X	12.87	PVS (breaker), Carlton - scrapped
1818	818DYE		2.64	AR	2203	11.89	FWt	6.90	PVS (breaker), Carlton - scrapped
1819	819DYE		2.64	AR	1778	5.87	NX	4.89	Nissho Iwai Corporation (agent), Japan
1820	820DYE		2.64	AR	1734	11.87	AF	1.88	United Counties Omnibus Co., 715
									10.91 Lister (dealer), Bolton
									11.91 Whiting (breaker), Ferrybridge - scrapped
1821	821DYE	YSL32B	2.64	AR	1176	6.86	NX	9.86	Strathtay Scottish SR6
									11.92 Cosgrove (breaker), Dundee - scrapped

Next page

The only provincial operator to purchase the Routemaster new was Northern General who took 50 front entrance 30ft. long variants in 1964/5. Representing these buses is now-preserved 2105 (EUP405B) which has been restored to its original livery. (K.A.Jenkinson)

One of two Routemasters used by Haven Bus on its Newhaven to Brighton service, RM933 is pictured here at the start of its day's duties. (L.Hough)

Routemasters have been a familiar sight in the yard of PVS at Carlton for over ten years. This view in March 1994 shows RM1141, former driver trainer RM2079 and ex.Clydeside Scottish RM1830 awaiting their final demise. (K.A.Jenkinson)

SHOP AT BINNS
HARTLEPOOL
45
2105
NORTHERN
SWALES MOOR ROAD
EUP 405B

H1
BRIGHTON
HAVEN BUS
RM 933
WLT 933

KNY © HARVEY NICHOLS
AMAZING
PALLADIUM
PRIVATE
LONDON GENERAL

Following its operation by Kelvin Scottish from 1986 to 1992, RM388 was converted to open staircase configuration for use on sightseeing duties in the historic city of York where it is seen in the summer of 1994. (K.A.Jenkinson)

Now preserved in Northern Ireland by McNeilly of Ballyclare, RM406 complete with a full London Transport blind display rests in Belfast in this night scene in 1994. (Paul Savage)

1822	822DYE		2.64	AR	1769	1.95	BN	1.95	South London Transport, London RM1822
1823	823DYE		2.64	AR	1754	5.87	NX	10.87	PVS (breaker), Carlton - scrapped
									10.87 some body parts sold to Clydeside Scottish
1824	824DYE		2.64	AR	1765	11.87	HT	8.88	PVS (breaker), Carlton - scrapped
1825	825DYE		2.64	AR	1745	4.93	AF	*3.95*	*London Transport Buses reserve fleet*
1826	826DYE		2.64	AR	1794	8.90	FW	1.91	PVS (breaker), Carlton - scrapped
1827	827DYE	*60-SRI-6627*	2.64	AR	1767	11.87	AG	12.88	Sri Lanka Transport Board
1828	828DYE		2.64	AR	1855	5.84	AR	9.84	PVS (breaker), Carlton
									9.84 Wigley (breaker), Carlton - scrapped
1829	829DYE		2.64	AR	1674	11.84	SW	12.84	PVS (breaker), Carlton - scrapped
1830	830DYE		2.64	AR	1756	10.87	X	2.88	Clydeside Scottish (for spares)
									5.89 Western Scottish (for spares)
									7.90 Wombwell Diesels (breaker), Wombwell
									3.94 PVS (breaker), Carlton - scrapped
1831	831DYE		2.64	AR	1751	12.84	AG	1.85	PVS (breaker), Carlton - scrapped
1832	832DYE		2.64	AR	1774	2.94	NX	5.94	PVS (breaker), Carlton - scrapped
1833	833DYE		2.64	AR	1907	11.84	AR	5.85	PVS (breaker), Carlton - scrapped
1834	834DYE		2.64	AR	1786	1.88	PD	5.88	MCW, Elmdon, Birmingham
									11.88 PVS (breaker), Carlton - scrapped
1835	835DYE		2.64	AR	1125	2.87	WD	4.87	PVS (breaker), Carlton - scrapped
1836	836DYE	EGF285B	2.64	AR	1752	4.93	GM	11.94	PVS (breaker), Carlton
									2.95 Chester Bus & Boat, Chester
1837	837DYE		2.64	AR	1766	3.87	PM	4.87	PVS (breaker), Carlton - scrapped
1838	838DYE		2.64	AR	1773	8.87	GM	11.87	Magicbus, Glasgow
									6.90 Wigley (breaker), Carlton - scrapped
1839	839DYE	GVS482	2.64	AR	1737	7.92	SW	7.92	PVS (breaker), Carlton - scrapped
1840	840DYE		2.64	AR	1750	10.94	HT	10.94	London Northern Bus Co., London RM1840
1841	841DYE		3.64	AR	1875	8.85	N	8.85	PVS (breaker), Carlton - scrapped
1842	842DYE		3.64	BK	1749	3.87	AV	10.87	Alston , London
		BFW544B							1.89 Haller, Rawby
									2.94 Rushfield, Langworth
									9.94 Rushby, Market Rasen
1843	843DYE		3.64	AR	1902	7.84	BW	10.85	William Jewel College, Liberty, Missouri, USA
1844	844DYE		3.64	AR	534	8.85	AF	8.85	PVS (breaker), Carlton
									8.85 Wigley (breaker), Carlton - scrapped
1845	845DYE		3.64	BK	1835	5.84	AR	8.84	PVS (breaker), Carlton - scrapped
1846	846DYE		3.64	BK	1755	11.87	WN	12.87	PVS (breaker), Carlton
									12.87 Wigley (breaker), Carlton - scrapped
1847	847DYE		3.64	BK	1831	4.84	AR	1.85	Stagecoach, Perth
									10.86 Magicbus, Glasgow
									1.89 Dunsmore (breaker), Larkhall - scrapped at Stagecoach Spittalfield depot
1848	848DYE		3.64	ON	62	7.86	SF	9.86	PVS (breaker), Carlton
									9.86 Wigley (breaker), Carlton - scrapped
1849	849DYE		3.64	BK	2040	2.87	T	4.88	PVS (breaker), Carlton - scrapped
1850	850DYE		3.64	BK	18	11.85	X	4.86	Clydeside Scottish (for spares)
									6.87 # W.Norths (dealer), Sherburn
									6.87 PVS (breaker), Carlton - scrapped
1851	851DYE	*60-Sri-6601*	3.64	BK	1781	1.88	BW	12.88	Sri Lanka Transport Board
1852	852DYE		3.64	BK	1824	3.85	BW	6.85	PVS (breaker), Carlton - scrapped
1853	853DYE		3.64	BK	1702	10.84	AR	1.85	PVS (breaker), Carlton
									1.85 Wigley (breaker), Carlton - scrapped
1854	854DYE		3.64	BK	1705	11.84	N	1.85	PVS (breaker), Carlton - scrapped
1855	855DYE		3.64	BK	450	4.85	MH	6.85	PVS (breaker), Carlton - scrapped
1856	856DYE		3.64	BK	1806	8.92	X	8.92	PVS (breaker), Carlton - scrapped *(collected by PVS from Nottingham)*
1857	857DYE		3.64	ON	1829	1.84	AR	8.84	PVS (breaker), Carlton - scrapped
1858	858DYE		3.64	BK	1867	11.84	WH	7.86	Stagecoach, Perth
		EDS561B							10.86 Magicbus, Glasgow 615
									4.92 Kelvin Central Buses 1925
									8.93 Watson, Chesterfield (for spares)
									8.94 PVS (breaker), Carlton - scrapped

1859	859DYE		3.64	BK	1872	7.84	AF	7.88	St.John Ambulance Brigade, London (following loan since 4.87)
									11.94 Greater Reading Omnibus, Reading 17
1860	860DYE		3.64	ON	1842	6.84	W	10.86	PVS (breaker), Carlton - scrapped
1861	861DYE		3.64	BK	1828	5.84	AG	1.85	PVS (breaker), Carlton - scrapped
1862	862DYE		3.64	ON	1822	9.84	AR	1.85	PVS (breaker), Carlton - scrapped
1863	863DYE		3.64	ON	1852	6.84	AG	8.84	PVS (breaker), Carlton - scrapped
1864	864DYE		3.64	ON	1874	9.84	W	5.86	Rees Industries, Liverpool
									6.87 London Buses RM1864
				B		5.92	WD	5.92	London Coaches, London RM1864
1865	865DYE		3.64	ON	365	2.85	WH	5.85	PVS (breaker), Carlton - scrapped
1866	ALD866B		4.64	U	960	5.87	NX	8.87	Beckett (breaker), Carlton
									8.87 Hardwick (breaker), Carlton - scrapped
1867	ALD867B		4.64	U	350	2.85	T	3.85	PVS (breaker), Carlton
									1.86 Rollinson (breaker), Carlton - scrapped
1868	ALD868B		4.64	U	1844	4.84	Q	9.84	PVS (breaker), Carlton
									9.84 Rollinson (breaker), Carlton - scrapped
1869	ALD869B		4.64	U	1825	9.84	TC	12.84	PVS (breaker), Carlton
									12.84 Wigley (breaker), Carlton - scrapped
1870	ALD870B		4.64	U	1612	8.83	TC	8.84	PVS (breaker), Carlton - scrapped
1871	ALD871B		4.64	U	1903	11.84	CT	10.87	Southampton Citybus 416
									1.89 Southend Transport 113
									10.93 Lister (dealer), Bolton
									10.93 Brakell (dealer), Cheam
									4.95 Hobson (preserved), Royston, Herts
1872	ALD872B		4.64	U	1870	1.95	BN	1.95	South London Transport, London RM1872
1873	ALD873B	*31-3833*	4.64	U	1863	5.84	BW	9.84	Far East demonstrator for LT Bus Sales
		ES4007							11.87 Citybus, Kowloon, Hong Kong 2
		HK1932							
1874	ALD874B		*4.64*	*U*	*9985*	*2.86*	*CT*	*6.86*	*Strathtay Scottish SR15*
									4.90 Kelbie (dealer), Turriff
									5.90 Ripley (breaker), Carlton - scrapped
1875	*ALD875B*		*4.64*	*ON*	*1843*	*6.84*	*NX*	*12.84*	
									12.84 Rollinson (breaker), Carlton - scrapped
1876	ALD876B		4.64	ON	1858	6.84	AL	8.84	PVS (breaker), Carlton
									8.84 Wigley (breaker), Carlton - scrapped
1877	ALD877B		4.64	U	1792	2.91	AK	8.92	PVS (breaker), Carlton - scrapped
1878	ALD878B		4.64	U	1717	6.84	AL	8.84	Hyper & Hyper, Kensington, London
									10.85 Turbeton (dealer), London
									2.86 Allmey (dealer), Eastcote
									10.86 London Borough of Wandsworth 1142
1879	ALD879B		4.64	U	30	3.85	T	6.85	PVS (breaker), Carlton - scrapped
1880	ALD880B		4.64	U	1834	10.84	W	2.85	PVS (breaker), Carlton - scrapped
1881	ALD881B		4.64	U	1628	10.85	SW	9.86	PVS (breaker), Carlton
									9.86 Wigley (breaker), Carlton - scrapped
1882	ALD882B		4.64	U	1782	1.95	BN	1.95	South London Transport, London RM1882
1883	ALD883B		4.64	U	1853	3.84	AR	6.84	Achimer Simonbrot Fabric, Germany
									10.91 Action Car Service, Koln, Germany
1884	ALD884B		4.64	U	1862	5.84	AR	6.84	P.Sykes (breaker), Barnsley - scrapped
1885	ALD885B	*YBB15167*	4.64	U	1871	6.84	T	9.84	King Food Corporation, Potchefstroom, South Africa
1886	ALD886B		4.64	U	1856	8.84	WH	9.84	PVS (breaker), Carlton
									9.84 Wigley (breaker), Carlton - scrapped

Vext page

ooking immaculate as it operates service 94 from Birmingham city centre to Chelmsley Wood in March 1993 s Frontline Buses KVS601, a well travelled Routemaster which had previously been a member of the Kelvin cottish fleet in which it was re-registered from WLT471 to EDS394A. (J.Whitmore)

fter first operating for Gash of Newark in its London red livery, WLT757 was repainted into its owner's fleet olours as seen here at its depot in May 1989 immediately after Gash's business had been purchased by incolnshire Road Car Co. Ltd. Two months later it was sold to East Yorkshire Motor Services by whom it is ill used in daily service. (K.A.Jenkinson)

94
Saltley Washwood Heath
Ward End Castle Bromwich
CHELMSLEY WOOD PINE SQUARE
KVS 601

GO GASH
W. GASH & SONS
TO HIRE
TEL. (0636) 702453
GO GASH
WLT 757
NO PARKING IN FRONT OF DOORS

Bucks Free Press
Bucks Free Press
Bucks Free Press Group
RM 238
VLT 238

Kelvin SCOTTISH
pirate in you
876R
SCOTTISH

1887	ALD887B		4.64	U	1868	7.84	AG	4.86	Hagle, Moss, Norway
		AX32911							8.92 Halden Traffik, Halden, Norway
1888	ALD888B	*BA4 850*	4.64	U	1861	5.84	T	4.85	Double Deck Tours, Niagara, Canada
1889	ALD889B		5.64	U	1914	11.85	TL	10.87	Southampton Citybus (not used)
									10.88 London Bus Export Co. (dlr), Chepstow
									5.89 Nichimen Corporation, Tokyo, Japan
1890	ALD890B		4.64	U	543	8.85	Q	10.85	Clydeside Scottish 262 (RM1890)
									5.89 Western Scottish C77
									8.90 PVS (breaker), Carlton
									9.90 Wigley (breaker), Carlton - scrapped
1891	ALD891B		5.64	U	1876	2.84	B	6.84	Booth (breaker), Rotherham - scrapped
1892	ALD892B		5.64	U	1816	10.84	WH	4.85	PVS (breaker), Carlton - scrapped
1893	ALD893B		5.64	U	1894	8.84	V	12.84	PVS (breaker), Carlton
									7.85 Rollinson (breaker), Carlton - scrapped
1894	ALD894B		5.64	U	2194	3.94	RA	1.95	London Central Buses, London (for spares)
									1.95 South London Transport (for spares)
									2.95 PVS (breaker), Carlton - scrapped
1895	ALD895B		5.64	U	1887	7.84	AG	4.85	PVS (breaker), Carlton
									4.85 Wigley (breaker), Carlton - scrapped
1896	ALD896B		5.64	U	1615	4.84	AR	8.84	PVS (breaker), Carlton - scrapped

1874	ALD874B		4.64	U	9985	2.86	CT	6.86	Strathtay Scottish SR15
									4.90 Kelbie (dealer), Turriff
									5.90 Ripley (breaker), Carlton - scrapped
1875	ALD875B		4.64	ON	1843	6.84	NX	12.84	PVS (breaker), Carlton
									12.84 Rollinson (breaker), Carlton - scrapped
1876	ALD876B		4.64	ON	1858	6.84	AL	8.84	PVS (breaker), Carlton
									8.84 Wigley (breaker), Carlton - scrapped
1877	ALD877B		4.64	U	1792	2.91	AK	8.92	PVS (breaker), Carlton - scrapped
1878	ALD878B		4.64	U	1717	6.84	AL	8.84	Hyper & Hyper, Kensington, London
									10.85 Turbeton (dealer), London
									2.86 Allmey (dealer), Eastcote
									10.86 London Borough of Wandsworth 1142
1879	ALD879B		4.64	U	30	3.85	T	6.85	PVS (breaker), Carlton - scrapped
1880	ALD880B		4.64	U	1834	10.84	W	2.85	PVS (breaker), Carlton - scrapped
1881	ALD881B		4.64	U	1628	10.85	SW	9.86	PVS (breaker), Carlton
									9.86 Wigley (breaker), Carlton - scrapped
1882	ALD882B		4.64	U	1782	1.95	BN	1.95	South London Transport, London RM1882
1883	ALD883B		4.64	U	1853	3.84	AR	6.84	Achimer Simonbrot Fabric, Germany
									10.91 Action Car Service, Koln, Germany
1884	ALD884B		4.64	U	1862	5.84	AR	6.84	P.Sykes (breaker), Barnsley - scrapped
1885	ALD885B	*YBB15167*	4.64	U	1871	6.84	T	9.84	King Food Corporation, Potchefstroom, South Africa
1886	ALD886B		4.64	U	1856	8.84	WH	9.84	PVS (breaker), Carlton
									9.84 Wigley (breaker), Carlton - scrapped

1887	ALD887B		4.64	U	1868	7.84	AG	4.86	Hagle, Moss, Norway
		AX32911							8.92 Halden Traffik, Halden, Norway
1888	ALD888B	*BA4 850*	4.64	U	1861	5.84	T	4.85	Double Deck Tours, Niagara, Canada

Previous page

Converted to semi open-top configuration for use as a promotional vehicle by Bucks Free Press, former RM238 is seen here carrying out its duties at the Coach & Bus Show at Birmingham's National Exhibition Centre in October 1989. (K.A.Jenkinson)

Its passenger-carrying days having ended, Kelvin Scottish 1922 (EDS295A, originally WLT741) was heavily cannibalised for spares at Old Kilpatrick depot during 1991 before being sold later that year to Lockhart (breaker) in whose Shaws Hill yard it is seen here three years later. (K.A.Jenkinson)

1889	ALD889B		5.64	U	1914	11.85	TL	10.87	Southampton Citybus (not used)
									10.88 London Bus Export Co. (dlr), Chepstow
									5.89 Nichimen Corporation, Tokyo, Japan
1890	ALD890B		4.64	U	543	8.85	Q	10.85	Clydeside Scottish 262 (RM1890)
									5.89 Western Scottish C77
									8.90 PVS (breaker), Carlton
									9.90 Wigley (breaker), Carlton - scrapped
1891	ALD891B		5.64	U	1876	2.84	B	6.84	Booth (breaker), Rotherham - scrapped
1892	ALD892B		5.64	U	1816	10.84	WH	4.85	PVS (breaker), Carlton - scrapped
1893	ALD893B		5.64	U	1894	8.84	V	12.84	PVS (breaker), Carlton
									7.85 Rollinson (breaker), Carlton - scrapped
1894	ALD894B		5.64	U	2194	3.94	RA	1.95	London Central Buses, London (for spares)
									1.95 South London Transport (for spares)
									2.95 PVS (breaker), Carlton - scrapped
1895	ALD895B		5.64	U	1887	7.84	AG	4.85	PVS (breaker), Carlton
									4.85 Wigley (breaker), Carlton - scrapped
1896	ALD896B		5.64	U	1615	4.84	AR	8.84	PVS (breaker), Carlton - scrapped
1897	ALD897B		5.64	U	1836	11.85	NX	9.86	Hernould, Antwerp, Belgium
1898	ALD898B		5.64	U	10	8.85	WN	8.85	PVS (breaker), Carlton
									8.85 Wigley (breaker), Carlton - scrapped
1899	ALD899B		5.64	U	499	8.85	ED	8.85	PVS (breaker), Carlton - scrapped
1900	ALD900B		5.64	TC	1873	10.84	AK	12.84	PVS (breaker), Carlton - scrapped
1901	ALD901B		5.64	TC	1904	1.85	E	3.85	PVS (breaker), Carlton - scrapped
1902	ALD902B		5.64	U	1909	6.84	GM	8.84	PVS (breaker), Carlton
									8.84 Wigley (breaker), Carlton - scrapped
1903	ALD903B		5.64	TC	527	4.85	WH	5.85	PVS (breaker), Carlton
									6.85 Wigley (breaker), Carlton - scrapped
1904	ALD904B	*BE9 679*	5.64	TC	1610	1.85	CF	5.86	Piccadilly Bus Tours, Ottowa, Canada
1905	ALD905B		5.64	U	459	8.85	T	9.85	PVS (breaker), Carlton - scrapped
1906	ALD906B		5.64	TC	1948	8.85	AG	9.85	PVS (breaker), Carlton
									9.85 Wigley (breaker), Carlton - scrapped
1907	ALD907B		5.64	TC	541	12.84	N	5.85	PVS (breaker), Carlton
									6.85 Wigley (breaker), Carlton - scrapped
1908	ALD908B		5.64	U	1864	6.84	AR	12.84	PVS (breaker), Carlton - scrapped
1909	ALD909B	*BD4 332*	5.64	U	1881	10.84	W	4.85	Copperfield Roadhouses, Ontario, Canada
		BA4 804							.89 Double Deck Tours, Niagara, Canada
1910	ALD910B		5.64	U	36	11.84	PM	12.84	PVS (breaker), Carlton - scrapped
1911	ALD911B	YSL76B	5.64	U	568	11.85	X	6.86	Strathtay Scottish SR14
									6.92 Lister (dealer), Bolton
									6.92 Southend Transport (not used)
									6.92 Anglo European Trade, Budapest, Hungary
1912	ALD912B		6.64	AF	73	8.85	Q	12.85	Videogram Tours, France
									.87 Vatoux, Bonnerville, France
									.91 Le Grons Pub, Araches, France
1913	ALD913B		6.64	AF	525	8.85	SF	10.85	Clydeside Scottish 263 (RM1913)
									5.89 Western Scottish C78
									9.90 PVS (breaker), Carlton
									9.91 Bentley & Worsnop (preserved), Halifax
1914	ALD914B	YSL75B	6.64	AF	22	10.85	N	7.86	Strathtay Scottish SR18
									10.91 Cosgrove (breaker), Dundee - scrapped
1915	ALD915B		6.64	AF	1448	12.87	AK	2.88	Clydeside Scottish (for spares)
									5.89 Western Scottish (for spares) - scrapped
1916	ALD916B		6.64	AF	2045	12.86	AV	9.87	W.Norths (dealer), Sherburn
									8.88 Queen Victoria Pub, Lloret de Mar, Spain
1917	ALD917B		6.64	AF	1905	5.84	CF	6.86	Kompas Touriftik, Frankfurt, Germany
									7.86 Kompas Touriftik, Portoroz, Yugoslavia
1918	ALD918B		6.64	AF	1901	6.84	T	9.84	King Food Corporation, Potchefstroom, South Africa
1919	ALD919B		6.64	AF	195	5.92	WD	5.92	London Coaches, London RM1919
1920	ALD920B		6.64	AF	1877	10.84	SW	12.84	PVS (breaker), Carlton
									12.84 Rollinson (breaker), Carlton - scrapped

White Rose of Glasshoughton was a short-lived operator of the Routemaster, running five Iveco-engined examples from December 1994 to May 1995. RM346 (SVS615) arrives in Leeds on the 164 service from Castleford in April 1995. (K.A.Jenkinson)

The short-lived Bournemouth area independent BHT Buses began operations with a fleet of Routemasters, many of which had previously served Kelvin Central Buses. One of these, 293 (YVS293) seen at The Square, Bournemouth in June 1993 had earlier operated for Clydeside Scottish who re-registered it LDS283A from its original WLT447 mark). (F.W.York)

Official London
Sightseeing Tour
Official London Sightseeing Tour
BLUE TRIANGLE
NMY632E

The Original LONDON TRANSPORT
SIGHTSEEING TOUR
THE ORIGINAL LONDON TRANSPORT SIGHTSEEING TOUR
LONDON TRANSPORT
WLT 450

1921	ALD921B		6.64	AF	1840	5.84	WH	6.87	Southampton Citybus (for spares)
									9.88 Morris (breaker), Carlton - scrapped
1922	ALD922B		7.64	AF	77	4.86	BN	9.86	PVS (breaker), Carlton
									9.86 Wigley (breaker), Carlton - scrapped
1923	ALD923B		6.64	AF	411	11.85	N	7.86	PVS (breaker), Carlton
									8.86 Wigley (breaker), Carlton - scrapped
1924	ALD924B		6.64	AF	1935	5.84	AG	4.85	Double Deck Bus Tours, Niagara, Canada
		BE1 823							5.87 McDonalds Restaurants, Toronto, Canada
1925	ALD925B		6,64	AF	1923	4.84	NX	8.84	PVS (breaker), Carlton
									8.84 Wigley (breaker), Carlton - scrappe
1926	ALD926B		6.64	AF	1946	11.84	SW	3.85	PVS (breaker), Carlton
									3.85 Wigley (breaker), Carlton - scrapped
1927	ALD927B		6.64	AF	463	4.85	T	6.85	PVS (breaker), Carlton - scrapped
1928	ALD928B		6.64	AF	1577	12.87	Q	2.88	PVS (breaker), Carlton - scrapped
1929	ALD929B		6.64	AF	1924	10.84	WH	10.88	PVS (breaker), Carlton - scrapped
1930	ALD930B		6.64	AF	1945	10.85	SW	4.87	Cabildo Insular de Lanzarote, Arrecife, Lanzarote
1931	ALD931B		6.64	AF	1933	10.84	NX	12.84	PVS (breaker), Carlton - scrapped
1932	ALD932B		6.64	AF	1927	7.87	V	7.87	PVS (breaker), Carlton - scrapped
1933	ALD933B		6.64	AF	1925	5.86	CF	8.86	Kelvin Scottish RM1933
									8.87 Stagecoach, Perth (not used)
									10.87 Cumberland Motor Services 904
1934	ALD934B		6.64	AF	2096	11.87	AD	12.87	PVS (breaker), Carlton
									12.87 Wigley (breaker), Carlton - scrapped
1935	ALD935B		7.64	H	2196	10.86	SF	4.87	PVS (breaker), Carlton - scrapped
1936	ALD936B		7.64	H	1936	2.85	BW	3.85	LT Bow garage Sports & Social Club
									.87 Hodgson (preserved), Collier Row
									4.95 Wright (dealer), Rainham
1937	ALD937B		7.64	H	1851	5.84	WH	6.84	Ensign (dealer), Purfleet
									6.84 PVS (breaker), Carlton - scrapped
1938	ALD938B		7.64	H	1823	12.84	AG	3.85	PVS (breaker), Carlton - scrapped
1939	ALD939B		7.64	H	1930	11.84	AG	1.86	PVS (breaker), Carlton - scrapped
1940	ALD940B		7.64	H	1952	9.85	NX	11.85	PVS (breaker), Carlton
									11.85 Wigley (breaker), Carlton - scrapped
1941	ALD941B		7.64	MH	1993	6.86	BN	9.86	Kelvin Scottish RM1941
									8.87 Stagecoach, Perth (not used)
									10.87 Cumberland Motor Services 902
1942	ALD942B		7.64	H	2004	2.91	AK	6.91	PVS (breaker), Carlton - scrapped
1943	ALD943B	*BB4 951*	7.64	H	1934	7.84	Q	5.86	Piccadilly Bus Tours, Ottowa, Canada
1944	ALD944B		7.64	H	1939	1.84	AR	6.84	Ripley (breaker), Carlton - scrapped
1945	ALD945B		7.64	H	1937	10.83	AP	12.83	Booth (breaker), Rotherham
									12.83 Goodwin (breaker), Carlton - scrapped
1946	ALD946B		7.64	H	2069	12.93	FY	4.94	PVS (breaker), Carlton - scrapped
1947	ALD947B		7.64	H	1932	5.84	Q	7.84	Herr Kustermann, Ulm, Germany
1948	ALD948B		7.64	H	2217	9.94	X	9.94	Centrewest, London RM1948
1949	ALD949B		7.64	H	1944	9.84	AG	6.85	Dolphin Internat'l Displays (agent), St.Albans
									7.85 Unknown, Los Angeles, USA
1950	ALD950B	*BB4 953*	7.64	MH	1926	11.85	B	5.86	Piccadilly Bus Tours, Ottowa, Canada

Previous page

New to British European Airways in 1967, front entrance Routemaster NMY632E was purchased by London Transport in November 1976 and numbered RMA49. Never used, it was sold for preservation in October 198 and was ultimately put into service in 1985 on Round London Sightseeing duties by Blue Triangle of Rainham who numbered it RMS49. It is seen here at Charing Cross station, London in April 1993. (P.T.Stokes)

Converted to open-top configuration in August 1988 for use on London Sightseeing duties, RM450 was at this same time fitted with a wheelchair lift to its nearside lower deck. Passing to London Coaches upon its privatisation in 1992, it is seen here at Gravesend away from its usual haunts. (D.W.Rhodes)

1951	ALD951B		7.64	MH	1947	11.91	PM	8.92	PVS (breaker), Carlton
									8.92 Parasel Society An'my, Montevideo, Uruguay
1952	ALD952B		7.64	H	1940	12.84	AG	2.85	PVS (breaker), Carlton
									2.85 Wigley (breaker), Carlton - scrapped
1953	ALD953B		7.64	H	1953	11.84	T	1.85	PVS (breaker), Carlton - scrapped
1954	ALD954B		7.64	H	1950	10.83	AK	7.84	PVS (breaker), Carlton
									7.84 Rollinson (breaker), Carlton - scrapped
1955	ALD955B		7.64	H	2089	10.94	NX	10.94	London Central Buses, London RM1955
1956	ALD956B		7.64	H	1942	3.84	AP	6.84	PVS (breaker), Carlton - scrapped
1957	ALD957B		7.64	MH	1912	4.84	B	8.84	PVS (breaker), Carlton - scrapped
1958	ALD958B		7.64	MH	2039	1.85	AG	3.85	PVS (breaker), Carlton - scrapped
1959	ALD959B		7.64	MH	2021	5.86	WD	9.86	Kelvin Scottish RM1959
		WLT984							8.87 Clydeside Scottish (for spares)
									9.87 # W.Norths (dealer), Sherburn
									3.89 PVS (breaker), Carlton - scrapped
1960	ALD960B		7.64	MH	1938	12.84	Q	10.86	PVS (breaker), Carlton
									11.86 Wigley (breaker), Carlton - scrapped
1961	ALD961B		7.64	MH	2018	10.86	HT	1.87	PVS (breaker), Carlton
									2.87 Wigley (breaker), Carlton - scrapped
1962	ALD962B		7.64	MH	1988	10.94	Q	10.94	London Central Buses, London RM1972
1963	ALD963B		7.64	MH	2092	9.86	N	9.86	PVS (breaker), Carlton - scrapped
1964	ALD964B		7.64	MH	2019	6.86	SF	9.86	PVS (breaker), Carlton - scrapped
1965	ALD965B		7.64	MH	1981	5.86	Q	10.86	PVS (breaker), Carlton - scrapped
1966	ALD966B		7.64	MH	1975	12.87	GM	4.88	Blackpool Transport 529
1967	ALD967B		7.64	MH	1951	9.84	NX	11.84	PVS (breaker), Carlton - scrapped
1968	ALD968B		7.64	MH	1153	2.87	TH	5.87	Hampshire Bus (not used)
									11.87 Magicbus, Glasgow 616
									10.90 Stagecoach, Perth 616
									10.94 Bluebird Buses 616
1969	ALD969B		7.64	MH	1966	3.87	Q	.88	Southampton Citybus
									10.89 Amex Trading (dealer), Buxton
									8.90 Unknown, USA
1970	ALD970B		7.64	MH	2076	6.92	PDt	10.94	PVS (breaker), Carlton *- for scrap*
1971	ALD971B		7.64	MH	2087	10.94	HT	10.94	London Northern Bus Co., London RM1971
1972	ALD972B		7.64	MH	2006	9.85	HT	11.85	PVS (breaker), Carlton
									11.85 Wigley (breaker), Carlton - scrapped
1973	ALD973B		7.64	MH	1989	8.87	E	9.87	PVS (breaker), Carlton
									9.87 Wigley (breaker), Carlton - scrapped
1974	ALD974B		8.64	PB	2027	5.86	GM	6.86	PVS (breaker), Carlton - scrapped
1975	ALD975B		7.64	J	1970	8.86	Q	3.87	Mooney (preserved), London
									6.90 North Mymms Coaches,Potters Bar
									11.92 Hemmings (preserved), St.Albans
									6.93 Wright (preserved), Paisley
1976	ALD976B		8.64	PB	2041	4.87	PM	6.87	PVS (breaker), Carlton - scrapped
1977	ALD977B		7.64	J	2114	10.94	NX	10.94	London Central Buses, London RM1977
1978	ALD978B		7.64	MH	1994	12.94	BN	12.94	South London Transport, London RM1978
1979	ALD979B		7.64	J	2081	10.94	HT	10.94	London Northern Bus Co., London RM1979
1980	ALD980B		7.64	J	1998	10.94	NX	10.94	London Central Buses, London RM1980
1981	ALD981B		8.64	PB	1943	11.84	NX	12.84	PVS (breaker), Carlton - scrapped

---

Next page

Although Clydeside Scottish purchased three ex.BEA front entrance Routemasters, only KGJ614D was placed in passenger service. This was given coach-type seating and the company's Quicksilver livery and was numbered SRMA1 before taking up its duties in 1988. (K.A.Jenkinson)

The first of a large number of Routemasters to be acquired by Clydeside Scottish, RM652 was initially evaluated by the company in July 1985 and was purchased three months later. Seen here in Paisley soon after being repainted into its new owner's fleet livery, it was adorned with the original style of promotional lettering applied to most buses in the fleet upon its formation from Western Scottish. (K.A.Jenkinson)

1
PRIVATE
Clydeside's
Welcome aboard. We're going your way.
SRMA 1
It'll bring out the pirate in you

613
Falside Road
Park Road
SMITHHILLS STREET
Clydeside
Best Bus with us
WLT 652

A comparative newcomer to the ranks of Routemaster operators is Greater Reading Omnibus whose fleet has grown considerably since the company's formation in 1994. No.10 (WYJ857, originally VLT172) fitted with body no.20 with fixed front upper deck glazing typifies this immaculate fleet which trades as Reading Mainline. (J.A.Godwin)

Amongst the most recent new British operators of the Routemaster is Chester Bus & Boat whose EGF285B (RM1836) is seen in Chester in June 1995 after being converted to open-top configuration for sightseeing duties. (B.Newsome)

1982	ALD982B		8.64	PB	2062	10.86	V	6.87	PVS (breaker), Carlton - scrapped
1983	ALD983B		8.64	PB	2005	6.86	CA	9.86	Kelvin Scottish RM1983
									8.87 Stagecoach, Perth (not used)
									10.87 Cumberland Motor Services 903
1984	ALD984B		8.64	PB	2079	6.87	AK	11.87	Clydeside Scottish (for spares)
									7.88 PVS (breaker), Carlton - scrapped
1985	ALD985B		8.64	PB	2050	2.87	CT	6.87	PVS (breaker), Carlton - scrapped
1986	ALD986B	*60-Sri-6618*	8.64	PB	2066	4.88	FY	12.88	Sri Lanka Transport Board
1987	ALD987B		7.64	PB	1997	2.87	AF	11.87	Clydeside Scottish (for spares)
									5.89 Western Scottish (for spares)
									8.89 Kelvin Central Buses (for spares)
									10.89 PVS (breaker), Carlton - scrapped
1988	ALD988B		7.64	PB	2048	11.88	HT	9.89	La Manda Diara Ponet, Lerida, Spain
1989	ALD989B		7.64	PB	1967	2.88	Q	4.88	Blackpool Transport 530
1990	ALD990B		7.64	PB	2028	6.86	SW	10.86	Gash, Newark RM19
									5.89 Lincolnshire Road Car Co., 1119
									7.89 East Yorkshire Motor Services 811
									3.95 Greater Reading Omnibus, Reading 25
1991	ALD991B		7.64	PB	2046	10.90	GMt	12.90	Antenna TV, Athens, Greece
1992	ALD992B		8.64	PB	1982	2.94	NX	12.94	PVS (breaker), Carlton - *for scrap*
1993	ALD993B		9.64	D	1965	8.86	ED	5.87	Southampton Citybus 403
									5.88 Durrant (preserved), Ilford
1994	ALD994B		8.64	PB	1977	6.87	PM	8.90	PVS (breaker), Carlton - scrapped
1995	ALD995B		8.64	PB	2102	10.84	EM	1.85	PVS (breaker), Carlton - scrapped
1996	ALD996B		8.64	PB	2017	6.90	AC+	8.90	PVS (breaker), Carlton
									8.90 Wigley (breaker), Carlton - scrapped
1998	ALD997B		9.64	D	1990	3.87	CT	6.87	PVS (breaker), Carlton - scrapped
1998	ALD998B		9.64	D	2120	10.83	CA	8.84	PVS (breaker), Carlton - scrapped
1999	ALD999B		9.64	D	2085	2.83	NX	12.83	Ensign (dealer), Purfleet
									6.84 PVS (breaker), Carlton - scrapped
2000	ALM200B		9.64	D	1971	7.94	NX	10.94	PVS (breaker), Carlton - *for scrap*
2001	ALM1B	EYY128B	9.64	D	2078	4.87	PM	6.87	PVS (breaker), Carlton - scrapped
2002	ALM2B	EGF299B	9.64	AE	2023	6.94	St	11.94	PVS (breaker), Carlton
									11.94 Brakell (dealer), Cheam - *for resale*
2003	ALM3B		9.64	D	2080	4.94	NXt	11.94	PVS (breaker), Carlton
									11.94 de la Parra, Vargas, Mexico City
2004	ALM4B		9.64	AE	1958	10.86	N	1.87	PVS (breaker), Carlton
									2.87 Wigley (breaker), Carlton - scrapped
2005	ALM5B		9.64	AE	1919	11.85	AL	5.87	Southampton Citybus 407
									1.89 Southend Transport 114
									8.93 Martin (dealer), Middlewich
		64 D 805							3.94 McConn, Rathcool, Eire
2006	ALM6B		9.64	AE	2007	6.86	N	9.86	Kelvin Scottish RM2006
									8.87 Clydeside Scottish (for spares)
									11.87 PVS (breaker), Carlton - scrapped
2007	ALM7B		9.64	AE	2106	12.86	T	2.87	PVS (breaker), Carlton
									2.87 Wigley (breaker), Carlton - scrapped
2008	ALM8B		9.64	AE	2116	2.94	NX	5.94	PVS (breaker), Carlton - scrapped
2009	ALM9B		9.64	AE	2119	4.89	HT	6.90	PVS (breaker), Carlton
									6.90 Wigley (breaker), Carlton - scrapped
2010	ALM10B		9.64	AE	1957	6.86	AL	12.86	Button Designs, London
									2.87 Natham, New Orleans, USA
2011	ALM11B		9.64	AE	1960	7.86	ED	6.87	Southampton Citybus 409
									2.91 Southend Transport 118
									2.94 Greater Reading Omnibus, Reading 4
2012	ALM12B		9.64	AE	2115	7.88	Q	1.90	PVS (breaker), Carlton - scrapped
2013	ALM13B		9.64	AE	2090	1.88	NX	3.88	Burnley & Pendle Transport (for spares)
									9.89 PVS (breaker), Carlton
									9.89 Wigley (breaker), Carlton - scrapped
2014	ALM14B		9.64	AE	2001	9.92	X	10.92	PVS (breaker), Carlton - scrapped
2015	ALM15B		9.64	AE	1985	7.92	GM	5.93	PVS (breaker), Carlton - scrapped
2016	ALM16B		10.64	GM	2057	4.91	Nt	6.91	PVS (breaker), Carlton - scrapped
2017	ALM17B		10.64	GM	1983	10.83	GM	5.84	Anglers Co., New York, USA
		7936H							6.88 Chicago Motor Coach Co, Chicago, USA

18	ALM18B		9.64	AE	1956	8.86	AL	10.87	Southampton Citybus (not used)
									10.88 London Bus Export Co. (dlr), Chepstow
									5.89 Nichimen Corporation, Tokyo, Japan
19	ALM19B		10.64	GM	2003	5.86	Q	9.86	PVS (breaker), Carlton
									9.86 Wigley (breaker), Carlton - scrapped
0	ALM20B		10.64	GM	1668	1.85	Q	2.85	PVS (breaker), Carlton - scrapped
1	ALM21B		9.64	AE	2031	8.94	AR	*3.95*	*London Transport Buses reserve fleet*
2	ALM22B		10.64	GM	2014	10.94	NX	10.94	London Central Buses, London RM2022
3	ALM23B		10.64	GM	2030	10.94	HT	10.94	London Northern Bus Co., London RM2023
4	ALM24B		10.64	GM	2072	2.87	AL	5.87	Stagecoach, Perth (not used)
									10.87 Cumberland Motor Services 901
5	ALM25B		10.64	GM	1928	10.84	WH	10.86	PVS (breaker), Carlton
									11.86 Wigley (breaker), Carlton - scrapped
6	ALM26B		10.64	GM	1961	2.87	AL	10.87	Southampton Citybus (not used)
									10.88 London Bus Export Co. (dealer), Chepstow
									7.89 Unknown, Japan
7	ALM27B		10.64	GM	2020	5.86	AG	8.86	Kelvin Scottish (for spares)
									7.87 PVS (breaker), Carlton - scrapped
8	ALM28B		10.64	GM	1962	6.86	NX	11.86	PVS (breaker), Carlton - scrapped
9	ALM29B		10.64	GM	2101	10.86	AC	3.87	PVS (breaker), Carlton - scrapped
0	ALM30B		10.64	GM	1995	6.86	CF	9.86	PVS (breaker), Carlton - scrapped
1	ALM31B		11.64	GM	1959	1.88	BW	9.89	PVS (breaker), Carlton - scrapped
2	ALM32B		10.64	GM	2104	11.87	V	1.88	Brakell (dealer), Cheam
		157-7-MJ59							8.90 Octobus SARL, Paris, France
	ALM33B		11.64	N	1987	5.94	X	*3.95*	*London Transport Buses reserve fleet*
	ALM34B		10.64	GM	2060	8.87	E	8.88	Southend Transport 110
									2.94 Clydeside 2000 (dealer), Paisley
									2.94 Greater Reading Omnibus, Reading 1
	ALM35B		10.64	GM	2011	6.86	E	9.86	Kelvin Scottish RM2035 (1952) (1940)
									4.89 Kelvin Cental Buses 1940
									10.92 Dunsmore (breaker), Larkhall - *for scrap*
	ALM36B		10.64	GM	2049	5.87	AK	8.87	Walthamstow Salvage (breaker), Walthamstow
									8.87 Hardwick (breaker), Carlton - scrapped
	ALM37B		10.64	GM	1980	3.87	N	5.87	Southampton Citybus 404
									3.89 Rayner (preserved), Reading
									6.91 Rayner (preserved), Wokingham
	ALM38B		12.64	N	2032	6.87	AK	10.87	PVS (breaker), Carlton - scrapped
	ALM39B		10.64	GM	1986	3.87	AG	6.87	PVS (breaker), Carlton - scrapped
	ALM40B		10.64	GM	2037	2.88	Q	3.88	United Counties Omnibus Co. (for spares)
									6.89 Smith (breaker), Bedford - scrapped at UCOCKettering depot
	ALM41B		10.64	GM	2016	10.94	HT	10.94	London Northern Bus Co., London RM2041
	ALM42B		11.64	GM	1973	4.86	N	9.89	PVS (breaker), Carlton
									9.89 Wigley (breaker), Carlton - scrapped
	ALM43B		11.64	GM	1949	12.86	N	6.87	Southampton Citybus 412
									10.88 London Bus Export Co. (dlr), Chepstow
									7.89 Unknown, Japan
	ALM44B		11.64	GM	2058	10.86	HT	1.87	PVS (breaker), Carlton
									2.87 Wigley (breaker), Carlton - scrapped
	ALM45B		11.64	GM	2022	6.86	X	8.86	Kelvin Scottish (for spares)
									7.87 PVS (breaker), Carlton - scrapped
	ALM46B		11.64	N	2008		PD	6.94	Unknown
	ALM47B		11.64	GM	1963	10.84	AR	11.84	PVS (breaker), Carlton
									12.84 Rollinson (breaker), Carlton - scrapped
	ALM48B		11.64	GM	2047	6.86	HT	9.86	Clydeside Scottish RM2048
									5.89 Western Scottish C80
									8.90 PVS (breaker), Carlton - scrapped
	ALM49B	*60-Sri-6617*	11.64	GM	2024	4.88	PM	12.88	Sri Lanka Transport Board
	ALM50B		11.64	N	1968		WD	11.87	Lever (preserved), Sutton
									8.89 London Buses, London RM2050
			9.90	U		11.93	BW	*3.95*	*London Transport Buses reserve fleet*
	ALM51B		11.64	GM	2036	10.94	NX	10.94	London Central Buses, London RM2051

Pictured at the Dunbar vintage vehicle rally in the late summer of 1994 is McGill of Barrhead's immaculate VYJ893 which was previously one of London's showbus Routemasters RM89. (C.Morrison)

One of a number of refurbished RMLs leased to BTS of Borehamwood for use on contracted service 13, RML2322 like its sisters carries a route diagram on its side panels.

2B
RM1909
D

PEAK TRAMWAYS
COMPANY LIMITED
PEAK TRAMWAY
COMPANY LIMITED
山頂纜車
山頂纜車
EZ 8347

2052	ALM52B		11.64	GM	2038	10.83	PM	7.84	PVS (breaker), Carlton - scrapped
2053	ALM53B		11.64	GM	2088	3.87	Q	11.87	Clydeside Scottish (for spares)
									3.90 Scrapped by Clydeside Scottish
2054	ALM54B		11.64	N	2091	11.86	AV	3.87	PVS (breaker), Carlton - scrapped
2055	ALM55B		11.64	N	2054	1.90	BNt	6.90	PVS (breaker), Carlton - scrapped
2056	ALM56B		11.64	GM	2073	5.86	AV	9.86	Kelvin Scottish (for spares)
									7.87 PVS (breaker), Carlton - scrapped
2057	ALM57B		11.64	N	2029	11.86	WD	2.87	PVS (breaker), Carlton - scrapped
2058	ALM58B		11.64	N	1000	6.86	Q	8.86	Kelvin Scottish RM2058
									8.87 Clydeside Scottish (for spares)
									9.87 # W.Norths (dealer), Sherburn
									3.89 PVS (breaker), Carlton - scrapped
2059	ALM59B		11.64	N	1929	2.86	CF	5.87	Southampton Citybus 413
									10.89 Amex Trading (dealer), Buxton
									9.92 Haywood (preserved), Shortlands
									5.93 Long term loan to Delaine, Bourne 113
2060	ALM60B		11.64	N	2107	11.87	V	1.88	United Counties Omnibus Co. 716
									10.92 Ribble Motor Services (not used)
2061	ALM61B		11.64	N	2003	2.92	TL	7.92	PVS (breaker), Carlton
									7.92 Wigley (breaker), Carlton - scrapped
2062	ALM62B		11.64	N	1972	7.84	Q	8.84	PVS (breaker), Carlton - scrapped
2063	ALM63B		11.64	N	2097	3.87	Q	11.87	Magicbus, Glasgow
									4.89 East Midland Motor Services RM2063
									7.92 Lister (dealer), Bolton
									7.92 Brakell (dealer), Cheam
		531 647B							8.93 Levy, Borrowdale, Harare, Zimbabwe
2064	ALM64B		11.64	N	1969	11.83	AP	9.84	PVS (breaker), Carlton - scrapped
2065	ALM65B		11.64	N	2012	8.86	Q	10.86	Gash, Newark RM20
									5.89 Lincolnshire Road Car Co. 1120
									7.89 East Yorkshire Motor Services 812
2066	ALM66B		11.64	N	1941	10.83	T	12.83	Booth (breaker), Rotherham - scrapped
2067	ALM67B		11.64	N	2025	6.86	Q	9.86	PVS (breaker), Carlton - scrapped
2068	ALM68B		11.64	N	1955	5.86	GM	7.86	PVS (breaker), Carlton - scrapped
2069	ALM69B		11.64	N	2034	8.86	Q	9.86	PVS (breaker), Carlton - scrapped
2070	ALM70B		11.64	N	2070	5.86	TC	9.86	Kelvin Scottish RM2070 (1954)
									1.89 PVS (breaker), Carlton - scrapped
2071	ALM71B		12.64	N	1954	10.87	HT	4.88	Blackpool Transport 531
2072	ALM72B		11.64	N	2055	5.86	BW	8.86	Kelvin Scottish RM2072 (1955)
									1.89 Scrapped by Kevin Scottish
2073	ALM73B		11.64	N	2010	5.86	GM	8.86	Kelvin Scottish RM2073 (1939)
									4.89 Kelvin Central Buses 1939
									6.93 Regal (dealer), Kirkintilloch
									1.95 PVS (breaker), Carlton
									2.95 Wigley (breaker), Carlton - *for scrap*
2074	ALM74B		11.64	N	2002	11.88	AD	1.89	PVS (breaker), Carlton
									2.89 Wigley (breaker), Carlton - scrapped
2075	ALM75B		11.64	N	1999	3.89	X	1.90	PVS (breaker), Carlton - scrapped
2076	ALM76B		12.64	N	1976	5.89	HT	1.90	PVS (breaker), Carlton - scrapped
2077	ALM77B		11.64	N	2042	2.87	N	8.87	Sargeant, Hanworth
									6.88 Bickers Action Enterprises, Codenham
									11.88 Brakell (dealer), Cheam
									2.95 Unknown, Montevideo, Uruguay
2078	ALM78B		12.64	N	2043	8.93	AC	*3.95*	*London Transport Buses reserve fleet*
2079	ALM79B		12.64	N	2067	12.91	Tt	3.94	PVS (breaker), Carlton - scrapped
2080	ALM80B		12.64	N	2059	10.86	AV	5.88	PVS (breaker), Carlton - scrapped

Previous page

Seen in the ownership of Copperfield Roadhouses of Ontario, Canada to whom it was sold in April 1985, RM1909 later passed to Double Deck Tours of Niagara, Canada for use on sightseeing services.

After leaving London in 1987, RM1703 spent a couple of years in service with Clydeside Scottish before being exported to Citybus, Hong Kong who converted it to open-top configuration in 1992. It is seen here in its new surrounds in April 1995 in Peak Tramways livery. (D.Bentley)

081	ALM81B		12.64	N	2068	5.86	NX	8.86	Kelvin Scottish RM2081 (1938)
									4.89 Kelvin Central Buses 1938
									1.93 Ripley (breaker), Carlton
									3.93 Mancunian Bus Co., Manchester RM2081
									2.94 Ripley (breaker), Carlton
									2.94 Wright (dealer), Rainham
082	ALM82B		12.64	N	2026	2.94	NX	11.94	PVS (breaker), Carlton - *for scrap*
083	ALM83B		12.64	N	2053	8.86	GM	12.86	SBG Engineering, Kilmarnock
									2.87 Kelvin Scottish RM2083
									8.87 Clydeside Scottish RM2083
									5.89 Western Scottish C81
									5.90 Kelvin Central Buses 1942
									2.93 Regal (dealer), Kirkintilloch
									3.93 BHT Buses, Parkstone 283
									8.94 BPTA, Bournemouth 283
084	ALM84B		12.64	N	2071	3.87	BN	4.87	PVS (breaker), Carlton
									6.87 Wigley (breaker), Carlton - scrapped
085	ALM85B		12.64	N	1974	7.85	NX	11.86	PVS (breaker), Carlton - scrapped
086	ALM86B		12.64	N	2074	5.86	AG	9.86	Kelvin Scottish RM2086
									8.87 Clydeside Scottish (for spares)
									9.87 # W.Norths (dealer), Sherburn
									3.89 PVS (breaker), Carlton - scrapped
087	ALM87B		12.64	N	2077	2.87	X	3.88	Burnley & Pendle Transport 187
									5.92 Lister (dealer), Bolton
									6.92 Southend Transport (dealer)
									6.92 Anglo European Trade, Budapest, Hungary
88	ALM88B	*60-Sri-6638*	12.64	N	2015	1.88	BW	12.88	Sri Lanka Transport Board
89	ALM89B		12.64	N	1984	11.87	GM	4.88	Blackpool Transport 533
90	ALM90B		12.64	N	2095	1.94	NX	4.94	PVS (breaker), Carlton - scrapped
91	ALM91B		12.64	CF	1979	11.84	NB	11.85	PVS (breaker), Carlton
									11.85 Wigley (breaker), Carlton - scrapped
92	ALM92B	*60-Sri-6616*	12.64	N	2105	1.88	BW	1.88	Sri Lanka Transport Board
93	ALM93B		12.64	CF	2009	7.85	CA	9.85	PVS (breaker), Carlton - scrapped
94	ALM94B		12.64	CF	1978	3.89	X	1.90	PVS (breaker), Carlton - scrapped
95	ALM95B		12.64	CF	2056	11.87	V	2.88	Clydeside Scottish (for spares)
									5.89 Western Scottish (for spares)
									10.89 PVS (breaker), Carlton - scrapped
96	ALM96B		12.64	N	2111	11.87	HT	2.88	Clydeside Scottish (for spares)
									4.89 Scrapped by Clydeside Scottish
97	ALM97B		12.64	N	2083	3.94	AR	*3.95*	*London Transport Buses reserve fleet*
98	ALM98B		12.64	CF	2064	11.86	AV	2.87	PVS (breaker), Carlton - scrapped
99	ALM99B		12.64	N	1964	4.93	PM	9.94	PVS (breaker), Carlton - *for scrap*
100	ALM100B		12.64	CF	2013	3.91	AR	6.91	Northcliffe Newsapapers, London
									6.91 K.K.B.Tarsasag, Istvan, Hungary
01	ALM101B		12.64	N	2109	6.87	WD	8.88	Southend Transport 111
									9.93 Lister (dealer), Bolton
									9.93 Brakell (dealer), Cheam
									.94 Unknown, Germany
02	ALM102B		12.64	CF	2033	6.86	Q	9.86	Kelvin Scottish RM2102
									8.87 Clydeside Scottish (for spares)
									9.87 # W.Norths (dealer), Sherburn
									3.89 PVS (breaker), Carlton - scrapped

Next page

cquired from United Counties in May 1989, East Midland RM980 seen here in its unique livery at Clipstone, Mansfield in October 1990 passed to the Stagecoach fleet at Perth in October 1992, taking the fleet number 605. (K.A.Jenkinson)

reshly repainted into EastEnders livery, Burnley & Pendle ALM87B rests in Burnley bus station whilst operating the trunk service to Colne in 1988. (K.A.Jenkinson)

ooking immaculate in its traditional blue & cream East Yorkshire livery in 1993 is CUV210C which had reviously operated for Clydeside Scottish and Western Scottish since its departure from London in May 1987. (K.A.Jenkinson)

16
Ravensdale
Forest Town
Garibaldi
MANSFIEI
EAST/MIDLAND
WLT 980

Burnley & Pendle
19
DOT COTTON
DOT COTTON
EastEnders
Burnley & Pendle

3
ORCHARD PARK
EAST YORKSHIRE

llowing Kentish Bus's winning of the contract for the operation of route 19, several RMLs were leased to
company for its operation. Above, RML2619 & RML2343 are seen undergoing refurbishment and
ainting at South Yorkshire Transport's Rotherham workshops on 3 April 1993 whilst below RML2574 shows
its route diagram on its side panels at Cobham bus rally. (K.A.Jenkinson / T.S.Blackman)

2103	ALM103B	12.64	CF	2113	9.94	FY	9.94	CentreWest, London RM2103
2104	ALM104B	12.64	CF	2061	6.92	PDt	12.93	PVS (breaker), Carlton - scrapped
2105	ALM105B	12.64	CF	1996	12.86	E	2.87	PVS (breaker), Carlton
								2.87 Wigley (breaker), Carlton - scrapped
2106	CUV106C	1.65	BW	2065	10.94	Q	10.94	London Central Buses, London RM2106
2107	CUV107C	2.65	BW	2093	8.86	Q	12.86	SBG Engineering, Kilmarnock
								1.87 Clydeside Scottish RM2107
								5.89 Western Scottish C82
								9.90 PVS (breaker), Carlton
								9.90 Wright (dealer), Rainham
								7.92 Dale (preserved), Streatham
2108	CUV108C	1.65	BW	2052	6.86	CA	8.86	Kelvin Scottish RM2108
								8.87 Clydeside Scottish (for spares)
								9.87 # W.Norths (dealer), Sherburn
								5.89 PVS (breaker), Carlton - scrapped
2109	CUV109C	1.65	BW	2108	10.94	NX	10.94	London Central Buses, London RM2109
2110	CUV110C	2.65	BW	2082	12.86	HT	10.87	PVS (breaker), Carlton
								10.87 Wigley (breaker), Carlton - scrapped
2111	CUV111C	1.65	BW	2100	8.86	N	10.86	PVS (breaker), Carlton - scrapped
2112	CUV112C	1.65	BW	2051	4.94	NXt	10.94	PVS (breaker), Carlton - *for scrap*
2113	CUV113C	2.65	BW	2084	11.88	HT	9.89	Burgsport International (agent), Harrow
								10.89 Unknown, Tokyo, Japan
2114	CUV114C	2.65	BW	2112	10.87	AF	3.88	Burnley & Pendle Transport 184
								5.92 Lister (dealer), Bolton
								5.92 Southend Transport (not used)
								6.92 Anglo European Trade, Budapest, Hungary
2115	CUV115C	1.65	BW	2035	6.86	S	8.86	Kelvin Scottish RM2115
								8.87 Clydeside Scottish (for spares)
								9.87 # W.Norths (dealer), Sherburn
								1.89 PVS (breaker), Carlton - scrapped
2116	CUV116C	1.65	BW	2117	5.84	AP	6.84	LT Sports Assoc'n., Seven Kings LT garage
								2.87 Newham Transport Group (preserved), Woolwich
								6.87 Lunn & Muir (preserved), Egham
2117	CUV117C	1.65	BW	2086	7.92	GM	3.93	PVS (breaker), Carlton - scrapped
2118	CUV118C	2.65	BW	2044	3.87	N	4.87	PVS (breaker), Carlton
								6.87 Wigley (breaker), Carlton - scrapped
2119	CUV119C	2.65	BW	2098	3.87	AK	6.87	PVS (breaker), Carlton
								6.87 Wigley (breaker), Carlton - scrapped
2120	CUV120C	2.65	BW	1992	2.87	SW	5.87	Lombard North Central(agent), London
	HH-ED-930							5.87 Teleticke GMBH, Bremerhaven, German[y]
2121	CUV121C	1.65	BW	2094	12.86	AV	5.87	Hampshire Bus (not used)
								11.87 Magicbus, Glasgow 618
								4.92 Kelvin Central Buses 1947
								8.93 Turner (preserved), Bridge of Weir
2122	CUV122C	1.65	BW	2121	.87	AD	12.87	United Counties Omnibus Co. 707
								10.92 Ribble Motor Services (not used)
2123	CUV123C	2.65	BW	1931	12.84	BW	1.85	PVS (breaker), Carlton - scrapped
2124	CUV124C	1.65	BW	2099	7.87	WD	8.88	Southend Transport 112
								11.93 Lister (dealer), Bolton
								11.93 Brakell (dealer), Cheam - *for resale*
2125	CUV125C	2.65	BW	2118	10.89	Xt	6.90	PVS (breaker), Carlton
								6.90 Wigley (breaker), Carlton - scrapped
2126	CUV126C	2.65	BW	2110	4.91	Qt	7.92	PVS (breaker), Carlton - scrapped
2127	CUV127C	2.65	BW	2075	7.86	CF	9.86	PVS (breaker), Carlton - scrapped
2128	CUV128C	1.65	BW	2187	10.94	Q	10.94	London Central Buses, London RM2128
2129	CUV129C	2.65	BW	2206	5.93	AF	11.94	PVS (breaker), Carlton
								12.94 Armitage, Barnsley
2130	CUV130C	2.65	AC	2168	2.87	AF	6.87	PVS (breaker), Carlton
								6.87 Wigley (breaker), Carlton - scrapped
2131	CUV131C	2.65	AC	2190	5.93	GM	8.93	Autopart International (agent), Banbury
								8.93 Fukunishi Co., Osaka, Japan

2132	CUV132C		1.65	BW 2177	4.93	GM	10.94	PVS (breaker), Carlton - *for scrap*
2133	CUV133C		1.65	BW 2201	4.88	PM	8.88	Burnley & Pendle Transport 183
								7.92 Southend Transport (dealer)
								8.93 Royal Blue Line Tours, Victoria, Canada
2134	CUV134C		2.65	BW 1293	9.82	CT	12.82	Berry (bkr), Leicester - scrapped at Aldenham
2135	CUV135C		2.65	BW 2149	11.88	AD	1.90	PVS (breaker), Carlton - scrapped
2136	CUV136C		2.65	BW 2189	10.94	HT	10.94	London Northern Bus Co., London RM2136
2137	CUV137C		2.65	BW 2192	6.87	BN	10.87	PVS (breaker), Carlton - scrapped
2138	CUV138C		2.65	AC 2163	2.87	TH	6.87	PVS (breaker), Carlton
								7.87 Wigley (breaker), Carlton - scrapped
2139	CUV139C		2.65	BW 2169	12.86	SW	8.87	PVS (breaker), Carlton - scrapped
2140	CUV140C		2.65	BW 2180	12.86	AV	2.87	PVS (breaker), Carlton - scrapped
2141	CUV141C		2.65	BW 2162	3.87	NX	6.87	PVS (breaker), Carlton - scrapped
2142	CUV142C		2.65	BW 2126	2.92	TL	7.92	PVS (breaker), Carlton
								7.92 Wigley (breaker), Carlton - scrapped
2143	CUV143C		2.65	BW 2202		Xt	3.91	PVS (breaker), Carlton - scrapped
2144	CUV144C		2.65	BW 2210	11.87	X	1.88	Sergeant, Hanworth
								3.88 Green Lane Auto Spares (breaker), Feltham - scrapped
2145	CUV145C		2.65	BW 2212	10.88	AD	1.89	Nissho Iwai Corporation (agent), Japan
2146	CUV146C		2.65	AC 2170	3.87	N	4.87	PVS (breaker), Carlton - scrapped
2147	CUV147C		2.65	AC 2205	10.86	AR	3.87	PVS (breaker), Carlton - scrapped
2148	CUV148C		2.65	AC 2186	9.88	Q	10.88	PVS (breaker), Carlton - scrapped
2149	CUV149C		2.65	AC 2184	2.87	TH	6.87	PVS (breaker), Carlton - scrapped
2150	CUV150C		2.65	AC 2122	10.88	HT	4.89	Burgsport International (agent), Harrow
								4.89 Unknown, Osaka, Japan
2151	CUV151C		3.65	AC 2143	10.94	NX	10.94	London Central Buses, London RM2151
2152	CUV152C		2.65	AC 2185	1.87	AD	6.87	PVS (breaker), Carlton
								5.87 Redbridge Truck & Bus (dlr), Wakefield
								7.87 Great Knight Tours, Atlanta, USA
								12.94 Double Deck Tours, Niagara, Canada
2153	CUV153C	*BA4 813*	3.65	AC 2155	10.94	HT	10.94	London Northern Bus Co., London RM2153
2154	CUV154C		3.65	AC 2197	10.86	AV	2.87	Brakell (dealer), Cheam
								3.87 Gowdy (preserved), Ballyclair, N.Ireland
								2.90 Ulster Engineering, Ballymena, N.Ireland
2155	CUV155C	*60-Sri-6605*	3.65	AC 2150	11.87	AK	12.88	Sri Lanka Transport Board
2156	CUV156C		2.65	AC 2198	11.87	X	2.88	Burnley & Pendle Transport 186
								7.92 Southend Transport (not used)
								11.92 Taffell, Ruislip
								11.94 Pring (Timebus), St.Albans
2157	CUV157C		2.65	AC 2144	3.88	WN	4.88	PVS (breaker), Carlton
								6.88 Wigley (breaker), Carlton - scrapped
2158	CUV158C	*60-Sri-6615*	1.66	WL 2171	10.86	E	12.88	Sri Lanka Transport Board
2159	CUV159C		1.66	WL 1049	2.92	TL	7.92	PVS (breaker), Carlton
								7.92 Wigley (breaker), Carlton - scrapped
2160	CUV160C	*60-Sri-6614*	3.65	AC 2207	11.87	V	12.88	Sri Lanka Transport Board
2161	CUV161C		3.65	AC 2165	7.92	SW	8.92	PVS (breaker), Carlton
								8.92 Wigley (breaker), Carlton - scrapped
2162	CUV162C		3.65	AC 2157	11.87	X	8.88	Gtr Manchester Buses, Manchester 2204
								7.90 Pegg (Rotherham & Dist.), Rotherham
								11.90 J.Sykes (breaker), Carlton
								6.91 Blackburn RM Group (pres'd), Blackburn
								11.91 Spence (dealer), Thorpe Bay
								11.91 Southend Transport 123
								2.94 Beach Bus Co., Kittyhawk, USA
2163	CUV163C		3.65	AC 2128	2.87	TH	4.87	PVS (breaker), Carlton
								6.87 Wigley (breaker), Carlton - scrapped
2164	CUV164C		3.65	AC 2123	8.90	S	12.90	PVS (breaker), Carlton - scrapped
2165	CUV165C	*BA4 814*	3.65	AC 2159	2.87	SW	4.87	Double Deck Tours, Niagara, Canada
2166	CUV166C		3.65	AC 2135	9.87	E	7.88	Bush & Meissner (agent), Elstree
								7.88 Fujisho Kunita, Fujishawa-shi, Japan
2167	CUV167C		3.65	AC 2131	6.87	WD	10.87	PVS (breaker), Carlton
								10.87 Wigley (breaker), Carlton - scrapped

2168	CUV168C	3.65	AC	2154	5.87	T	8.87	PVS (breaker), Carlton - scrapped
2169	CUV169C	3.65	AC	2124	5.87	NX	8.87	J.Sykes (breaker), Carlton - scrapped
2170	CUV170C	3.65	AC	2161	1.88	NX	2.91	PVS (breaker), Carlton - scrapped
2171	CUV171C	3.65	AC	2158	9.87	AF	4.89	Pepsi Cola, Oman
								11.90 Royal Oman Police, Oman
2172	CUV172C	3.65	AC	2174	5.87	PM	10.87	PVS (breaker), Carlton - scrapped
2173	CUV173C	3.65	AC	2146	6.94	X	*3.95*	*London Transport Buses reserve fleet*
2174	CUV174C	3.65	AC	2147	11.87	AF	6.89	Nissho Iwai Corporation, Japan (not collected)
								4.93 Ensign (dealer), Rainham
								7.93 Brakell (dealer), Cheam
								12 .94 Beach Bus Co., Kittyhawk, USA
2175	CUV175C	3.65	AC	2193	12.86	GM	4.87	LRT Bus Engineering, Chiswick
								3.88 PVS (breaker), Carlton - scrapped
2176	CUV176C	3.65	AC	2134	10.87	AK	12.87	PVS (breaker), Carlton - scrapped
								1.88 Some body parts to Stagecoach, Perth
2177	CUV177C	4.65	AC	2166	3.87	AK	6.87	PVS (breaker), Carlton
								6.87 Wigley (breaker), Carlton - scrapped
2178	CUV178C	3.65	AC	2127	6.91	St	.92	Pan Brittanica Industries, Waltham Abbey
2179	CUV179C	4.65	AC	2133	1.95	BN	1.95	South London Transport, London RM2179
2180	CUV180C	4.65	H	2175	10.87	AF	3.88	Burnley & Pendle Transport 180
								7.92 Southend Transport (dealer)
								1.93 Pring (Timebus), St.Albans
2181	CUV181C	4.65	AC	2141	4.93	GM	4.95	Unknown
2182	CUV182C	4.65	AC	2125	2.87	AR	5.87	PVS (breaker), Carlton - scrapped
2183	CUV183C	4.65	AC	2173	3.88	SW	4.89	Pepsi Cola. Oman
								2.90 Rahman & Taher, Dubai
	23428							
2184	CUV184C	4.65	AC	2129	3.87	NX	6.87	PVS (breaker), Carlton - scrapped
2185	CUV185C	4.65	H	2160	1.95	BN	1.95	South London Transport RM2185
2186	CUV186C	4.65	D	2132	10.94	HT	10.94	London Northern Bus Co., London RM2186
2187	CUV187C	4.65	AC	2152		AC	11.94	PVS (breaker), Carlton
								6.95 Daly (agent), London
								6.95 Exported
2188	CUV188C	4.65	AC	2142	2.92	TL	7.92	PVS (breaker), Carlton - scrapped
2189	CUV189C	4.65	H	2183	7.92	SW	3.93	PVS (breaker), Carlton - scrapped
2190	CUV190C	4.65	AC	2176	4.89	HT	1.90	PVS (breaker), Carlton - scrapped
2191	CUV191C	4.65	AC	2140	11.87	V	2.89	PVS (breaker), Carlton - scrapped
2192	CUV192C	4.65	AC	2211	11.87	V	1.88	United Counties Omnibus Co. 708
								7.95 Stagecoach Selkent, London RM2192
2193	CUV193C	4.65	AC	2145	12.86	WD	8.87	Matsui & Co. (agent), London
								9.87 Unknown, Japan
2194	CUV194C	4.65	AC	2172	9.87	V	12.87	PVS (breaker), Carlton - scrapped
2195	CUV195C	4.65	AC	2148	2.88	AD	3.88	United Counties Omnibus Co. (for spares)
								6.89 Smith (breaker), Bedford - scrapped
								at UCOC Kettering depot
2196	CUV196C	9.65	AC	2199	6.87	PM	10.87	PVS (breaker), Carlton - scrapped
2197	CUV197C	4.65	H	2167	2.87	AG	3.87	PVS (breaker), Carlton - scrapped
2198	CUV198C	4.65	H	2137	2.87	TH	3.87	Andrew Treagus Association, London
								5.87 Brakell (dealer), Cheam
								10.87 Drabwell (preserved), Bushey
2199	CUV199C	4.65	H	1360	12.84	PM	1.85	PVS (breaker), Carlton - scrapped
2200	CUV200C	5.65	H	2178	12.86	AR	8.88	Gtr Manchester Buses, Manchester 2200
								7.90 Pegg (Rotherham & Dist.), Rotherham
								12.90 J.Sykes (breaker), Carlton
								3.91 Wombwell Diesels (breaker), Wombwell
								11.92 Wright (dealer), Rainham
								6.93 Octobus SARL, Paris, France
2201	CUV201C	4.65	H	2153	7.94	St	11.94	PVS (breaker), Carlton
								2.95 Greater Reading Omnibus, Reading 21
2202	CUV202C	4.65	H	2200	2.87	V	4.87	PVS (breaker), Carlton - scrapped
2203	CUV203C	12.65	SF	2204	10.86	ED	11.87	Clydeside Scottish (for spares)
								6.88 Nelson Cladding Ltd., Penicuik
								3.95 Kenmore Investments, Edinburgh
2204	CUV204C	5.65	H	2138	12.91	Tt	10.94	PVS (breaker), Carlton - *for scrap*

2205	CUV205C		5.65	H	2215	11.88	WN	9.89	Hori & Partners, Budapest, Hungary
2206	CUV206C	*BA4 803*	5.65	H	2181	2.87	AL	4.87	Double Deck Tours, Niagara, Canada
2207	CUV207C	*60-Sri-6602*	5.65	H	2156	11.87	AF	12.88	Sri Lanka Transport Board
2208	CUV208C		5.65	H	2130	2.87	TH	5.87	SBG Engineering, Kilmarnock
									5.87 Clydeside Scottish RM2208
									5.89 Western Scottish C83
									9.90 PVS (breaker), Carlton
									9.90 Ripley (breaker), Carlton
									2.91 Black Prince, Morley RM2208
									5.93 King (preserved), Leeds
2209	CUV209C		5.65	H	2191	5.93	BW	3.94	Beach Bus Co., Kittyhawk, N.Carolina, USA
2210	CUV210C		5.65	H	2208	11.86	AC	5.87	Clydeside Scottish RM2210
									5.89 Western Scottish C84
									9.90 PVS (breaker), Carlton
									6.92 East Yorkshire Motor Services 816
2211	CUV211C		5.65	H	2179	3.87	NX	7.87	PVS (breaker), Carlton
									7.87 Wigley (breaker), Carlton - scrapped
2212	CUV212C	*HH-DC-1232*	5.65	H	2182	5.87	HT	10.87	Clark, Hamburg, Germany
2213	CUV213C		5.65	H	2136	5.94	AC	*3.95*	*London Transport Buses reserve fleet*
2214	CUV214C		2.66	R	2213	6.87	E	10.87	PVS (breaker), Carlton - scrapped
2215	CUV215C		9.65	AC	2188	12.86	SF	3.87	PVS (breaker), Carlton
									3.87 Wigley (breaker), Carlton - scrapped
2216	CUV216C		5.65	H	2209	1.88	BW	1.90	PVS (breaker), Carlton - scrapped
2217	CUV217C		9.65	AC	2139	12.95	BN	1.95	South London Transport, London RM2217
RCL									
2218	CUV218C		6.65	RE	2218	12.69	RE	1.70	London Country Bus Services RCL2218
									3.78 London Transport RCL2218
			2.79	SEt		3.84	SF	3.85	London Borough of Redbridge
2219	CUV219C		6.65	RE	2219	12.69	RE	1.70	London Country Bus Services RCL2219
									3.78 London Transport RCL2219
			12.78	Mt		7.84	EM	2.85	LT Disrtict Line Athletic Club, Acton Town
									6.87 BaMMOT (Preserved), Wythall
2220	CUV220C		6.65	RE	2220	12.69	RE	1.70	London Country Bus Services RCL2220
									3.79 Wombwell Diesels (breaker), Wombwell
									7.79 London Transport RCL2220
			11.80	EM		5.92	WD	5.92	London Coaches, London RCL2220
2221	CUV221C		6.65	RE	2221	12.69	RE	1.70	London Country Bus Services RCL2221
									3.78 London Transport RCL2221
			12.78	Mt		1.79	Mt	4.79	LTE mobile cinema/exhibition bus
									4.85 London U'ground Dist'n Services, Acton
2222	CUV222C		6.65	RE	2222	12.69	RE	1.70	London Country Bus Services RCL2222
									6.79 London Transport RCL2222
			6.80	SF		11.84	SF	5.85	PVS (breaker), Carlton
									10.85 Rollinson (breaker), Carlton - scrapped
2223	CUV223C		6.65	RE	2223	12.69	RE	1.70	London Country Bus Services RCL2223
									12.77 London Transport RCL2223
			6.80	SF		3.84	SF	9.84	Payne (preserved), Maidstone
									4.85 Brakell (dealer), Cheam
									8.86 Gillespie, London
									4.88 Lavender (PAG Ltd.), Raynes Park
									8.94 Unknown, London
2224	CUV224C		6.65	RE	2224	12.79	RE	1.70	London Country Bus Services RCL2224
									12.77 London Transport RCL2224
			1.78	PRt		2.84	EM	8.84	PVS (breaker), Carlton - scrapped
2225	CUV225C		6.65	RE	2225	12.79	RE	1.70	London Country Bus Services RCL2225
									12.77 London Transport (not used)
									1.78 Wombwell Diesels (breaker) - scrapped
2226	CUV226C		6.65	RE	2226	12.69	GD	1.70	London Country Bus Services RCL2226
									3.79 Wombwell Diesels (breaker), Wombwell
									7.79 London Transport RCL2226
			9.80	EM		6.84	EM	9.85	Wenmay (Willys Wheels), Egham
									1.89 Convoy Film Transport Services, Ascot
									2.93 Powell & Elsey (Abada Film Services), Weybrdge

2227	CUV227C	6.65	RE	2227	12.69	RE	1.70	London Country Bus Services RCL2227
								12.77 London Transport (not used)
								1.78 Wombwell Diesels (breaker) - scrapped
2228	CUV228C	6.65	RE	2228	12.69	GY	1.70	London Country Bus Services RCL2228
								7.79 London Transport RCL2228
		9.80	EM		4.84	EM	8.84	PVS (breaker), Carlton - scrapped
2229	CUV229C	6.65	RE	2229	12.69	RE	1.70	London Country Bus Services RCL2229
								8.78 London Transport RCL2229
		9.78	Rt		5.84	SF	4.85	London Transport Museum (pres'd), London
2230	CUV230C	6.65	RE	2230	12.69	RE	1.70	London Country Bus Services RCL2230
								8.78 London Transport RCL2230
		8.78	Mt		4.83	SF	9.84	PVS (breaker), Carlton - scrapped
2231	CUV231C	6.65	RE	2231	12.69	RE	1.70	London Country Bus Services RCL2231
								3.79 Wombwell Diesels (breaker), Wombwell
								7.79 London Transport RCL2231
		9.80	EM		8.84	EM	12.84	PVS (breaker), Carlton
								12.84 Rollinson (breaker), Carlton - scrapped
2232	CUV232C	6.65	RE	2232	12.69	RE	1.70	London Country Bus Services RCL2232
								12.77 London Transport RCL2232
		1.78	BWt		12.83	EM	8.84	PVS (breaker), Carlton - scrapped
2233	CUV233C	6.65	RE	2233	12.69	RE	1.70	London Country Bus Services RCL2233
								12.77 London Transport RCL2233
		1.78	WHt		12.82	SF	10.83	W.Norths (dealer), Sherburn-in-Elmet
								1.84 Moore (preserved), London
								2.84 Brown & Sherwood (pres'd), Barking
								10.86 Brown (preserved), Romford
2234	CUV234C	6.65	RE	2234	12.69	GY	1.70	London Country Bus Services RCL2234
								10.78 London Transport RCL2234
		10.78	AWt		3.84	SF	8.84	PVS (breaker), Carlton
								8.84 Wigley (breaker), Carlton - scrapped
2235	CUV235C	6.65	RE	2235	12.69	DG	1.70	London Country Bus Services RCL2235
								12.77 London Transport RCL2235
		1.78	Mt		5.92	WD	5.92	London Coaches, London RCL2235
2236	CUV236C	6.65	RE	2236	12.69	DG	1.70	London Country Bus Services RCL2236
								12.77 London Transport RCL2236
		1.78	GMt		4.84	EM	9.84	PVS (breaker), Carlton - scrapped
2237	CUV237C	6.65	RE	2237	12.69	GD	1.70	London Country Bus Services RCL2237
								7.79 London Transport RCL2237
		10.80	EM		5.84	EM	12.84	PVS (breaker), Carlton - scrapped
2238	CUV238C	6.65	RE	2238	12.69	DG	1.70	London Country Bus Services RCL2238
								6.79 London Transport RCL2238
		10.80	EM		5.84	EM	9.85	Wenmay (Willys Wheels), Egham
								1.89 Convoy Film Transport Services, Ascot
								2.93 Powell & Elsey (Abada Film Services), Weybridge
2239	CUV239C	6.65	RE	2239	12.69	DG	1.70	London Country Bus Services RCL2239
								6.79 London Transport RCL2239
		4.80	Mt		9.83	SF	11.83	Biddell (preserved), Woodford Bridge
								10.85 Wright (Blue Triangle), Rainham
								2.94 Wright & Biddell, Rainham
2240	CUV240C	6.65	RE	2240	12.69	DG	1.70	London Country Bus Services RCL2240
								6.79 London Transport RCL2240
		7.80	SF		5.92	WD	5.92	London Coaches, London RCL2240
2241	CUV241C	6.65	RE	2241	12.69	DG	1.70	London Country Bus Services RCL2241
								3.79 Wombwell Diesels (breaker), Wombwell
								7.79 London Transport RCL2241
		10.80	EM		5.92	WD	5.92	London Coaches, London RCL2241
2242	CUV242C	6.65	RE	2242	12.69	DG	1.70	London Country Bus Services RCL2242
								6.79 London Transport RCL2242
		8.80	SF		4.84	SF	12.84	PVS (breaker), Carlton
								12.84 Wigley (breaker), Carlton - scrapped
2243	CUV243C	6.65	RE	2243	12.69	GY	1.70	London Country Bus Services RCL2243
								3.79 Wombwell Diesels (breaker), Wombwell
								7.79 London Transport RCL2243
		11.80	SF		5.92	WD	5.92	London Coaches, London RCL2243

2244	CUV244C		6.65	RE	2244	12.69	RE	1.70	London Country Bus Services RCL2244
									9.78 London Transport RCL2244
			9.78	Rt		11.82	EM	10.83	W.Norths (dealer), Sherburn - scrapped
2245	CUV245C		6.65	RE	2245	12.69	GY	1.70	London Country Bus Services RCL2245
									10.78 London Transport RCL2245
			10.78	Qt		5.92	WD	5.92	London Coaches, London RCL2245
2246	CUV246C		7.65	HG	2246	12.69	GY	1.70	London Country Bus Services RCL2246
									6.79 London Transport RCL2246
			6.80	SF		7.83	SF	10.83	W.Norths (dealer), Sherburn - scrapped
2247	CUV247C		7.65	GY	2247	12.69	DG	1.70	London Country Bus Services RCL2247
									11.78 London Transport RCL2247
			10.80	EM		12.84	EM	5.85	PVS (breaker), Carlton
									10.85 Rollinson (breaker), Carlton - scrapped
2248	CUV248C		7.65	HG	2248	12.69	GY	1.70	London Country Bus Services RCL2248
									9.78 London Transport RCL2248
			9.78	FWt		5.92	WD	5.92	London Coaches, London RCL2248
2249	CUV249C		7,65	HG	2249	12.69	WR	1.70	London Country Bus Services RCL2249
									2.79 London Transport RCL2249
			2.79	BNt		8.84	SF	12.84	PVS (breaker), Carlton - scrapped
2250	CUV250C		7.65	GY	2250	12.69	GD	1.70	London Country Bus Services RCL2250
									3.79 London Transport RCL2250
			3.79	WNt		5.92	WD	5.92	London Coaches, London RCL2251
2251	CUV251C		7.65	GY	2251	12.69	DG	1.70	London Country Bus Services RCL2251
									11.78 LondonTransport RCL2251
			6.80	SF		10.84	SF	5.85	PVS (breaker), Carlton - scrapped
2252	CUV252C		7.65	GY	2252	12.69	DG	1.70	London Country Bus Services RCL2252
									11.78 London Transport RCL2252
			10.80	EM		11.84	EM	4.85	Karajin, Kenora, Ontario, Canada
		BC8 559							6.88 Double Deck Tours, Niagara, Canada
2253	CUV2253		7.65	GY	2253	12.69	DG	1.70	London Country Bus Services RCL2253
									7.79 London Transport RCL2253
			9.80	EM		5.92	WD	5.92	London Coaches, London RCL2253
2254	CUV254C		7.65	GY	2254	12.69	WR	1.70	London Country Bus Services RCL2254
									12.77 London Transport RCL2254
			1.78	GMt		7.84	EM	12.84	Bonay Window Services, High Wycombe
									4.90 Hart, Harrow - on loan to BEL, Willesden
									2.93 Hart (preserved), Harrow
2255	CUV255C		7,65	GY	2255	12.69	WR	1.70	London Country Bus Services RCL2255
									6.79 London Transport RCL2255
		BC8 555	6.80	SF		8.83	SF	10.83	Double Deck Tours, Niagara, Canada
2256	CUV256C		7.65	GY	2256	12.69	WR	1.70	London Country Bus Services RCL2256
									12.78 London Transport RCL2256
			12.78	PRt		9.84	SF	5.85	Brakell (dealer), Cheam
									8.90 Southend Transport 121
2257	CUV257C		7.65	GY	2257	12.69	WR	1.70	London Country Bus Services RCL2257
									6.79 London Transport RCL2257
			6.80	SF		5.83	SF	10.83	W.Norths (dealer), Sherburn - scrapped
2258	CUV258C		7.65	HG	2258	12.69	WR	1.70	London Country Bus Services RCL2258
									12.77 London Transport RCL2258
			1.78	WWt		8.83	SF	10.83	W.Norths (dealer), Sherburn - scrapped
2259	CUV259C		7.65	HG	2259	12.69	WR	1.70	London Country Bus Services RCL2259
									1.79 London Transport RCL2259
			1.79	SEt		5.92	WD	5.92	London Coaches, London RCL2259
2260	CUV260C		7.65	HG	2260	12.69	WR	1.70	London Country Bus Services RCL2260
									3.79 Wombwell Diesels (breaker), Wombwell
									7.79 London Transport RCL2260
			11.80	EM		5.92	WD	5.92	London Coaches, London RCL2260

RML

2261	CUV261C	2.66	WH	2391	9.94	AR	9.94	Leaside Bus Co., London RML2261
2262	CUV262C	11.66	AF	2686	10.94	RA	10.94	London General Transport, London RML2262
2263	CUV263C	11.65	AR	2539	10.94	RA	10.94	London General Transport, London RML2263
2264	CUV264C	11.65	AR	2551	1.95	BN	1.95	South London Transport, London RML2264
2265	CUV265C	11.65	AR	2520	7.93	FY	10.93	Leased to BTS, Borehamwood RML2265

2266	CUV266C	11.65	AR	2393	3.93	AF	4.93	Leased to Kentish Bus RML2266
2267	CUV267C	11.65	AR	2699	9.94	AR	9.94	Leaside Bus Co., London RML2267
2268	CUV268C	11.65	AR	2515	9.94	X	9.94	CentreWest, London RML2268
2269	CUV269C	11.65	AR	2558	11.94	S	11.94	London United Busways, London RML2269
2270	CUV270C	11.65	AR	2521	10.94	Q	10.94	London Central Buses, London RML2270
2271	CUV271C	11.65	AR	2682	10.94	NX	10.94	London Central Buses, London RML2271
2272	CUV272C	11.65	AR	2688	9.94	U	9.94	Stagecoach East London, London RML2272
2273	CUV273C	11.65	AR	2544	10.94	Q	10.94	London Central Buses, London RML2273
2274	CUV274C	11.65	AR	2531	10.94	AC	10.94	Metroline Travel, London RML2274
2275	CUV275C	11.65	AR	2553	10.94	Q	10.94	London Central Buses, London RML2275
2276	CUV276C	11.65	AR	2303	10.94	Q	10.94	London Central Buses, London RML2276
2277	CUV277C	11.65	AR	2395	9.94	AR	9.94	Leaside Bus Co., London RML2277
2278	CUV278C	10.65	GD	2364	9.94	X	9.94	CentreWest, London RML2278
2279	CUV279C	10.65	GD	2381	10.94	Q	10.94	London Central Buses, London RML2279
2280	CUV280C	10.65	GD	2357	9.94	CT	9.94	Leaside Bus Co., London RML2280
2281	CUV281C	11.65	AR	2468	9.94	X	9.94	CentreWest, London RML2281
2282	CUV282C	1.66	SF	2392	10.94	HT	10.94	London Northern Bus Co., London RML2282
2283	CUV283C	11.65	AR	2723	10.94	NX	10.94	London Central Buses, London RML2283
2284	CUV284C	10.66	AC	2721	10.94	HT	10.94	London Northern Bus Co., London RML2284
2285	CUV285C	11.65	AR	2361	10.94	AC	10.94	Metroline Travel, London RML2285
2286	CUV286C	11.65	AR	2445	9.94	U	9.94	Stagecoach East London, London RML2286
2287	CUV287C	10.65	GD	2394	9.94	CT	9.94	Leaside Bus Co. London RML2287
2288	CUV288C	10.65	GD	2304	10.94	AC	10.94	Metroline Travel, London RML2288
2289	CUV289C	11.65	AR	2289	10.94	AC	10.94	Metroline Travel, London RML2289
2290	CUV290C	11.65	AR	2377	11.94	AF	11.94	London General Transport, London RML2290
2291	CUV291C	11.65	AR	2710	9.94	X	9.94	CentreWest, London RML2291
2292	CUV292C	11.65	AR	2404	9.94	AR	9.94	Leaside Bus Co., London RML2292
2293	CUV293C	10.65	GD	2403	11.94	S	11.94	London United Busways, London RML2293
2294	CUV294C	11.65	AR	2294	9.94	AR	9.94	Leaside Bus Co., London RML2294
2295	CUV295C	10.65	GD	2368	10.94	HT	10.94	London Northern Bus Co., London RML2295
2296	CUV296C	10.65	GD	2373	10.94	HT	10.94	London Northern Bus Co, London RML2296
2297	CUV297C	10.65	GD	2388	11.94	AF	11.94	London General Transport, London RML2297
2298	CUV298C	10.65	GD	2739	11.94	S	11.94	London United Busways, London RML2298
2299	CUV299C	10.65	GD	2371	10.94	AC	10.94	Metroline Travel, London RML2299
2300	CUV300C	10.65	GD	2406	9.94	BW	9.94	Stagecoach East London, London RML2300
2301	CUV301C	10.65	GD	2399	4.93	WW	4.93	Leased to Kentish Bus RML2301
2302	CUV302C	10.65	GD	2366	10.94	NX	10.94	London Central Buses, London RML2302
2303	CUV303C	10.65	GD	2758	9.94	BW	9.94	Stagecoach East London, London RML2303
2304	CUV304C	10.65	GD	2314	9.94	CT	9.94	Leaside Bus Co., London RML2304
2305	CUV305C	10.65	GD	2390	11.94	RA	11.94	London General Transport, London RML2305
2306	CUV306C	10.65	EG	2306	12.69	EG	1.70	London Country Bus Services RML2306 12.77 London Transport (not used) 2.78 Wombwell Diesels (breaker) - scrapped
2307	CUV307C	10.65	GD	2746	12.69	GD	1.70	London Country Bus Services RML2307 12.77 London Transport RML2307
		5.78	HT		1.95	BN	1.95	South London Transport, London RML2307
2308	CUV308C	10.65	RG	2263	12.69	RG	1.70	London Country Bus Services RML2308 6.79 London Transport RML2308
		2.80	AC		10.94	AC	10.94	Metroline Travel, London RML2308
2309	CUV309C	10.65	GD	2309	12.69	HA	1.70	London Country Bus Services RML2309 7.79 London Transport RML2309
		2.80	H		9.94	X	9.94	CentreWest, London RML2309
2310	CUV310C	10.65	GD	2310	12.69	GD	1.70	London Country Bus Services RML2310 12.77 London Transport RML2310
		4.78	U		10.94	HT	10.94	London Northern Bus Co., London RML2310
2311	CUV311C	10.65	GD	2293	12.69	GD	1.70	London Country Bus Services RML2311 12.77 London Transport RML2311
		3.78	NX		9.94	U	9.94	Stagecoach East London, London RML2311
2312	CUV312C	10.65	GD	2312	12.69	GD	1.70	London Country Bus Services RML2312 12.77 London Transport RML2312
		4.78	AF		10.94	AC	10.94	Metroline Travel, London RML2312

2313	CUV313C	10.65	GD	2313	12.69	GD	1.70	London Country Bus Services RML2313
								6.79 London Transport RML2313
		4.80	W		9.94	X	9.94	CentreWest, London RML2313
2314	CUV314C	10.65	GD	2379	12.69	GD	1.70	London Country Bus Services RML2314
								7.79 London Transport RML2314
		2.80	H		10.94	Q	10.94	London Central Buses, London RML2314
2315	CUV315C	10.65	GD	2271	12.69	GD	1.70	London Country Bus Services RML2315
								12.77 London Transport RML2315
		1.78	U		9.94	AR	9.94	Leaside Bus Co., London RML2315
2316	CUV316C	10.65	GD	2385	12.69	GD	1.70	London Country Bus Services RML2316
								7.79 London Transport RML2316
		2.80	AC		11.94	AF	11.94	London General Transport, London RML2316
2317	CUV317C	10.65	GD	2317	12.69	GD	1.70	London Country Bus Services RML2317
								12.77 London Transport RML2317
		3.78	AE		11.94	RA	11.94	London General Transport, London RML2317
2318	CUV318C	11.65	NF	2318	12.69	GR	1.70	London Country Bus Services RML2318
								12.77 London Transport RML2318
		3.78	WH		10.94	Q	10.94	London Central Buses, London RML2318
2319	CUV319C	10.65	GD	2319	12.69	GD	1.70	London Country Bus Services RML2319
								12.77 London Transport (not used)
								1.78 Wombwell Diesels (breaker) - scrapped
2320	CUV320C	11.65	NF	2320	12.69	GR	1.70	London Country Bus Services RML2320
								12.77 London Transport (not used)
								1.78 Wombwell Diesels (breaker) - scrapped
2321	CUV321C	11.65	NF	2292	11.94	AF	11.94	London General Transport, London RML2321
2322	CUV322C	11.65	NF	2322	12.69	NF	1.70	London Country Bus Services RML2322
								7.79 London Transport RML2322
		12.80	HL		9.93	Q	*12.93*	*Leased to BTS, Borehamwood RML2322*
2323	CUV323C	11.65	NF	2323	12.69	NF	1.70	London Country Bus Services RML2323
								7.79 London Transport RML2323
		11.80	HL		9.94	AR	9.94	Leaside Bus Co., London RML2323
2324	CUV324C	11.65	NF	2324	12.69	NF	1.70	London Country Bus Services RML2324
								7.79 London Transport RML2324
		2.80	FY		1.95	BN	1.95	South London Transport, London RML2324
2325	CUV325C	11.65	NF	2325	12.69	NF	1.70	London Country Bus Services RML2325
								7.79 London Transport RML2325
		4.80	W		9.94	CT	9.94	Leaside Bus Co., London RML2325
2326	CUV326C	11.65	NF	2326	12.69	NF	1.70	London Country Bus Services RML2326
								10.79 London Transport RML2326
		11.80	HT		9.94	CT	9.94	Leaside Bus Co., London RML2326
2327	CUV327C	11.65	NF	2327	12.69	NF	1.70	London Country Bus Servces RML2327
								7.79 London Transport RML2327
		2.80	AC		10.94	Q	10.94	London Central Buses, London RML2327
2328	CUV328C	11.65	NF	2328	12.69	NF	1.70	London Country Bus Services RML2328
								10.79 London Transport RML2328
		2.80	AC		9.94	CT	9.94	Leaside Bus Co., London RML2328
2329	CUV329C	11.65	GD	2329	12.69	GD	1.70	London Country Bus Services RML2329
								7.79 London Transport RML2329
		3.80	BW		9.94	CT	9.94	Leaside Bus Co., London RML2329
2330	CUV330C	11.65	GD	2330	12.69	GD	1.70	London Country Bus Services RML2330
								7.79 London Transport RML2330
		11.80	HL		9.94	AR	9.94	Leaside Bus Co., London RML2330
2331	CUV331C	11.65	GD	2331	12.69	GD	1.70	London Country Bus Services RML2331
								12.77 London Transport RML2331
		5.78	AF		10.94	AC	10.94	Metroline Travel, London RML2331
2332	CUV332C	11.65	GD	2269	12.69	GD	1.70	London Country Bus Services RML2332
								12.77 London Transport RML2332
		1.78	T		10.94	NX	10.94	London Central Buses, London RML2332
2333	CUV333C	11.65	GD	2375	12.69	GD	1.70	London Country Bus Services RML2333
								12.77 London Transport RML2333
		4.78	U		1.95	BN	1.95	South London Transport, London RML2333
2334	CUV334C	11.65	GD	2334	12.69	GD	1.70	London Country Bus Services RML2334
								10.79 London Transport RML2334
		4.80	FY		9.94	CT	9.94	Leaside Bus Co., London RML2334

2335	CUV335C	11.65	GD	2335	12.69	GD	1.70	London Country Bus Services RML2335
								12.77 London Transport RML2335
		4.78	HT		10.94	Q	10.94	London Central Buses, London RML2335
2336	CUV336C	11.65	GD	2336	12.69	GD	1.70	London Country Bus Services RML2336
								10.79 London Transport RML2336
		2.80	CF		10.94	Q	10.94	London Central Buses, London RML2336
2337	CUV337C	11.65	NF	2337	12.69	NF	1.70	London Country Bus Services RML2337
								12.77 London Transport (not used)
								1.78 Wombwell Diesels (breaker) - scrapped
2338	CUV338C	11.65	NF	2338	12.69	NF	1.70	London Country Bus Services RML2338
								10.79 London Transport RML2338
		11.80	HL		10.94	Q	10.94	London Central Buses, London RML2338
2339	CUV339C	11.65	NF	2463	12.69	NF	1.70	London Country Bus Services RML2339
								10.79 London Transport RML2339
		2.80	F		10.94	NX	10.94	London Central Buses, London RML2339
2340	CUV340C	11.65	NF	2340	12.69	NF	1.70	London Country Bus Services RML2340
								10.79 London Transport RML2340
		2.80	NX		9.94	AR	9.94	Leaside Bus Co., London RML2340
2341	CUV341C	11.65	NF	2341	12.69	NF	1.70	London Country Bus Services RML2341
								7.79 London Transport RML2341
		4.80	W		8.93	FY	*10.93*	*Leased to BTS, Borehamwood RML2341*
2342	CUV342C	11.65	NF	2342	12.69	NF	1.70	London Country Bus Services RML2342
								10.79 London Transport RML2342
		1.80	H		11.94	RA	11.94	London General Transport, London RML2342
2343	CUV343C	11.65	NF	2343	12.69	NF	1.70	London Country Bus Services RML2343
								10.79 London Transport RML2343
		2.80	H		4.94	WW	*4.93*	*Leased to Kentish Bus RML2343*
2344	CUV344C	11.65	NF	2344	12.69	NF	1.70	London Country Bus Services RML2344
								12.79 London Transport RML2344
		3.80	AF		9.94	CT	9.94	Leaside Bus Co., London RML2344
2345	CUV345C	11.65	N	2345	12.69	NF	1.70	London Country Bus Services RML2345
								3.79 Wombwell Diesels (breaker)
								7.79 London Transport RML2345
		5.81	HL		10.94	NX	10.94	London Central Buses, London RML2345
2346	CUV346C	12.65	GD	2346	12.69	GD	1.70	London Country Bus Services RML2346
								6,79 London Transport RML2346
		1.80	Tt		9.94	AR	9.94	Leaside Bus Co., London RML2346
2347	CUV347C	12.65	GD	2347	12.69	GD	1.70	London Country Bus Services RML2347
								12.77 London Transport RML2347
		1.78	HTt		4.93	AF	*4.93*	*Leased to Kentish Bus RML2347*
2348	CUV348C	12.65	GD	2387	12.69	GD	1.70	London Country Bus Services RML2348
								2.80 London Transport RML2348
		3.80	WH		10.94	AC	10.94	Metroline Travel, London RML2348
2349	CUV349C	12.65	GD	2349	12.69	GD	1.70	London Country Bus Services RML2349
								12.79 London Transport RML2349
		4.80	W		11.94	S	11.94	London United Busways, London RML2349
2350	CUV350C	12.65	GD	2350	12.69	GD	1.70	London Country Bus Services RML2350
								7.79 London Transport RML2350
		9.80	HL		9.94	AR	9.94	Leaside Bus Co., London RML2350
2351	CUV351C	12.65	GD	2351	12.69	GD	1.70	London Country Bus Services RML2351
								12.77 London Transport RML2351
		1.78	U		1.95	BN	1.95	South London Transport, London RML2351
2352	CUV352C	12.65	GD	2285	12.69	GD	1.70	London Country Bus Services RML2352
								1.80 London Transport RML2352
		2.80	U		9.94	X	9.94	CentreWest, London RML2352
2353	CUV353C	12.65	GD	2353	12.69	GD	1.70	London Country Bus Services RML2353
								7.79 London Transport RML2353
		9.79	BWt		11.94	S	11.94	London United Busways, London RML2353
2354	CUV354C	12.65	GD	2464	12.69	GD	1.70	London Country Bus Services RML2354
								9.78 London Transport RML2354
		9.78	HT		9.94	CT	9.94	Leaside Bus Co., London RML2354
2355	CUV355C	3.66	GR	2355	12.69	NF	1.70	London Country Bus Services RML2355
								12.78 London Transport RML2355
		1.79	SEt		9.94	CT	9.94	Leaside Bus Co., London RML2355

2356	CUV356C	12,65	SF	2386	9.94	CT	9.94	Leaside Bus Co., London RML2356
2357	CUV357C	12.65	SF	2376	9.94	X	9.94	CentreWest, London RML2357
2358	CUV358C	12.65	SF	2261	11.94	RA	11.94	London General Transport, London RML2358
2359	CUV359C	12.65	SF	2273	9.94	CT	9.94	Leaside Bus Co. London RML2359
2360	CUV360C	12.65	SF	2332	11.94	RA	11.94	London General Transport, London RML2360
2361	CUV361C	12.65	SF	2720	11.94	AF	11.94	London General Transport, London RML2361
2362	CUV362C	12.65	SF	2282	10.94	Q	10.94	London Central Buses, London RML2362
2363	CUV363C	12.65	SF	2356	11.94	RA	11.94	London General Transport, London RML2363
2364	CUV364C	11.66	AF	2759	11.94	AF	11.94	London General Transport, London RML2364
2365	CUV365C	11.66	AF	2276	9.94	X	9.94	CentreWest, London RML2365
2366	CUV366C	2.66	WH	2279	1.95	BN	1.95	South London Transport, London RML2366
2367	CUV367C	2.66	WW	2295	10.94	HT	10.94	London Northern Bus Co., London RML2367
2368	CUV368C	7.66	U	2266	10.94	AC	10.94	Metroline Travel, London RML2368
2369	CUV369C	3.66	WH	2408	9.94	X	9.94	CentreWest, London RML2369
2370	CUV370C	2.66	WW	2278	9.94	CT	9.94	Leaside Bus Co., London RML2370
2371	CUV371C	6.66	SW	2358	11.94	AF	11.94	London General Transport, London RML2371
2372	CUV372C	3.66	WH	2748	9.94	AR	9.94	Leaside Bus Co., London RML2372
2373	CUV373C	2.66	WH	2362	9.94	AR	9.94	Leaside Bus Co., London RML2373
2374	CUV374C	11.66	AF	2409	9.94	X	9.94	CentreWest, London RML2374
2375	CUV375C	3.66	WH	2281	1.95	BN	1.95	South London Transport, London RML2375
2376	CUV376C	2.66	WW	2315	11.94	AF	11.94	London General Transport, London RML2376
2377	CUV377C	2.66	WH	2665	10.94	AC	10.94	Metroline Travel, London RML2377
2378	CUV378C	2.66	WW	2291	9.94	X	9.94	CentreWest, London RML2378
2379	CUV379C	2.66	PR	2272	9.94	X	9.94	CentreWest, London RML2379
2380	CUV380C	2.66	WH	2288	9.94	AR	9.94	Leaside Bus Co., London RML2380
2381	JJD381D	3.66	WH	2713	10.94	Q	10.94	London Central Buses, London RML2381
2382	JJD382D	3.66	WH	2741	4.93	AF	*4.93*	*Leased to Kentish Bus RML2382*
2383	JJD383D	2.66	WW	2270	4.93	WW	*4.93*	*Leased to Kentish Bus RML2383*
2384	JJD384D	2.66	PR	2400	10.94	AC	10.94	Metroline Travel, London RML2384
2385	JJD385D	4.66	WH	2283	11.94	RA	11.94	London General Transport, London RML2385
2386	JJD386D	2.66	WH	2299	9.94	CT	9.94	Leaside Bus Co., London RML2386
2387	JJD387D	2.66	WW	2374	4.93	WW	*4.93*	*Leased to Kentish Bus RML2387*
2388	JJD388D	2.66	WW	2284	9.94	X	9.94	CentreWest, London RML2388
2389	JJD389D	2.66	PR	2286	11.94	RA	11.94	London General Transport, London RML2389
2390	JJD390D	2.66	WW	2321	9.94	X	9.94	CentreWest, London RML2390
2391	JJD391D	3.66	WH	2369	9.94	AR	9.94	Leaside Bus Co., London RML2391
2392	JJD392D	3.66	WH	2290	9.94	BW	9.94	Stagecoach East London, London RML2392
2393	JJD393D	2.66	WH	2737	10.94	HT	10.94	London Northern Bus Co., London RML2393
2394	JJD394D	2.66	WH	2264	9.94	AR	9.94	Leaside Bus Co., London RML2394
2395	JJD395D	3.66	WH	2757	10.94	HT	10.94	London Northern Bus Co., London RML2395
2396	JJD396D	11.66	AF	2461	10.94	Q	10.94	London Central Buses, London RML2396
2397	JJD397D	9.66	H	2297	10.94	Q	10.94	London Central Buses, London RML2397
2398	JJD398D	2.66	PR	2751	11.94	AF	11.94	London General Transport, London RML2398
2399	JJD399D	2.66	WH	2275	9.95	BW	9.94	Stagecoach East London, London RML2399
2400	JJD400D	2.66	WH	2389	10.94	Q	10.94	London Central Buses, London RML2400
2401	JJD401D	2.66	PR	2747	9.94	CT	9.94	Leaside Bus Co., London RML2401
2402	JJD402D	2.66	WH	2287	9.94	BW	9.94	Stagecoach East London, London RM2402
2403	JJD403D	2.66	PR	2733	11.94	RA	11.94	London General Transport, London RML2403
2404	JJD404D	2.66	WH	2302	7.93	AC	*10.93*	*Leased to BTS, Borehamwood RML2404*
2405	JJD405D	1.66	FY	2365	9.94	X	9.94	CentreWest, London RML2405
2406	JJD406D	2.66	PR	2401	9.94	CT	9.94	Leaside Bus Co., London RML2406
2407	JJD407D	1.66	FY	2396	1.95	BN	1.95	South London Transport, London RML2407
2408	JJD408D	2.66	WH	2301	9.94	AR	9.94	Leaside Bus Co., London RML2408
2409	JJD409D	2.66	PR	2360	9.94	CT	9.94	Leaside Bus Co., London RML2409
2410	JJD410D	2.66	PR	2308	4.93	AF	*4.93*	*Leased to Kentish Bus RML2410*
2411	JJD411D	2.66	HE	2411	12.69	HE	1.70	London Country Bus Services RML2411
								2.80 London Transport RML2411
		6.80	SW		10.94	Q	10.94	London Central Buses RML2411
2412	JJD412D	2.66	HE	2412	12.69	HE	1.70	London Country Bus Services RML2412
								12.79 London Transport RML2412
		4.80	W		11.94	AF	11.94	London General Transport, London RML2412

2413 JJD413D	3.66	GR	2413	12.69	HA	1.70	London Country Bus Services RML2413
							7.79 London Transport RML2413
	9.79	Dt		10.94	HT	10.94	London Northern Bus Co., London RML2413
2414 JJD414D	3.66	HH	2414	12.69	HH	1.70	London Country Bus Services RML2414
							11.78 London Transport RML2414
	3.79	FWt		11.94	S	11.94	London United Busways, London2414
2415 JJD415D	2.66	HE	2415	12.69	HE	1.70	London Country Bus Services RML2415
							7.79 London Transport RML2415
	12.80	HL		9.94	BW	9.94	Stagecoach East London, London RML2415
2416 JJD416D	2.66	HE	2416	12.69	HE	1.70	London Country Bus Services RML2416
							3.79 Wombwell Diesels (breaker), Wombwell
							7.79 London Transport RML2416
	12.80	HL		9.94	CT	9.94	Leaside Bus Co., London RML2416
2417 JJD417D	2.66	HE	2417	12.69	HE	1.70	London Country Bus Services RML2417
							12.77 London Transport (not used)
							1.78 Wombwell Diesels (breaker) - scrapped
2418 JJD418D	2.66	HE	2418	12.69	HE	1.70	London Country Bus Services RML2418
							3.79 Wombwell Diesels (breaker), Wombwell
							7.79 London Transport RML2418
	12.80	HT		9.94	AR	9.94	Leaside Bus Co., London RML2418
2419 JJD419D	2.66	HE	2419	12.69	HE	1.70	London Country Bus Services RML2419
							12.77 London Transport RML2419
	1.78	AE		10.94	HT	10.94	London Northern Bus Co., London RML2419
2420 JJD420D	3.66	GR	2420	12.69	GR	1.70	London Country Bus Services RML2420
							12.77 London Transport (not used)
							1.78 Wombwell Diesels (breaker) - scrapped
2421 JJD421D	3.66	GR	2421	12.69	GR	1.70	London Country Bus Services RML2421
							12.77 London Transport (not used)
							1.78 Wombwell Diesels (breaker) - scrapped
2422 JJD422D	3.66	GR	2422	12.69	GR	1.70	London Country Bus Services RML2422
							3.80 London Transport RML2422
	6.80	U		11.94	AF	11.94	London General Transport, London RML2422
2423 JJD423D	3.66	GR	2423	12.69	GR	1.70	London Country Bus Services RML2423
							3.79 Wombwell Diesels (breaker) - scrapped
2424 JJD424D	3.66	GR	2424	12.69	GR	1.70	London Country Bus Services RML2424
							3.79 Wombwell Diesels (breaker) - scrapped
2425 JJD425D	3.66	GR	2425	12.69	GR	1.70	London Country Bus Services RML2425
							12.77 London Transport (not used)
							1.78 Wombwell Diesels (breaker) - scrapped
2426 JJD426D	3.66	HH	2426	12.69	NF	1.70	London Country Bus Services RML2426
							12.77 London Transport (not used)
							1.78 Wombwell Diesels (breaker) - scrapped
2427 JJD427D	3.66	GR	2427	12.69	GR	1.70	London Country Bus Services RML2427
							12.77 London Transport (not used)
							2.78 Wombwell Diesels (breaker) - scrapped
2428 JJD428D	3.66	GR	2454	12.69	GR	1.70	London Country Bus Services RML2428
							6.79 London Transport RML2428
	2.80	H		9.94	X	9.94	CentreWest, London RML2428
2429 JJD429D	3.66	GR	2429	12.69	GR	1.70	London Country Bus Services RML2429
							3.79 Wombwell Diesels (breaker), Wombwell
							7.79 London Transport RML2429
	2.81	HL		9.94	BW	9.94	Stagecoach East London, London RML2429
2430 JJD430D	3.66	GR	2430	12.69	GR	1.70	London Country Bus Services RML2430
							12.77 London Transport RML2430
	4.78	AE		10.94	AC	10.94	Metroline Travel, London RML2430
2431 JJD431D	3.66	GR	2431	12.69	GR	1.70	London Country Bus Services RML2431
							3.79 Wombwell Diesels (breaker), Wombwell
							7.79 London Transport RML2431
	2.81	AF		10.94	AC	10.94	Metroline Travel, London RML2431
2432 JJD432D	3.66	GR	2432	12.69	GR	1.70	London Country Bus Services RML2432
							3.79 Wombwell Diesels (breaker), Wombwell
							7.79 London Transport RML2432
	2.81	CS		11.94	S	11.94	London United Busways, London RML2432

2433	JJD433D	3.66	GR	2433	12.69	GR	1.70	London Country Bus Services RML2433
								12.77 London Transport (not used)
								1.78 Wombwell Diesels (breaker) - scrapped
2434	JJD434D	3.66	GR	2434	12.69	GR	1.70	London Country Bus Services RML2434
								12.77 London Transport RML2434
		5.78	BW		9.94	AR	9.94	Leaside Bus Co., London RML2434
2435	JJD435D	3.66	GR	2265	12.69	GR	1.70	London Country Bus Services RML2435
								12.77 London Transport RML2435
		1.78	AC		9.94	BW	9.94	Stagecoach East London, London RML2435
2436	JJD436D	5.66	WR	2436	12.69	WR	1.70	London Country Bus Services RML2436
								12.77 London Transport (not used)
								1.78 Wombwell Diesels (breaker) - scrapped
2437	JJD437D	3.66	GR	2437	12.69	GR	1.70	London Country Bus Services RML2437
								6.79 London Transport RML2437
		2.80	AF		9.94	BW	9.94	Stagecoach East London, London RML2437
2438	JJD438D	3.66	GR	2438	12.69	GR	1.70	London Country Bus Services RML2438
								12.77 London Transport (not used)
								1.78 Wombwell Diesels (breaker) - scrapped
2439	JJD439D	3.66	GR	2439	12.69	GR	1.70	London Country Bus Services RML2439
								12.77 London Transport RML2439
		4.78	HT		10.94	AC	10.94	Metroline Travel, London RML2439
2440	JJD440D	3.66	GR	2440	12.69	GR	1.70	London Country Bus Services RML2440
								7.79 London Transport RML2440
		8.80	HL		10.94	Q	10.94	London Central Buses, London RML2440
2441	JJD441D	3.66	GR	2367	11.94	AF	11.94	London General Transport, London RML2441
2442	JJD442D	5.66	HA	2442	12.69	HA	1.70	London Country Bus Services RML2442
								10.78 London Transport RML2442
		3.79	Rt		9.94	X	9.94	CentreWest, London RML2442
2443	JJD443D	3.66	GR	2384	7.93	AC	*10.93*	*Leased to BTS, Borehamwood RML2443*
2444	JJD444D	5.66	HA	2444	12.69	HA	1.70	London Country Bus Services RML2444
								12.77 London Transport RML2444
		1.78	SE		9.94	BW	9.94	Stagecoach East London, London RML2444
2445	JJD445D	5.66	HA	2372	12.69	HA	1.70	London Country Bus Services RML2445
								2.80 London Transport RML2445
		4.80	W		9.94	U	9.94	Stagecoach East London, London RML2445
2446	JJD446D	5.66	NF	2446	12.69	NF	1.70	London Country Bus Services RML2446
								3.80 London Transport RML2446
		6.80	U		10.94	AC	10.94	Metroline Travel, London RML2446
2447	JJD447D	5.66	WR	2447	12.69	NF	1.70	London Country Bus Services RML2447
								1.80 London Transport RML2447
		2.80	AF		11.94	S	11.94	London United Busways, London RML2447
2448	JJD448D	5.66	HA	2448	12.69	HA	1.70	London Country Bus Services RML2448
								12.77 London Transport (not used)
								1.78 Wombwell Diesels (breaker) - scrapped
2449	JJD449D	5.66	HA	2449	12.69	HA	1.70	London Country Bus Services RML2449
								12.77 London Transport (not used)
								2.78 Wombwell Diesels (breaker) - scrapped
2450	JJD450D	5.66	HA	2450	12.69	HA	1.70	London Country Bus Services RML2450
								7.79 London Transport RML2450
		11.80	HL		9.94	BW	9.94	Stagecoach East London, London RML2450
2451	JJD451D	5.66	NF	2451	12.69	NF	1.70	London Country Bus Services RML2451
								7.79 London Transport RML2451
		9.79	NSt		9.94	BW	9.94	Stagecoach East London, London RML2451
2452	JJD452D	5.66	NF	2452	12.69	NF	1.70	London Country Bus Services RML2452
								2.80 London Transport RML2452
		6.80	NX		4.93	AF	*4.93*	*Leased to Kentish Bus RML2452*
2453	JJD453D	5.66	HA	2453	12.69	HA	1.70	London Country Bus Services RML2453
								3.80 London Transport RML2453
		6.80	SW		11.94	AF	11.94	London General Transport, London RML2453
2454	JJD454D	5.66	NF	2428	12.69	NF	1.70	London Country Bus Services RML2454
								12.77 London Transport RML2454
		1.78	SWt		10.94	Q	10.94	London Central Buses, London RML2454
2455	JJD455D	5.66	NF	2455	12.69	NF	1.70	London Country Bus Services RML2455
								8.78 London Transport RML2455
		8.78	Qt		11.94	S	11.94	London United Busways, London RML2455

2456	JJD456D	5.66	HA	2456	12.69	HA	1.70	London Country Bus Services RML2456 7.79 London Transport RML2456
		11.80	HL		9.94	U	9.94	Stagecoach East London, London RML2456
2457	JJD457D	5.66	WR	2457	12.69	NF	1.70	London Country Bus Services RML2457 7.79 London Transport RML2457
		1.81	WH		9.94	CT	9.94	Leaside Bus Co., London RML2457
2458	JJD458D	5.66	HA	2458	12.69	HA	1.70	London Country Bus Services RML2458 12.77 London Transport (not used) 2.78 Wombwell Diesels (breaker) - scrapped
2459	JJD459D	5.66	NF	2459	12.69	HA	1.70	London Country Bus Services RML2459 12.77 London Transport (not used) 1.78 Wombwell Diesels (breaker) - scrapped
2460	JJD460D	5.66	NF	2460	12.69	HA	1.70	London Country Bus Services RML2460 12.77 London Transport RML2460
		1.78	HT		9.94	AR	9.94	Leaside Bus Co., London RML2460
2461	JJD461D	5.66	AR	2405	11.94	AF	11.94	London General Transport, London RML2461
2462	JJD462D	5.66	FY	2267	9.94	BW	9.94	Stagecoach East London, London RML2462
2463	JJD463D	5.66	FY	2462	11.94	S	11.94	London United Busways, London RML2463
2464	JJD464D	5.66	FY	2397	11.94	S	11.94	London United Busways, London RML2464
2465	JJD465D	5.66	AF	2465	11.94	RA	11.94	London General Transport, London RML2465
2466	JJD466D	5.66	AF	2492	11.94	AF	11.94	London General Transport, London RML2466
2467	JJD467D	5.66	AF	2470	9.94	X	9.94	CentreWest, London RML2467
2468	JJD468D	5.66	FY	2370	9.94	AR	9.94	Leaside Bus Co., London RML2468
2469	JJD469D	5.66	AF	2728	10.94	Q	10.94	London Central Buses, London RML2469
2470	JJD470D	5.66	AF	2316	9.94	BW	9.94	Stagecoach East London, London RML2470
2471	JJD471D	5.66	FY	2477	10.94	AC	10.94	Metroline Travel, London RML2471
2472	JJD472D	5.66	AF	2486	11.94	AF	11.94	London General Transport, London RML2472
2473	JJD473D	5.66	AF	2407	9.94	X	9.94	CentreWest, London RML2473
2474	JJD474D	5.66	AF	2466	10.94	Q	10.94	London Central Buses, London RML2474
2475	JJD475D	5.66	AF	2382	11.94	AF	11.94	London General Transport, London RML2475
2476	JJD476D	6.66	SW	2441	9.94	X	9.94	CentreWest, London RML2476
2477	JJD477D	5.66	AF	2469	1.95	BN	1.95	South London Transport, London RML2477
2478	JJD478D	5.66	AF	2383	10.94	AC	10.94	Metroline Travel, London RML2478
2479	JJD479D	5.66	AF	2512	10.94	HT	10.94	London Northern Bus Co., London RML2479
2480	JJD480D	5.66	AF	2471	9.94	X	9.94	CentreWest, London RML2480
2481	JJD481D	6.66	SW	2473	9.94	BW	9.94	Stagecoach East London, London RML2481
2482	JJD482D	6.66	SW	2756	10.94	Q	10.94	London Central Buses, London RML2482
2483	JJD483D	5.66	AF	2402	9.94	CT	9.94	Leaside Bus Co., London RML2483
2484	JJD484D	6.66	SW	2490	10.94	Q	10.94	London Central Buses, London RML2484
2485	JJD485D	6.66	SW	2443	11.94	S	11.94	London United Busways, London RML2485
2486	JJD486D	6.66	SW	2478	9.94	X	9.94	CentreWest, London RML2486
2487	JJD487D	6.66	SW	2472	10.93	FY	*10.93*	*Leased to BTS, Borehamwood RML2487*
2488	JJD488D	6.66	SW	2501	9.94	BW	9.94	Stagecoach East London, London RML2488
2489	JJD489D	6.66	SW	2475	11.94	S	11.94	London United Busways, London RML2489
2490	JJD490D	6.66	SW	2507	9.94	X	9.94	CentreWest, London RML2490
2491	JJD491D	6.66	SW	2483	1.95	BN	1.95	South London Transport RML2491
2492	JJD492D	6.66	SW	2510	9.94	CT	9.94	Leaside Bus Co., London RML2492
2493	JJD493D	6.66	SW	2491	9.94	BW	9.94	Stagecoach East London, London RML2493
2494	JJD494D	6.66	SW	2514	9.94	CT	9.94	Leaside Bus Co., London RML2494
2495	JJD495D	6.66	SW	2504	9.94	U	9.94	Stagecoach East London, London RML2495
2496	JJD496D	6.66	FY	2354	9.94	U	9.94	Stagecoach East London, London RML2496
2497	JJD497D	6.66	SW	2410	9.94	U	9.94	Stagecoach East London, London RML2497
2498	JJD498D	6.66	SW	2545	9.94	X	9.94	CentreWest, London RML2498
2499	JJD499D	7.66	U	2476	10.94	Q	10.94	London Central Buses, London RML2499
2500	JJD500D	6.66	FY	2262	11.94	S	11.94	London United Busways, London RML2500
2501	JJD501D	6.66	FY	2497	9.94	X	9.94	CentreWest, London RML2501
2502	JJD502D	6.66	SW	2538	11.94	AF	11.94	London General Transport, London RML2502
2503	JJD503D	7.66	U	2480	9.94	AR	9.94	Leaside Bus Co., London RML2503
2504	JJD504D	7.66	U	2494	9.94	AR	9.94	Leaside Bus Co., London RML2504
2505	JJD505D	7.66	U	2528	4.93	AF	*4.93*	*Leased to Kentish Bus RML2505*
2506	JJD506D	6.66	SW	2523	9.94	X	9.94	CentreWest, London RML2506
2507	JJD507D	7.66	U	2555	10.94	NX	10.94	London Central Buses, London RML2507

2508	JJD508D		7.66	U	2530	10.94	AC	10.94	Metroline Travel, London RML2508
2509	JJD509D		7.66	U	2511	10.94	AC	10.94	Metroline Travel, London RML2509
2510	JJD510D		7.66	U	2537	9.94	AR	9.94	Leaside Bus Co., London RML2510
2511	JJD511D		7.66	U	2488	10.94	HT	10.94	London Northern Bus Co., London RML2511
2512	JJD512D		7.66	U	2559	12.92	AF	*4.93*	*Leased to Kentish Bus RML2512*
2513	JJD513D		7.66	U	2546	10.94	Q	10.94	London Central Buses, London RML2513
2514	JJD514D		7.66	U	2352	12.92	BW	*4.93*	*Leased to Kentish Bus RML2514*
2515	JJD515D		7.66	U	2498	10.94	Q	10.94	London Central Buses, London RML2515
2516	JJD516D	WLT516	7.66	U	2516	11.94	RA	11.94	London General Transport, London DRM2516
2517	JJD517D		7.66	U	2280	11.94	RA	11.94	London General Transport, London RML2517
2518	JJD518D		7.66	U	2519	9.94	AR	9.94	Leaside Bus Co., London RML2518
2519	JJD519D		7.66	U	2540	11.94	S	11.94	London United Busways, London RML2519
2520	JJD520D		7.66	U	2549	11.94	AF	11.94	London General Transport, London RML2520
2521	JJD521D		7.66	U	2534	1.95	BN	1.95	South London Transport, London RML2521
2522	JJD522D		7.66	U	2522	9.94	X	9.94	CentreWest, London RML2522
2523	JJD523D		7.66	U	2474	4.93	WW	*4.93*	*Leased to Kentish Bus RML2523*
2524	JJD524D		7.66	U	2524	12.92	B	*4.93*	*Leased to Kentish Bus RML2524*
2525	JJD525D		7.66	U	2554	9.94	AR	9.94	Leaside Bus Co., London RML2525
2526	JJD526D		7.66	U	2526	9.94	CT	9.94	Leaside Bus Co., London RML2526
2527	JJD527D		7.66	U	2650	7.93	AC	*12.93*	*Leased to BTS, Borehamwood RML2527*
2528	JJD528D		7.66	U	2467	9.94	AR	9.94	Leaside Bus Co., London RML2528
2529	JJD529D		9.66	H	2529	10.94	Q	10.94	London Central Buses, London RML2529
2530	JJD530D		7.66	U	2502	9.94	X	9.94	CentreWest, London RML2530
2531	JJD531D		7.66	U	2487	4.93	AF	*4.93*	*Leased to Kentish Bus RML2531*
2532	JJD532D		7.66	U	2499	10.94	AC	10.94	Metroline Travel, London RML2532
2533	JJD533D		7.66	U	2489	4.93	AF	*4.93*	*Leased to Kentish Bus RML2533*
2534	JJD534D		7.66	U	2532	9.94	CT	9.94	Leaside Bus Co., London RML2534
2535	JJD535D		7.66	U	2543	11.94	AF	11.94	London General Transport, London RML2535
2536	JJD536D		7.66	U	2508	4.93	WW	*4.93*	*Leased to Kentish Bus RML2536*
2537	JJD537D		7.66	U	2542	10.94	AC	10.94	Metroline Travel, London RML2537
2538	JJD538D		7.66	U	2548	7.93	AC	*12.93*	*Leased to BTS, Borehamwood RML2538*
2539	JJD539D		9.66	H	2479	10.94	NX	10.94	London Central Buses, London RML2539
2540	JJD540D		7.66	U	2484	11.94	AF	11.94	London General Transport, London RML2540
2541	JJD541D		9.66	H	2482	9.94	U	9.94	Stagecoach East London, London RML2541
2542	JJD542D		9.66	H	2560	9.94	X	9.94	CentreWest, London RML2542
2543	JJD543D		10.66	AC	2503	11.94	AF	11.94	London General Transport, London RML2543
2544	JJD544D		9.66	H	2570	9.94	AR	9.94	Leaside Bus Co., London RML2544
2545	JJD545D		9.66	H	2496	1.95	BN	1.95	South London Transport, London RML2545
2546	JJD546D		9.66	H	2541	9.94	AR	9.94	Leaside Bus Co., London RML2546
2547	JJD547D		9.66	H	2745	10.94	AC	10.94	Metroline Travel, London RML2547
2548	JJD548D		4.68	HL	2550	12.92	BN	*4.93*	*Leased to Kentish Bus RML2548*
2549	JJD549D		9.66	H	2518	1.95	BN	1.95	South London Transport, London RML2549
2550	JJD550D		9.66	H	2485	9.94	U	9.94	Stagecoach East London, London RML2550
2551	JJD551D		10.66	AC	2509	10.94	Q	10.94	London Central Buses, London RML2551
2552	JJD552D		9.66	H	2552	9.94	CT	9.94	Leaside Bus Co., London RML2552
2553	JJD553D		9.66	H	2481	9.94	X	9.94	CentreWest, London RML2553
2554	JJD554D		9.66	SW	2495	10.94	Q	10.94	London Central Buses, London RML2554
2555	JJD555D		9.66	H	2500	9.94	X	9.94	CentreWest, London RML2555
2556	JJD556D		9.66	H	2506	10.94	Q	10.94	London Central Buses, London RML2556
2557	JJD557D		9.66	H	2557	8.83	J	2.83	Ensign (dealer), Purfleet
									6.83 PVS (breaker), Carlton - scrapped
2558	JJD558D		10.66	AC	2505	10.94	AC	10.94	Metroline Travel, London RML2558
2559	JJD559D		10.66	AC	2556	9.94	X	9.94	CentreWest, London RML2559
2560	JJD560D		10.66	AC	2493	10.94	Q	10.94	London Central Buses, London RML2560
2561	JJD561D		9.66	H	2571	10.94	HT	10.94	London Northern Bus Co., London RML2561
2562	JJD562D		9.66	H	2577	9.94	AR	9.94	Leaside Bus Co., London RML2562
2563	JJD563D		9.66	H	2573	6.93	FY	*10.93*	*Leased to BTS, Borehamwood RML2563*
2564	JJD564D		9.66	H	2645	11.94	AF	11.94	London General Transport, London RML2564
2565	JJD565D		10.66	H	2566	9.94	U	9.94	Stagecoach East London, London RML2565
2566	JJD566D		9.66	H	2574	10.94	AC	10.94	Metroline Travel, London RML2566
2567	JJD567D		9.66	H	2611	9.94	CT	9.94	Leaside Bus Co., London RML2567
2568	JJD568D		10.66	AC	2533	11.94	AF	11.94	London General Transport, London RML2568

2569	JJD569D	10.66	AC	2585	7.93	FY	*10.93*	*Leased to BTS, Borehamwood RML2569*
2570	JJD570D	10.66	AC	2575	11.94	AF	11.94	London General Transport, London RML2570
2571	JJD571D	10.66	AC	2631	9.94	AR	9.94	Leaside Bus Co., London RML2571
2572	JJD572D	10.66	AC	2593	1.95	BN	1.95	South London Transport, London RML2572
2573	JJD573D	10.66	AC	2594	1.95	BN	1.95	South London Transport, London RML2573
2574	JJD574D	10.66	AC	2603	12.92	BN	*4.93*	*Leased to Kentish Bus RML2574*
2575	JJD575D	11.66	AF	2579	11.94	AF	11.94	London General Transport, London RML2575
2576	JJD576D	10.66	AC	2643	11.94	AF	11.94	London General Transport, London RML2576
2577	JJD577D	11.66	AF	2535	1.93	AF	*4.93*	*Leased to Kentish Bus RML2577*
2578	JJD578D	11.66	AF	2572	10.94	NX	10.94	London Central Buses, London RML2578
2579	JJD579D	11.66	AF	2536	10.94	AC	10.94	Metroline Travel, London RML2579
2580	JJD580D	11.66	AF	2513	11.94	AF	11.94	London General Transport, London RML2580
2581	JJD581D	11.66	AF	2561	9.94	U	9.94	Stagecoach East London, London RML2581
2582	JJD582D	11.66	AF	2576	6.93	FY	*10.93*	*Leased to BTS, Borehamwood RML2582*
2583	JJD583D	11.66	AF	2578	10.94	NX	10.94	London Central Buses, London RML2583
2584	JJD584D	11.66	AF	2568	10.94	NX	10.94	London Central Buses, London RML2584
2585	JJD585D	11.66	AF	2588	10.94	AC	10.94	Metroline Travel, London RML2585
2586	JJD586D	11.66	AF	2586	1.93	AF	*4.93*	*Leased to Kentish Bus RML2586*
2587	JJD587D	11.66	AF	2580	10.94	Q	10.94	London Central Buses, London RML2587
2588	JJD588D	11.66	AF	2584	9.94	AR	9.94	Leaside Bus Co., London RML2588
2589	JJD589D	11.66	AF	2565	9.94	AR	9.94	Leaside Bus Co., London RML2589
2590	JJD590D	11.66	AF	2563	11.94	AF	11.94	London General Transport, London RML2590
2591	JJD591D	11.66	AF	2589	12.92	BN	*4.93*	*Leased to Kentish Bus RML2591*
2592	JJD592D	11.66	AF	2569	9.94	BW	9.94	Stagecoach East London, London RML2592
2593	JJD593D	11.66	AC	2587	11.94	AF	11.94	London General Transport, London RML2593
2594	JJD594D	11.66	AC	2567	10.94	AC	10.94	Metroline Travel, London RML2594
2595	JJD595D	12.66	U	2598	9.94	AR	9.94	Leaside Bus Co., London RML2595
2596	JJD596D	12.66	U	2590	10.94	NX	10.94	London Central Buses, London RML2596
2597	JJD597D	12.66	U	2583	9.94	CT	9.94	Leaside Bus Co., London RML2597
2598	JJD598D	12.66	U	2582	9.93	Q	*12.93*	*Leased to BTS, Borehamwood RML2598*
2599	NML598E	5.67	J	2658	10.94	AC	10.94	Metroline Travel, London RML2599
2600	NML600E	5.67	J	2655	11.94	S	11.94	London United Busways, London RML2600
2601	NML601E	5.67	J	2648	10.94	Q	10.94	London Central Buses, London RML2601
2602	NML602E	5.67	J	2652	9.94	X	9.94	CentreWest, London RML2602
2603	NML603E	5.67	J	2637	10.94	HT	10.94	London Northern Bus Co., London RML2603
2604	NML604E	5.67	J	2646	10.94	NX	10.94	London Central Buses, London RML2604
2605	NML605E	5.67	J	2636	11.94	AF	11.94	London General Transport, London RML2605
2606	NML606E	5.67	J	2627	11.94	RA	11.94	London General Transport, London RML2606
2607	NML607E	5.67	J	2618	9.94	BW	9.94	Stagecoach East London, London RML2607
2608	NML608E	5.67	J	2621	1.95	BN	1.95	South London Transport, London RML2608
2609	NML609E	5.67	J	2649	9.94	X	9.94	CentreWest, London RML2609
2610	NML610E	5.67	J	2600	9.94	U	9.94	Stagecoach East London, London RML2610
2611	NML611E	5.67	J	2591	9.94	AR	9.94	Leaside Bus Co., London RML2611
2612	NML612E	5.67	J	2630	11.94	AF	11.94	London General Transport, London RML2612
2613	NML613E	5.67	J	2581	10.94	Q	10.94	London Central Buses, London RML2613
2614	NML614E	5.67	J	2596	10.94	Q	10.94	London Central Buses, London RML2614
2615	NML615E	6.67	J	2620	11.94	AF	11.94	London General Transport, London RML2615
2616	NML616E	6.67	J	2616	9.94	U	9.94	Stagecoach East London, London RML2616
2617	NML617E	6.67	J	2634	9.94	AR	9.94	Leaside Bus Co., London RML2617
2618	NML618E	6.67	J	2651	11.94	RA	11.94	London General Transport, London RML2618
2619	NML619E	5.67	J	2602	1.93	AF	*4.93*	*Leased to Kentish Bus RML2619*
2620	NML620E	5.67	J	2605	10.94	HT	10.94	London Northern Bus Co., London RML2620
2621	NML621E	6.67	J	2640	11.94	S	11.94	London United Busways, London RML2621
2622	NML622E	5.67	J	2617	11.94	S	11.94	London United Busways, London RML2622
2623	NML623E	5.67	J	2595	9.94	X	9.94	CentreWest, London RML2623
2624	NML624E	5.67	J	2635	9.94	BW	9.94	Stagecoach East London, London RML2624
2625	NML625E	5.67	J	2601	9.94	AR	9.94	Leaside Bus Co., London RML2625
2626	NML626E	5.67	J	2562	11.94	AF	11.94	London General Transport, London RML2626
2627	NML627E	6.67	J	2642	7.93	FY	*12.93*	*Leased to BTS, Borehamwood RML2627*
2628	NML628E	5.67	J	2604	9.94	AR	9.94	Leaside Bus Co., London RML2628
2629	NML629E	5.67	J	2607	10.94	Q	10.94	London Central Buses, London RML2629

2630	NML630E	5.67	J	2608	10.94	Q	10.94	London Central Buses, London RML2630
2631	NML631E	5.67	J	2647	11.94	AF	11.94	London General Transport, London RML2631
2632	NML632E	5.67	J	2599	9.94	AR	9.94	Leaside Bus Co., London RML2632
2633	NML633E	5.67	J	2615	6.93	AC	*10.93*	*Leased to BTS, Borehamwood RML2633*
2634	NML634E	6.67	AF	2639	10.94	AC	10.94	Metroline Travel, London RML2634
2635	NML635E	6.67	AF	2619	9.94	AR	9.94	Leaside Bus Co., London RML2635
2636	NML636E	6.67	AF	2657	1.95	BN	1.95	South London Transport, London RML2636
2637	NML637E	6.67	AF	2625	11.94	AF	11.94	London General Transport, London RML2637
2638	NML638E	7.67	R	2654	9.94	AR	9.94	Leaside Bus Co., London RML2638
2639	NML639E	6.67	AF	2609	9.94	U	9.94	Stagecoach East London, London RML2639
2640	NML640E	6.67	AF	2622	11.94	AF	11.94	London General Transport, London RML2640
2641	NML641E	6.67	AF	2612	9.94	U	9.94	Stagecoach East London, London RML2641
2642	NML642E	6.67	AF	2606	9.94	U	9.94	Stagecoach East London, London RML2642
2643	NML643E	6.67	AF	2656	9.94	AR	9.94	Leaside Bus Co., London RML2643
2644	NML644E	9.67	UX	2614	11.94	AF	11.94	London General Transport, London RML2644
2645	NML645E	7.67	R	2564	11.94	S	11.94	London United Busways, London RML2645
2646	NML646E	7.67	R	2629	11.94	S	11.94	London United Busways, London RML2646
2647	NML647E	7.67	R	2632	9.94	X	9.94	CentreWest, London RML2647
2648	NML648E	7.67	R	2527	11.94	RA	11.94	London General Transport, London RML2648
2649	NML649E	7.67	R	2633	10.94	AC	10.94	Metroline Travel, London RML2649
2650	NML650E	7.67	HL	2628	11.94	S	11.94	London United Busways, London RML2650
2651	NML651E	7.67	R	2626	10.94	AC	10.94	Metroline Travel, London RML2651
2652	NML652E	7.67	R	2660	10.94	AC	10.94	Metroline Travel, London RML2652
2653	NML653E	7.67	R	2641	1.95	BN	1.95	South London Transport, London RML2653
2654	NML654E	7.67	R	2597	11.94	AF	11.94	London General Transport, London RML2654
2655	NML655E	7.67	R	2624	9.94	AR	9.94	Leaside Bus Co., London RML2655
2656	NML656E	7.67	HL	2592	9.94	X	9.94	CentreWest, London RML2656
2657	NML657E	7.67	R	2653	9.94	BW	9.94	Stagecoach East London, London RML2657
2658	SMK658F	9.67	UX	2623	9.94	AR	9.94	Leaside Bus Co., London RML2658
2659	SMK659F	9.67	UX	2610	6.93	AC	*12.93*	*Leased to BTS, Borehamwood RML2659*
2660	SMK660F	9.67	HL	2613	9.94	AR	9.94	Leaside Bus Co., London RML2660
2661	SMK661F	9.67	HL	2695	9.94	U	9.94	Stagecoach East London, London RML2661
2662	SMK662F	11.67	TC	2638	11.94	S	11.94	London United Busways, London RML2662
2663	SMK663F	10.67	HL	2670	6.93	FY	*10.93*	*Leased to BTS, Borehamwood RML2663*
2664	SMK664F	11.67	TC	2659	9.94	X	9.94	CentreWest, London RML2664
2665	SMK665F	11.67	TC	2685	9.94	BW	9.94	Stagecoach East London, London RML2665
2666	SMK666F	11.67	TC	2666	9.94	AR	9.94	Leaside Bus Co., London RML2666
2667	SMK667F	11,67	TC	2663	9.94	X	9.94	CentreWest, London RML2667
2668	SMK668F	11.67	CF	2708	7.93	AC	*10.93*	*Leased to BTS, Borehamwood RML2668*
2669	SMK669F	9.67	HL	2547	11.94	RA	11.94	London General Transport, London RML2669
2670	SMK670F	9.67	HL	2724	9.94	U	9.94	Stagecoach East London, London RML2670
2671	SMK671F	9.67	HL	2398	9.94	U	9.94	Stagecoach East London, London RML2671
2672	SMK672F	9.67	HL	2754	9.94	X	9.94	CentreWest, London RML2672
2673	SMK673F	9.67	HL	2738	10.94	NX	10.94	London Central Buses, London RML2673
2674	SMK674F	9.67	HL	2719	7.93	FY	*10.93*	*Leased to BTS, Borehamwood RML2674*
2675	SMK675F	9.67	HL	2339	9.94	CT	9.94	Leaside Bus Co., London RML2675
2676	SMK676F	9.67	HL	2683	10.94	Q	10.94	London Central Buses, London RML2676
2677	SMK677F	9.67	HL	2363	9.94	X	9.94	CentreWest, London RML2677
2678	SMK678F	9.67	HL	2680	9.94	AR	9.94	Leaside Bus Co., London RML2678
2679	SMK679F	9.67	HL	2672	10.94	HT	10.94	London Northern Bus Co., London RML2679
2680	SMK680F	9.67	HL	2300	11.94	RA	11.94	London General Transport, London RML2680
2681	SMK681F	9.67	HL	2744	10.94	AC	10.94	Metroline Travel, London RML2681
2682	SMK682F	9.67	HL	2307	9.94	CT	9.94	Leaside Bus Co., London RML2682
2683	SMK683F	9.67	HL	2755	10.94	Q	10.94	London Central Buses, London RML2683
2684	SMK684F	9.67	HL	2752	9.94	AR	9.94	Leaside Bus Co., London RML2684
2685	SMK685F	9.67	HL	2311	9.94	CT	9.94	Leaside Bus Co., London RML2685
2686	SMK686F	9.67	HL	2333	6.93	AC	*10.93*	*Leased to BTS, Borehamwood RML2686*
2687	SMK687F	9.67	HL	2753	9.94	X	9.94	CentreWest, London RML2687
2688	SMK688F	9.67	HL	2706	9.94	CT	9.94	Leaside Bus Co., London RML2688
2689	SMK689F	9.67	HL	2725	10.94	AC	10.94	Metroline Travel, London RML2689
2690	SMK690F	9.67	HL	2662	10.94	AC	10.94	Metroline Travel, London RML2690

2691	SMK691F	9.67	HL	2691	9.72	HL	9.72	Gala Cosmetics (International), Surbiton
								.73 Used by Gala Cosmetics in Canada
								.74 Used by Gala Cosmetics in Finland
2692	SMK692F	9.67	UX	2740	1.95	BN	1.95	South London Transport, London RML2692
2693	SMK693F	9.67	UX	2750	11.94	RA	11.94	London General Transport, London RML2693
2694	SMK694F	9.67	HL	2742	7.93	AC	*10.93*	*Leased to BTS, Borehamwood RML2694*
2695	SMF695F	9.67	HL	2743	10.94	AC	10.94	Metroline Travel, London RML2695
2696	SMK696F	9.67	HL	2684	9.94	Ut	9.94	Stagecoach East London, London RML2696
2697	SMK697F	9.67	HL	2661	11.94	S	11.94	London United Busways, London RML2697
2698	SMK698F	9.67	HL	2687	10.94	AC	10.94	Metroline Travel, London RML2698
2699	SMK699F	9.67	HL	2675	10.94	HT	10.94	London Northern Bus Co., London RML2699
2700	SMK700F	10.67	HL	2664	11.94	S	11.94	London United Busways, London RML2700
2701	SMK701F	10.67	HL	2669	10.94	AC	10.94	Metroline Travel, London RML2701
2702	SMK702F	10.67	HL	2712	11.94	S	11.94	London United Busways, London RML2702
2703	SMK703F	10.67	HL	2701	10.94	AC	10.94	Metroline Travel, London RML2703
2704	SMK704F	9.67	UX	2690	11.94	S	11.94	London United Busways, London RML2704
2705	SMK705F	10.67	HL	2698	9.94	U	9.94	Stagecoach East London, London RML2705
2706	SMK706F	10.67	HL	2727	10.94	AC	10.94	Metroline Travel, London RML2706
2707	SMK707F	10.67	HL	2694	11.94	S	11.94	London United Busways, London RML2707
2708	SMK708F	10.67	HL	2674	9.94	AR	9.94	Leaside Bus Co., London RM2708
2709	SMK709F	10.67	UX	2693	9.94	BW	9.94	Stagecoach East London, London RML2709
2710	SMK710F	10.67	UX	2668	10.94	AC	10.94	Metroline Travel, London RML2710
2711	SMK711F	10.67	HL	2711	10.94	Q	10.94	London Central Buses, London RML2711
2712	SMK712F	10.67	HL	2709	10.94	Q	10.94	London Central Buses, London RML2712
2713	SMK713F	10.67	HL	2679	10.94	AC	10.94	Metroline Travel, London RML2713
2714	SMK714F	10.67	HL	2673	10.94	Q	10.94	London Central Buses, London RML2714
2715	SMK715F	10.67	HL	2525	12.91	AF	*4.93*	*Leased to Kentish Bus RML2715*
2716	SMK716F	11.67	TC	2681	9.94	CT	9.94	Leaside Bus Co., London RML2716
2717	SMK717F	11.67	TC	2716	9.94	AC	9.94	CentreWest, London RML2717
2718	SMK718F	11.67	TC	2677	1.95	BN	1.95	South London Transport, London RML2718
2719	SMK719F	11.67	TC	2722	7.93	FY	*12.93*	*Leased to BTS, Borehamwood RML2719*
2720	SMK720F	11.67	TC	2689	11.94	S	11.94	London United Busways, London RML2720
2721	SMK721F	11.67	TC	2692	11.94	S	11.94	London United Busways, London RML2721
2722	SMK722F	11.67	TC	2704	11.94	S	11.94	London United Busways, London RML2722
2723	SMF723F	11.67	TC	2705	9.94	U	9.94	Stagecoach East London, London RML2723
2724	SMK724F	11.67	HL	2717	9.94	X	9.94	CentreWest, London RML2724
2725	SMK725F	11.67	TC	2671	11.94	RA	11.94	London General Transport, London RML2725
2726	SMK726F	11.67	TC	2700	1.95	BN	1.95	South London Transport, London RML2726
2727	SMK727F	11.67	TC	2298	10.94	AC	10.94	Metroline Travel, London RML2727
2728	SMK728F	11.67	HL	2667	10.94	AC	10.94	Metroline Travel, London RML2728
2729	SMK729F	11.67	TC	2696	11.94	S	11.94	London United Busways, London RML2729
2730	SMK730F	11.67	TC	2678	1.95	BN	1.95	South London Transport, London RML2730
2731	SMK731F	11.67	TC	2697	10.94	HT	10.94	London Northern Bus Co., London RML2731
2732	SMK732F	11.67	TC	2732	11.94	RA	11.94	London General Transport, London RML2732
2733	SMK733F	11.67	TC	2274	10.94	Q	10.94	London Central Buses, London RML2733
2734	SMK734F	11.67	HL	2702	11.94	S	11.94	London United Busways, London RML2734
2735	SMK735F	11.67	HL	2277	9.94	X	9.94	CentreWest, London RML2735
2736	SMK736F	11.67	HL	2729	11.94	RA	11.94	London General Transport, London RML2736
2737	SMK737F	11.67	HL	2348	10.94	AC	10.94	Metroline Travel, London RML2737
2738	SMK738F	11.67	HL	2714	9.94	BW	9.94	Stagecoach East London, London RML2738
2739	SMK739F	12.67	TC	2676	11.94	S	11.94	London United Busways, London RML2739
2740	SMK740F	12.67	TC	2707	9.94	X	9.94	CentreWest, London RML2740
2741	SMK741F	12.67	TC	2718	1.95	BN	1.95	South London Transport, London RML2741
2742	SMK742F	12.67	TC	2715	9.94	AR	9.94	Leaside Bus Co., London RML2742
2743	SMK743F	12.67	TC	2435	9.94	U	9.94	Stagecoach East London, London RML2743
2744	SMK744F	12.67	TC	2296	11.94	S	11.94	London United Busways, London RML2744
2745	SMK745F	12.67	TC	2380	11.94	AF	11.94	London General Transport, London RML2745
2746	SMK746F	12.67	TC	2268	9.94	AC	9.94	Leaside Bus Co., London RML2746
2747	SMK747F	12.67	TC	2726	9.94	AR	9.94	Leaside Bus Co., London RML2747
2748	SMK748F	1.68	TC	2359	9.94	U	9.94	Stagecoach East London, London RML2748
2749	SMK749F	12.67	TC	2730	9.94	BW	9.94	Stagecoach East London, London RML2749
2750	SMK750F	1.68	TC	2378	9.94	CT	9.94	Leaside Bus Co., London RML2750

2751	SMK751F	1.68	TC	2731	11.94	S	11.94	London United Busways, London RML2751
2752	SMK752F	1.68	TC	2305	11.94	RA	11.94	London General Transport, London RML2752
2753	SMK753F	1.68	TC	2517	1.95	BN	1.95	South London Transport, London RML2753
2754	SMK754F	3.68	TC	2749	9.94	CT	9.94	Leaside Bus Co., London RML2754
2755	SMK755F	3.68	TC	2703	10.94	AC	10.94	Metroline Travel, London RML2755
2756	SMK756F	5.68	HL	2735	7.93	FY	*12.93*	*Leased to BTS, Borehamwood RML2756*
2757	SMK757F	2.68	TC	2736	11.94	S	11.94	London United Busways, London RML2757
2758	SMK758F	2.68	TC	2734	9.94	CTt	9.94	Leaside Bus Co., London RML2758
2759	SMK759F	2.68	TC	2644	1.95	BN	1.95	South London Transport, London RML2759
2760	SMK760F	3.68	U	2760	9.94	U	9.94	Stagecoach East London, London RML2760

BRITISH EUROPEAN AIRWAYS / RMA

1	KGJ601D	10.66				6.79	London Transport RMA28 (not used)
							11.82 Blackwell (preserved), Ilford
2	KGJ602D	10.66				11.76	London Transport RMA14
		1.78	ALDs	8.85	ALD	8.85	BEL, Aldenham RMA14
							7.87 Graves (preserved), Watford
							.91 Green Rover, Watford RMA2
3	KGJ603D	11.66				6.79	London Transport RMA29
		6.81	PMt			2.88	Clydeside Scottish (for spares)
							5.89 Western Scottish (for spares)
							7.90 Wombwell Diesels (bkr), Wombwell
							3.92 J.Sykes (breaker), Carlton
							3.92 Brown, Motcombe
4	KGJ604D	11.66				6.79	London Transport RMA30
		6.79	CTs	10.85	CTs	10.85	BEL, Aldenham RMA30
							8.87 PVS (breaker), Carlton - scrapped
	KGJ605D	11.66				6.79	London Transport RMA31
		11.79	ACs	7.80	ACs	10.81	Wombwell Diesels (breaker), Wombwell - scrapped
	KGJ606D	11.66				6.79	London Transport RMA32
		11.79	Ws	10.85	SEs	10.85	BEL, Aldenham RMA32
							8.87 PVS (breaker), Carlton - scrapped
	KGJ607D	11.66				6.79	London Transport RMA33
		12.80	ONs	10.85	ONs	10.85	BEL, Aldenham RMA33
							8.87 PVS (breaker), Carlton
							8.87 Wigley (breaker), Carlton - scrapped
	KGJ608D	11.66				6.79	London Transport RMA34
		6.79	Vs	10.85	Vs	10.85	BEL, Aldenham RMA34
							8.87 PVS (breaker), Carlton - scrapped
	KGJ609D	11.66				6.79	London Transport RMA35 (not used)
							1.82 Wombwell Diesels (bkr) - scrapped
0	KGJ610D	11.66				6.79	London Transport RMA36
		11.79	Ss	10.85	Ss	10.85	BEL, Aldenham RMA36
							8.87 PVS (breaker), Carlton - scrapped
1	KGJ611D	12.66				11.76	London Transport RMA15
		3.78	ALDs	9.85	ALD	9.85	BEL, Aldenham RMA15
							10.86 London Transport RMA15
		4.87	B	5.92	WD	5.92	London Coaches, London RMA15
							10.94 Wright (dealer), Rainham
2	KGJ612D	12.66				6.79	London Transport RMA37
		8.79	AVs	10.85	AVs	10.85	BEL, Aldenham RMA37
							8.87 PVS (breaker), Carlton
							10.87 Brown, Motcombe
3	KGJ613D	12.66				6.79	London Transport RMA38
		6.81	AGt	10.90	Ut	8.91	PVS (breaker), Carlton - scrapped
4	KGJ614D	12.66				11.76	London Transport RMA16
		1.78	ALDs	8.85	AVs	8.85	BEL, Aldenham RMA16
							2.88 Clydeside Scottish SRMA1
							5.89 Western Scottish SRMA1
							10.91 Clydeside 2000 100

15	KGJ615D	12.66				6.79	London Transport RMA39 (not used)
							9.81 Wombwell Diesels (bkr) - scrapped
16	KGJ616D	12.66				6.79	London Transport RMA40
		4.81	PMt	2.91	Ut	6.91	PVS (breaker), Carlton - scrapped
17	KGJ617D	12.66				11.76	London Transport RMA17 (not used)
							10.82 Gooch (preserved), Seven Kings
							6.92 Wright (dealer), Rainham
							6.92 Octobus SARL, Paris, France
18	KGJ618D	12.66				11.76	London Transport RMA18
		3.78	ALDs	8.85	ALD	8.85	BEL, Aldenham RMA18
							8.87 PVS (breaker), Carlton
							8.87 Wigley (breaker), Carlton - scrapped
19	KGJ619D	12.66				6.79	London Transport RMA41
		6.79	SPs	9.85	ALD	9.85	BEL, Aldenham RMA41
							1.87 PVS (breaker), Carlton - scrapped
20	KGJ620D	12.66				6.79	London Transport RMA42
		4.81	PMt	5.91	FWt	5.92	PVS (breaker), Carlton - scrapped
21	KGJ621D	12.66				8.75	London Transport RMA1
		10.75	NS	10.85	Rs	10.85	BEL, Aldenham RMA1
							1.94 Henderson (preserved), Cambridge
22	KGJ622D	12.66				11.76	London Transport RMA19
		3.78	ALDs	8.85	ALD	8.85	BEL, Aldenham RMA19
							1.87 PVS (breaker), Carlton
							6.88 Munton, York
							6.91 Horder, Daventry
23	KGJ623D	12.66				6.79	London Transport RMA43 (not used)
							9.81 Wombwell Diesels (breaker) - scrapped
24	KGJ624D	12.66				6.79	London Transport RMA44
		6.79	Ss	12.82	Rs	6.83	Ensign (dealer), Grays
							7.83 PVS (breaker), Carlton
							8.83 Wigley (breaker), Carlton - scrapped
25	KGJ625D	12.66				6.79	London Transport RMA45 (not used)
							11.81 Wombwell Diesels (bkr) - scrapped
26	NMY626E	1.67				8.75	London Transport RMA2
		10.75	NS	7.79	AVs	9.81	Wombwell Diesels (breaker), Wombwell - scrapped
27	NMY627E	1.67				8.75	London Transport RMA3
		10.75	NS	9.90	Ut	5.92	PVS (breaker), Carlton - scrapped
28	NMY628E	1.67				6.79	London Transport RMA46
		6.79	AWs	6.84	SPs	12.86	Morgan (preserved), Coulsdon
							10.94 Time, Thornton Heath
							1.95 PVS (breaker), Carlton - *for scrap*
29	NMY629E	1.67				8.75	London Transport RMA4
		10.75	NS	9.90	Ut	5.92	PVS (breaker), Carlton - scrapped
30	NMY630E	1.67				6.79	London Transport RMA47
		6.81	CTt		Ut	9.89	Higgins (preserved), Bracknell
31	NMY631E	1.67				6.79	London Transport RMA48
		11.81	AGs	10.85	Hs	10.85	BEL, Aldenham RMA48
							8.87 PVS (breaker), Carlton
							9.87 Wright (Blue Triangle), Rainham
							2.94 Wright & Biddell, Rainham
32	NMY632E	1.67				6.79	London Transport RMA49 (not used)
							10.82 Biddell (preserved), Woodford Bridge
							10.85 Wright (Blue Triangle), Rainham
							2.94 Wright & Biddell, Rainham
33	NMY633E	1.67				11.76	London Transport RMA20
		3.78	ALDs	9.85	ALD	9.85	BEL, Aldenham RMA20
							6.87 Stagecoach, Perth (not used)
							11.87 Magicbus, Glasgow 620
							4.92 Kelvin Central Buses 1948 (0994)
							8.93 Stagecoach, Perth 606 (not used)
							10.94 Chaboud, Lavoux, France

34	NMY634E	2.67				6.79	London Transport RMA50
		11.79	FWs	11.84	NBs	1.87	Stagecoach, Perth
							3.87 Magicbus, Glasgow 621
							4.92 Kelvin Central Buses 1949
							8.93 Stagecoach (preserved), Perth 608
							10.94 Bluebird Buses (preserved) 651
35	NMY635E	1.67				8.75	London Transport RMA5
		10.75	NS	9.94	U	9.94	Stagecoach East London, London RMA5
36	NMY636E	1.67				6.79	London Transport RMA51
		3.85	AVs	8.85	FWs	8.85	BEL, Aldenham RMA51
							10.86 London Transport RMA51
		4.87	B	5.92	WD	5.92	London Coaches, London RMA51
							10.94 Wright (dealer), Rainham
37	NMY637E	1.67				6.79	London Transport RMA52
		7.79	AWs	8.85	ALD	9.85	BEL, Aldenham RMA52
							1.87 Pegg (preserved), Rotherham
							7.91 J.Sykes (breaker), Carlton
							9.91 North Mimms Coaches, Potters Bar
							8.92 Time, Thornton Heath RMA52
38	NMY638E	1.67				8.75	London Transport RMA6
		10.75	NS	8.85	Xs	8.85	BEL, Aldenham RMA6
							8.87 PVS (breaker), Carlton
							8.87 Wigley (breaker), Carlton
							9.87 Higgins (preserved), Bracknell
39	NMY639E	1.67				8.75	London Transport RMA7
		10.75	NS	8.85	WWs	8.85	BEL, Aldenham RMA7
							8.87 PVS (breaker), Carlton - scrapped
40	NMY640E	1.67				8.75	London Transport RMA8
		10.75	NS	8.85	AVs	8.85	BEL, Aldenham RMA8
							8.88 London Buses, London RMA8
			U	9.94	U	9.94	Stagecoach East London, London RMA8
41	NMY641E	2.67				6.79	London Transport RMA53
		6.79	NXs	10.85	ALD	10.85	BEL, Aldenham RMA53
							7.87 Bertin, Hounslow
							Boath, Norwood Green
42	NMY642E	2.67				11.76	London Transport RMA21 (not used)
							9.81 Wombwell Diesels (breaker) - scrapped
43	NMY643E	2.67				6.79	London Transport RMA54 (not used)
							10.81 Wombwell Diesels (breaker) - scrapped
44	NMY644E	2.67				6.79	London Transport RMA55
		6.81	ARt	11.94	St	11.94	London United Busways, London RMA55
45	NMY645E	2.67				11.76	London Transport RMA22
		3.78	ALDs	8.85	ALD	8.85	BEL, Aldenham RMA22
							10.86 London Transport RMA22
		2.87	B	5.92	WD	5.92	London Coaches, London RMA22
							10.94 Wright (dealer), Rainham
							11.94 Wright & Biddell, Rainham
							4.95 Kavanagh, Urlingford, Eire
46	NMY646E	2.67				8.75	London Transport RMA9
		10.75	NS	10.85	TLs	10.85	BEL, Aldenham RMA9
							3.88 Wembley Stadium, London
47	NMY647E	2.67				8.75	London Transport RMA10
		10.75	NS	8.85	Vs	8.85	BEL, Aldenham RMA10
							2.87 Lemon (preserved), Romford
							9.92 Taffell (preserved), Woodford Bridge
48	NMY648E	2.67				8.75	London Transport RMA11
		10.75	NS	9.85	ALD	9.85	BEL, Aldenham RMA11
							2.87 Verwood Transport, Poole
							1.89 Legg, Aylesbury
							11.91 Green Rover, Watford RMA48
							1.93 Graves (preserved), Watford

49	NMY649E		2.67				11.76	London Transport RMA23
			5.78	ALDs	8.85	NBs	8.85	BEL, Aldenham RMA23
								3.87 Lever Bros., Northolt
								5.89 Ireland (dealer), Hull
								4.91 Unknown, West Midlands
50	NMY650E		2.67				11.76	London Transport RMA24
			7.78	Xs	6.82	ALD	7.84	PVS (breaker), Carlton
								7.84 Wigley (breaker), Carlton - scrapped
51	NMY651E		2.67				6.79	London Transport RMA56 (not used)
								10.82 LT PD garage Sports & Social Club
								2.88 Doggett (preserved), Purley
								Wright (dealer), Rainham
								3.92 Octobus SARL, Paris, France
52	NMY652E		2.67				8.75	London Transport RMA12
			10.75	NS	11.82	AVs	10.83	W.Norths (dealer), Sherburn - scrapped
53	NMY653E		2.67				11.76	London Transport RMA25
			1.78	ALDs	9.85	ALD	9.85	BEL, Aldenham RMA25
								10.86 London Transport RMA25
			12.86	B	5.92	WD	5.92	London Coaches, London RMA25
								10.94 Wright (dealer), Rainham
		67 D 813						10.94 McConn, Rathcool, Eire
54	NMY654E		3.67				6.79	London Transport RMA57 (not used)
								10.82 Mooney (preserved), London
								10.85 Blake (preserved), Palmers Green
								10.92 Rowe & Smith (preserved), Fulham
								12.94 Adler (preserved), Clacton
55	NMY655E		3.67				6.79	London Transport RMA58
			10.79	AVs	10.85	AVs	10.85	BEL Aldenham RMA58
								7.87 Verwood Transport, Poole
								1.89 Spence (dealer), Southend
								9.89 Brakell (dealer), Cheam
								11.91 Forrest (Blue Triangle), Bootle
								5.94 Merseyrider, Liverpool 0655
								10.94 Merseybus, Liverpool 0655
								2.95 Forrest (preserved), Bootle
56	NMY656E		3.67				8.75	London Transport RMA13
			10.75	NS	10.85	Vs	10.85	BEL, Aldenham RMA13
								2.87 Murray-Roberts (preserved), Truro
								12.88 Murray-Roberts (preserved), Croydon
								7.90 Murray-Roberts (pres'd), Kentish Town
57	NMY657E		3.67				6.79	London Transport RMA59
			3.85	SPs	10.85	SPs	10.85	BEL, Aldenham RMA59
								8.87 PVS (breaker), Carlton
								8.87 Wigley (breaker), Carlton - scrapped
58	NMY658E		3.67				6.79	London Transport RMA60
			6.81	Et	12.87		2.88	Clydeside Scottish (driver trainer)
								9.89 PVS (breaker), Carlton - scrapped
59	NMY659E		3.67				6.79	London Transport RMA61
			6.79	Ss	9.80	Ss	11.81	Wombwell Diesels (breaker) - scrapped
60	NMY660E		3.67				11.76	London Transport RMA26
			8.78	HLs	10.85	HLs	10.85	BEL, Aldenham RMA26
								10.86 London Transport RMA26
			11.86	B	5.92	WD	5.92	London Coaches, London RMA26
								10.94 Wright (dealer), Rainham
		67-D-816						11.94 McConn, Rathcool, Eire
61	NMY661E		3.67				11.76	London Transport RMA27
			1.78	ALDs	8.85	AVs	2.86	PVS (breaker), Carlton - scrapped
62	NMY662E		4.67				6.79	London Transport RMA62
			6.79	Ts	8.85	WWs	8.85	BEL, Aldenham RMA62
								12.87 London Borough of Ealing
63	NMY663E		4.67				6.79	London Transport RMA63
			6.79	ALDs	8.85	ALD	8.85	BEL, Aldenham RMA63
								8.87 PVS (breaker), Carlton - scrapped

64	NMY664E	3.67				6.79	London Transport RMA64
		6.79	AVs	7.79	AVs	11.81	Wombwell Diesels (breaker) - scrapped
65	NMY665E	4.67				6.79	London Transport RMA65
		6.79	HDs	9.85	ALD	9.85	BEL, Aldenham RMA65
							10.86 London Transport RMA65
		12.86	B	5.92	WD	5.92	London Coaches, London RMA65
							11.93 Letts, Wincanton

RM581 is seen here in open-top form in use as a promotional vehicle for a Hertford newspaper. (T.G.Walker)

Circumnavigating Trafalgar Square, London is pre-privatised London Central's refurbished 30ft. long RML2454.

NORTHERN GENERAL TRANSPORT / RMF

2085	RCN685		3069	4.64	.78	10.78	Martin (dealer), Middlewich
							10.78 Goodwin (breaker), Carlton - scrapped
2086	RCN686		3070	4.64	.77	12.77	Martin (dealer), Middlewich
							12.77 Goodwin (breaker), Carlton
							3.78 Brakell (dealer), Cheam
							5.80 Moore (preserved), Beckenham
							1.82 Scrapped
2087	RCN687		3071	4.64	.79	12.79	London Transport RMF2768 (not used)
							10.81 Wombwell Diesels (breaker) - scrapped
2088	RCN688		3072	4.64	.77	12.77	Martin (dealer), Middlewich
							12.77 Goodwin (breaker), Carlton - scrapped
2089	RCN689		3073	4.64	.77	12.77	Martin (dealer), Middlewich
							12.77 Brakell (dealer), Cheam
							3.78 Ashton, Epsom
							8.84 Page Motors, Epsom
2090	RCN690		3074	4.64	.77	1.78	London Transport (for spares)+
							1.78 Wombwell Diesels (breaker) - scrapped
2091	RCN691		3075	4.64	.80	10.80	Booth (breaker), Rotherham - scrapped
2092	RCN692		3076	4.64	.77	12.77	Martin (dealer), Middlewich
							2.78 Brakell (dealer), Cheam
							7.78 Ashton, Epsom
							12.81 Heaver Models Museum, Maidstone
							6.84 Rollinson (breaker), Carlton - scrapped
2093	RCN693		3077	4.64	.77	6.77	Scrapped by Northern General Transport
2094	RCN694		3078	4.64	.80	10.80	Booth (breaker), Rotherham - scrapped
2095	RCN695		3079	4.64	1.81	2.81	Mendez & Wade (preserved), Welling
							9.86 Stagecoach, Perth
							6.87 Scrapped by Stagecoach at Glasgow dep
2096	RCN696		3080	4.64	.79	12.79	London Transport RMF2679 (not used)
							10.81 Wombwell Diesels (breaker) - scrapped
2097	RCN697		3081	4.64	.80	8.80	London Transport RMF2772 (not used)
							7.81 Ashton, Epsom
2098	RCN698		3082	4.64	.77	12.77	Martin (dealer), Middlewich
							12.77 Goodwin (breaker), Carlton
							3.79 Capel (preserved), Nottingham
							7.79 Goodwin (breaker), Carlton - scrapped
2099	RCN699		3083	4.64	.80	11.80	Wombwell Diesels (breaker), Wombwell
							1.81 Stevensons, Spath 52
							5.86 Stagecoach, Perth
		EDS508B					10.86 Magicbus, Glasgow 617
							12.91 Go-Ahead Northern Bus Enthusiast Association (preserved), Gateshead
2100	RCN700		3084	4.64	.80	10.80	Hartwood Exports (bkr), Birdwell - scrapped
2101	RCN701		3085	5.64	.80	8.80	London Transport RMF2771 (not used)
							7.81 Ashton, Epsom
2102	RCN702		3086	5.64	.80	10.80	Booth (breaker), Rotherham
2103	DUP294B		3087	10.64	9.77	9.77	Scrapped by Northern General Transport
2104	EUP404B		3088	12.64	.77	12.77	Martin (dealer), Middlewich
							12.77 London Bus Pres. Group (dlr), Cobham
							5.78 Brakell (dealer), Cheam
							12.79 London Transport RMF2767
2105	EUP405B		3089	12.64	.80	11.80	Slater (preserved), Newcastle
2106	EUP406B		3090	12.64	.77	12.77	Martin (dealer), Middlewich
							12.77 London Bus Pres. Group (dlr), Cobham
							5.78 Brakell (dealer), Cheam
							11.81 Obsolete Fleet, London
							10.83 Omnibus Promotions (dealer), London
							.84 Lever (preserved), Sutton
							6.87 London Transport RMT2793
							Brakell (dealer), Cheam
							1.91 Lamming, Coulsdon

2107	EUP407B	3091	12.64	.77	12.77	Martin (dealer), Middlewich
						12.77 Brakell, Cheam RMF2792
						.84 Greater London Council, London
						Green, Knockholt
						7.86 Copeland, London
2108	FPT578C	3092	1.65	.77	2.82	APT (dealer), Lincoln
						1.83 PVS (breaker), Carlton - scrapped
2109	FPT579C	3093	1.65	10.76	10.76	Scrapped by Northern General Transport
2110	FPT580C	3094	1.65	.77	12.77	Martin (dealer), Middlewich
						2.78 Brakell (dealer), Cheam
						3.78 Ashton, Epsom
2111	FPT581C	3095	1.65	.80	10.80	Booth (breaker), Rotherham
						12.80 Brakell (dealer), Cheam
						.81 Taffle (preserved), Ruislip
						Brakell (dealer), Cheam
						.84 New Cross Playbus Association, London
2112	FPT582C	3096	1.65	.77	12.77	Martin (dealer), Middlewich
						2.78 Brakell (dealer), Cheam
						12.79 London Transport RMF2761 (not used)
						10.81 Wombwell Diesels (breaker) - scrapped
2113	FPT583C	3097	1.65	2.78	6.78	Ensign (dealer), Grays
						7.78 Jones (breaker), Carlton
						8.78 Wigley (breaker), Carlton - scrapped
2114	FPT584C	3098	1.65	3.78	7.78	Ensign (dealer), Grays
						9.78 Brakell (dealer), Cheam
						12.79 London Transport RMF2762 (not used)
						9.81 Wombwell Diesels (breaker) - scrapped
2115	FPT585C	3099	1.65	3.78	7.78	Ensign (dealer), Grays
						9.78 Brakell (dealer), Cheam
						12.79 London Transport RMF2763 (not used)
						10.81 Wombwell Diesels (breaker) - scrapped
2116	FPT586C	3100	1.65	.80	10.80	Booth (breaker), Rotherham - scrapped
2117	FPT587C	3101	2.65	12.77	1.78	London Transport (for spares) +
						1.78 Wombwell Diesels (breaker) - scrapped
2118	FPT588C	3102	2.65	.78	7.78	Ensign (dealer), Grays
						9.78 Brakell, Cheam RMF2794
						11.81 Obsolete Fleet, London
						10.83 Omnibus Promotions (dealer), London
						1.85 Tower Hamlets Christian Fellowship, London
						1.87 Biddell, Woodford Bridge
						Wright (Blue Triangle), Rainham
						.92 Maybury (Big Bus Co.), London
						.95 Ensign Bus Services (London Pride), London
2119	FPT589C	3103	1.65	.77	12.77	Martin (dealer), Middlewich
						12.77 Brakell, Cheam RMF2791
						11.78 Omnibus Promotions (dealer), London
						12.83 Promobus Bus, Madrid, Spain
2120	FPT590C	3104	1.65	12.80	12.80	Booth (breaker), Rotherham
						12.80 Brakell (dealer), Cheam
						8.86 Stagecoach, Perth
						12.86 Magicbus, Glasgow 619
						9.92 Matthews (preserved), Sidcup
2121	FPT591C	3105	1.65	12.80	1.81	Allmey (preserved), Eastcote
						Brakell (dealer), Cheam
						10.84 Hotelli Taipale, Varkaus, Finland
2122	FPT592C	3106	1.65	.80	1.81	Wright & Humphries (preserved), Dagenham
						7.91 Owen (preserved), Upper Norwood
2123	FPT593C	3107	1.65	.80	5.81	Wright & Humphries (preserved), Dagenham
						10.81 Wombwell Diesels (breaker) - scrapped
2124	FPT594C	3108	2.65	12.80	2.82	APT (dealer), Lincoln
						1.83 PVS (breaker), Carlton - scrapped
2125	FPT595C	3109	2.65	.77	11.77	Beck (breaker), Burnopfield - scrapped

2126	FPT596C	3110	2.65	.78	6.78	Ensign (dealer), Grays
						7.78 Jones (breaker), Carlton - scrapped
2127	FPT597C	3111	2.65	.78	6.78	Ensign (dealer), Grays
						7.78 Jones (breaker), Carlton - scrapped
2128	FPT598C	3112	2.65	.80	3.81	Davies (preserved), Redhill
						4.82 Frampton Jones (preserved), Carshalton
						3.87 Magicbus, Glasgow
						1.89 Dunsmore (breaker), Larkhall - scrapped
2129	FPT599C	3113	3.65	.77	9.77	Scrapped by Northern General Transport
2130	FPT600C	3114	4.65	.79	7.79	Ensign (dealer), Grays
						1.80 London Transport RMF2770 (not used)
						10.81 Wombwell Diesels (breaker) - scrapped
2131	FPT601C	3115	6.65	.78	6.78	Ensign (dealer), Grays
						6.78 Brakell, Cheam RMF2765
						12.79 London Transport RMF2764 (not used)
						9.81 Wombwell Diesels (breaker) - scrapped
2132	FPT602C	3116	3.65	.78	6.78	Ensign (dealer), Grays
						7.78 Brakell (dealer), Cheam
						12.79 London Transport RMF2765 (not used)
						10.81 Wombwell Diesels (breaker) - scrapped
2133	FPT603C	3117	3.65	.78	6.78	Ensign (dealer), Grays
						6.78 Brakell (dealer), Cheam
						9.78 Reid & Turpin (preserved), Slough
						3.82 Booth (breaker), Rotherham
						5.82 Bailey (preserved), Burgh Heath
						5.83 Ashton, Epsom
						.90 Watson (pres'd), Chesterfield RMF2809
						1.95 Pegg, Rotherham
2134	FPT604C	3118	3.65	.78	6.78	Ensign (dealer), Grays
						7.78 Brakell, Cheam RMF2766
						12.79 London Transport RMF2766 (not used)
						10.81 Wombwell Diesels (breaker) - scrapped

Seen enroute to the Epsom Derby in 1984 whilst used as a mobile restaurant/hospitality suite is former Northern General FPT580C.

ROUTEMASTERS RE-REGISTERED IN BRITAIN

New Reg.No.	Fleet No.	Date Re-reg'd
GVS447	RM284	5.92
GVS448	RM1229	5.92
GVS479	RM379	7.92
GVS480	RM474	7.92
GVS481	RM1614	7.92
GVS482	RM1839	7.92
GVS483	RM532	7.92
GVS490	RM954	7.92
GVS491	RM916	7.92
GVS492	RM47	7.92
GVS497	RM277	8.92
GVS498	RM1166	8.92
HVS710	RM512	6.92
HVS935	RM255	1.93
HVS936	RM51	1.93
HVS937	RM682	1.93
KFF239	RM659	3.94
KFF240	RM1133	3.94
KFF252	RM826	4.94
KFF257	RM646	4.94
KFF276	RML893	7.94
KFF277	RM342	7.94
KFF367	RM1101	11.94
KVS599	RM408	1.93
KVS601	RM471	1.93
LFF875	RMC1456	8.94
LFF881	RM113	10.94
MFF503	RM599	1.94
MFF505	RM470	1.94
MFF509	RM1312	2.94
MFF510	RM598	2.94
MFF518	RM516	2.94
MFF577	RM946	8.94
MFF578	RM329	8.94
MFF579	RM1236	8.94
MFF580	R931	8.94
MFF581	RM804	8.94
MFF582	RM339	8.94
NVS405	RM1055	10.92
NVS485	RM1292	2.93
NVS804	RM982	8.92
NVS855	RM757	1.93
OVS940	RM875	12.92
PSK819	RM1049	2.92
PSK820	RM461	2.92
PSK821	RM491	2.92
PSK822	RM575	2.92
PSK823	RM240	2.92
PVS828	RM1018	4.93
PVS829	RM1019	4.93
PVS830	RM1020	4.93
RSK254	RM1271	1.92
RSK572	RM110	10.91
RSK605	RM694	3.92
SVS615	RM346	12.92
SVS616	RM1352	12.92
SVS617	RM431	12.92
SVS618	RM548	12.92
TSK269	RM706	12.92
TSK270	RM713	12.92
TSK271	RM824	12.92
VLT89	RM994	1.94
VYJ542	RM797	1.93
VYJ806	RM1124	8.93
VYJ807	RM1324	8.93
VYJ808	RM1361	8.93
VYJ809	RM1304	8.93
VYJ876	RM1262	10.93
VYJ892	RM395	1.94
VYJ893	RM89	1.94
USK625	RM980	6.93
UYJ654	RM1224	7.93
WLT371	RM371	11.88
WLT516	RML2516	2.94
WLT652	RM652	11.93
WLT675	RM17	5.91
WLT759	RM759	6.93
WLT984	RM1959	5.88
WSK219	RM528	4.92
WVS423	RM999	6.93
WYJ857	RM172	12.93
XFF528	RM10	10.94
XFF813	RML898	1.95
XFF814	RML890	1.95
XVS319	RM949	4.93
XVS826	RM648	4.93
XVS827	RM487	4.93
XVS828	RM843	4.93
XVS829	RM696	4.93
XVS830	RM180	4.93
XVS839	RM244	5.93
XVS850	RM1083	6.93
XVS851	RM467	6.93
XVS875	RM1186	7.93
XVS876	RM920	7.93
XYJ417	RM735	1.94
XYJ418	RM736	1.94
XYJ419	RM625	1.94
XYJ427	RM1185	2.94
XYJ428	RM32	2.94
XYJ429	RM1205	2.94
XYJ430	RM1070	2.94
XYJ440	RM838	4.94
XYJ441	RM1170	4.94
XYJ442	RM1257	4.94
XYJ443	RM990	4.94
YVS285	RM1134	3.93
YVS287	RM1053	3.93
YVS288	RM357	3.93
YVS289	RM55	3.93
YVS290	RM1149	3.93
YVS291	RM219	3.93
YVS292	RM1032	5.93
YVS293	RM447	5.93
YVS294	RM229	5.93
YVS296	RM809	5.93
71AWN	RM1397	4.95
324CLT	RM1324	4.94
449CLT	RM1449	8.93
691DYE	RM1691	9.90
276KVS	RMC1486	11.92
ABD892A	RM1068	4.91
AEW440A	RM1421	5.90
ALA814A	RM100	10.85
ALC179A	RM1089	5.90
ALC290A	RM1005	1.91
ALC338A	RM675	5.91
ALC368A	RMC1500	6.91
ALC459A	RM1585	2.94
ALC464A	RM902	7.94
AST415A	RM45	10.88
AST416A	RM191	11.88
BHU987A	RM832	9.91
BMJ919A	RM908	10.91
BNK31A	RM1685	8.92
BNK32A	RM1647	8.92
DFH806A	RM969	7.90
EDS48A	RM504	3.87
EDS50A	RM560	4.87
EDS98A	RM1006	6.87
EDS107A	RM1053	7.87
EDS109A	RM1040	7.87
EDS111A	RM22	7.87
EDS117A	RM149	7.87
EDS120A	RM290	7.87

New Reg.No.	Fleet No.	Date Re-reg'd
EDS125A	RM288	8.87
EDS128A	RM55	8.87
EDS129A	RM290	8.87
EDS130A	RM177	8.87
EDS134A	RM229	8.87
EDS143A	RM667	8.87
EDS146A	RM1596	8.87
EDS147A	RM293	9.87
EDS157A	RM250	9.87
EDS221A	RM1010	12.87
EDS247A	RM43	3.88
EDS277A	RM770	3.88
EDS278A	RM357	3.88
EDS281A	RM408	3.88
EDS282A	RM408	3.88
EDS285A	RM415	3.88
EDS288A	RM910	3.88
EDS293A	RM678	3.88
EDS295A	RM741	3.88
EDS297A	RM760	3.88
EDS300A	RM388	3.88
EDS312A	RM799	8.88
EDS320A	RM606	8.88
EDS341A	RM831	8.88
EDS352A	RM987	8.88
EDS362A	RM858	8.88
EDS379A	RM1601	8.88
EDS381A	RM480	8.88
EDS392A	RM439	8.88
EDS393A	RM419	8.88
EDS394A	RM471	8.88
EDS395A	RM538	8.88
EDS396A	RM809	8.88
EDS397A	RM774	8.88
EDS401A	RM915	8.88
KGH26A	RM1977	10.87
KGH602A	RM15	8.89
KGH856A	RM173	12.90
KGH859A	RM1188	12.90
KGH883A	RM554	5.91
KGH887A	RM1217	5.91
KGH889A	RM751	5.91
KGH899A	RM463	6.91
KGH925A	RM1078	6.91
KGH932A	RM1656	6.91
KGH934A	RM27	6.91
KGH936A	RM1319	6.91
KGH956A	RM1023	11.90
KGH969A	RM1101	12.90
KGH975A	RM1330	8.91
KGH991A	RMC1519	12.91
KGJ24A	RM803	12.90
KGJ28A	RM98	12.90
KGJ29A	RM1197	12.90
KGJ37A	RM1545	1.91
KGJ41A	RM818	1.91
KGJ43A	RM1007	1.91
KGJ52A	RMC1480	2.91
KGJ61A	RM179	2.91
KGJ62A	RM837	2.91

New Reg.No.	Fleet No.	Date Re-reg'd
KGJ65A	RM60	2.91
KGJ69A	RM807	3.91
KGJ83A	RM13	4.91
KGJ84A	RM372	4.91
KGJ116A	RM1772	7.93
KGJ117A	RM1528	7.93
KGJ142A	RM311	12.91
KGJ164A	RM1542	12.91
KGJ167A	RM1700	5.92
KGJ173A	RM1698	5.92
KGJ184A	RM1435	1.93
KGJ187A	RM1621	4.93
KGJ188A	RM1619	4.93
LDS67A	RM1274	5.89
LDS68A	RM1056	5.89
LDS136A	RM495	7.89
LDS148A	RM485	9.89
LDS150A	RM444	10.89
LDS152A	RM526	10.89
LDS153A	RM501	10.89
LDS161A	RM652	10.89
LDS162A	RM794	11.89
LDS164A	RM978	11.89
LDS173A	RM37	11.89
LDS184A	RM550	12.89
LDS190A	RM1449	12.89
LDS199A	RM48	12.89
LDS201A	RM1607	12.89
LDS206A	RM303	12.89
LDS210A	RM1245	1.90
LDS214A	RM17	2.90
LDS232A	RM154	2.90
LDS233A	RM204	2.90
LDS234A	RM226	2.90
LDS235A	RM234	2.90
LDS236A	RM272	2.90
LDS237A	RM416	2.90
LDS238A	RM697	2.90
LDS239A	RM727	2.90
LDS247A	RM859	2.90
LDS248A	RM830	2.90
LDS253A	RM1013	2.90
LDS254A	RM1032	2.90
LDS255A	RM206	3.90
LDS256A	RM305	3.90
LDS257A	RM666	3.90
LDS258A	RM720	3.90
LDS259A	RM919	3.90
LDS260A	RM924	3.90
LDS261A	RM956	3.90
LDS279A	RM54	4.90
LDS280A	RM104	4.90
LDS281A	RM219	4.90
LDS282A	RM245	4.90
LDS283A	RM447	4.90
LDS284A	RM546	4.90
LDS285A	RM1054	4.90
LDS286A	RM1703	4.90
LDS317A	RM367	5.90
LDS334A	RM73	8.90
LDS335A	RM81	8.90

New Reg no.	Fleet No.	Date Re-reg'd
LDS336A	RM166	8.90
LDS337A	RM364	8.90
LDS338A	RM874	8.90
LDS339A	RM974	8.90
LDS341A	RM441	7.90
LDS402A	RM1145	12.90
LDS475A	RM1134	7.91
NKH807A	RM1366	6.90
NRH801A	RM732	11.90
NRH802A	RM798	11.90
NRH803A	RM871	11.90
NRH805A	RM1041	11.90
NSG636A	RM1164	8.89
OKU34A	RM391	6.91
OKU105A	RM1618	9.92
OWJ871A	RM1397	2.90
OYM368A	RM1002	10.87
OYM374A	RM9	6.87
OYM378A	RM20	6.87
OYM413A	RM12	10.87
OYM424A	RM14	12.87
OYM432A	RM88	2.88
OYM453A	RM29	6.88
OYM503A	RM77	4.89
OYM518A	RM400	5.89
OYM579A	RM434	8.89
OYM580A	RM46	8.89
OYM582A	RM53	9.89
OYM583A	RM136	10.89
OYM611A	RM31	6.89
PAG809A	RM1741	11.94
WTS87A	RM1691	12.87
WTS97A	RM42	1.88
WTS101A	RM183	1.88
WTS102A	RM917	1.88
WTS109A	RM93	2.88
WTS128A	RM221	2.88
WTS131A	RM217	2.88
WTS163A	RM1149	3.88
WTS164A	RM677	3.88
WTS177A	RM223	3.88
WTS186A	RM1143	3.88
WTS225A	RM943	4.88
WTS245A	RM298	5.88
WTS268A	RM743	6.88
WTS316A	RM610	8.88
WTS329A	RM759	8.88
WTS333A	RM316	8.88
WTS404A	RM702	10.88
WTS418A	RM909	10.88
WTS887A	RM699	6.89
WTS973A	RM1017	10.87
XMC223A	RM456	9.85
XMD79A	RM110	6.91

New Reg.No.	Fleet No.	Date Re-reg'd
XMD81A	RM429	6.91
XSL220A	RM26	4.90
XSL596A	RM1289	11.90
YTS565A	RM784	4.87
YTS820A	RM1599	7.87
YTS824A	RM321	7.87
YTS867A	RM427	7.87
YTS892A	RM921	7.87
ALD959B	RM984	5.88

New Reg.No.	Fleet No.	Date Re-reg'd
BFW544B	RM1842	1.89
EBY247B	RM1810	3.90
EBY257B	RM1809	5.90
EBY315B	RM1555	.92
EDS508B	NGT2099	5.87
EDS537B	RM1630	8.88
EDS561B	RM1858	12.89
EDS567B	RM1768	5.90
EDS568B	RM1803	5.90

New Reg no.	Fleet No.	Date Re-reg'd
EGF220B	RM1811	3.90
EGF282B	RM1046	7.91
EGF285B	RM1836	7.91
EGF286B	RM1815	8.91
EGF299B	RM2002	6.94
EVM132B	RM1807	4.92
EYY128B	RM2001	6.87
YSL32B	RM1821	12.87
YSL76B	RM1911	7.90
LGH31T	RM23	8.94

Several Routemasters were used as test rigs before gaining their bus bodies. This view of rig 002 in December 1958 shows the bodywork used for this purpose. (LT)

Converted at Aldenham works to offside rear platform configuration in 1984 prior to embarking on a demonstration tour to China, RM1288 was later sold to Citybus, Hong Kong. (J.Whitmore)

Still wearing its Northern General livery, Stagecoach's RCN695 is seen here in Glasgow accompanied by corporate-liveried 602DYE on Magicbus duties in Glasgow early in 1987. Sadly RCN695 was burnt out a few months later. (P.McElroy)

OPEN TOP / CONVERTIBLE OPEN TOP LONDON BUSES ROUTEMASTERS

Fleet No.	Wdn as closed top	Last Dep.	Conv. to open top	Conv. to conv. open top	Conv. to ERM	Parts used from RM	
RM							
49	2.86	X	3.86				
68	11.85	AF	4.86				
80	7.85	Q	2.86		5.90	1329	
84	2.86	NB	3.86		5.90	1616	
90	10.85	T	3.86		5.90	2170	
94	1.86	Q	3.86		7.90	253	
143	2.86	WN	4.86		6.90	1114	
163	10.85	HT	3.86		11.89	458	
235	2.86	X	3.86		6.90	1745	
237	1.86	BW	3.86		6.90	580	
242	12.85	CT	4.86		7.90	2216	
281	2.86	NB	3.86		7.90	1664	
307	4.88	WD	8.88				*Fitted with wheelchair lift*
313	11.85	NX	3.86	1.91			
377	4.88	WD	7.88				
398	12.85	WD	4.86	1.91			
428	12.85	CT	3.86				
438	10.85	TH	3.86				
450	4.88	WD	10.88				*Fitted with wheelchair lift*
479	6.91	WD		9.91			
562	2.86	SF	4.86				
572	4.88	WD	7.88				
644	5.88	WD	7.88				
658	1.86	CF	4.86				
704	8.85	B	4.86				
710	6.91	WD		9.91			
752	11.85	BW	4.86				
753	4.88	WD	7.88				
762	2.86	X	4.86				
811	2.86	GM	4.86				
925	11.85	WD	4.86				
1919	9.85	BN	4.86				
RMC							
1510	7.89	Xt	8.89				
1515	7.87	Ut	8.87				
RCL							
2220	3.90	WD	5.90	1.91			
2235	8.90	WD		1.91			
2240	12.90	WD		3.91			
2241	12.90	WD		3.91			
2243	8.90	WD		1.91			
2245	3.90	WD	5.90	1.91			
2248	12.90	WD		4.91			
2250	12.90	WD		4.91			
2253	12.90	WD		4.91			
2259	12.90	WD		7.91			

RM1768 blazes uncontrollably after a flywheel gland burst in a traffic jam at Marble Arch and sent hot oil gushing on to the exhaust. Unbelievably, after being fitted with a new body, this bus was returned to service, eventually being sold to Clydeside Scottish in 1988. (LT)

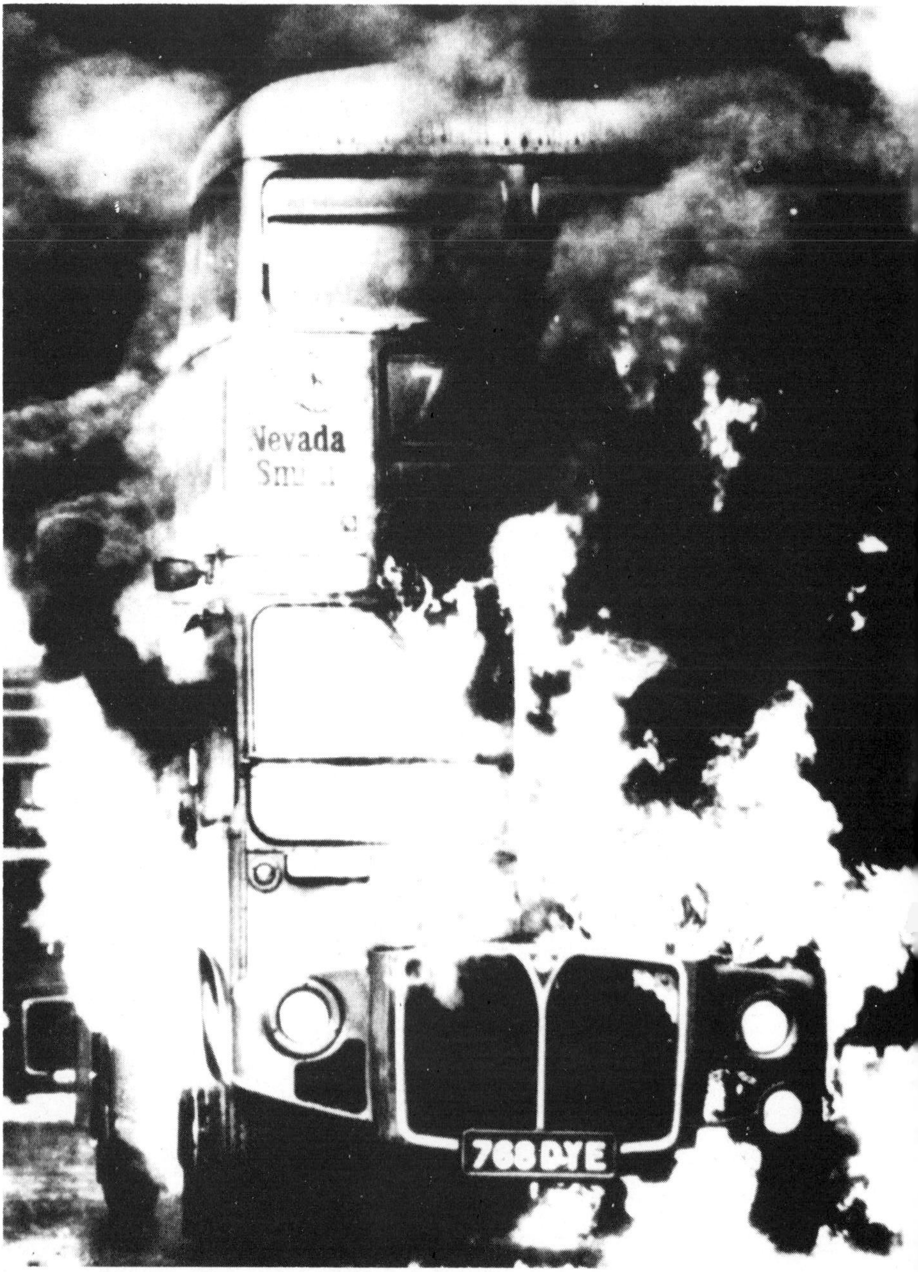

RCL2221 never entered passenger service after its return from London Country and instead has served in a variety of non-PSV roles. Here it is seen painted in Shillibeer livery as a mobile exhibition and cinema in May 1979. (T.G.Walker)

Nearing the end of its life, engineless RM68 which had been converted to open-top format in 1986 for London sightseeing duties awaits the breakers torch in the yard of PVS, Carlton in September 1991. (P.T.Stokes)

LONDON TRANSPORT GARAGES

Country Area garages are shown in italics

A Sutton
AC Willesden
AD Palmers Green
AE Hendon
AF Putney (Chelverton Road)
AG Ash Grove
AK Streatham
AL Merton
ALD Aldenham Works
AM Plumstead
AP Seven Kings
AR Tottenham
AV Hounslow

B Battersea
BEA British Airways
BK Barking
BN Brixton
BW Bow
BX Bexleyheath

CA Clapham
CF Chalk Farm
CM *Chelsham*
CS Chiswick Works
CT Clapton
CY *Crawley*

D Dalston
DG *Dunton Green*
DS *Dorking*
DT *Dartford*

E Enfield
ED Elmers End
EG *East Grinstead*
EM Edmonton
EP *Epping*
EW Edgware

FW Fulwell
FY Finchley

GF *Guildford*
GM Victoria
GR *Garston*
GY *Grays*

H Hackney
HA *Harlow*
HD Harrow Weald
HE *High Wycombe*
HF *Hatfield*
HG *Hertford*
HH *Hemel Hempstead*
HL Hanwell
HT Highgate
HW Hanwell

J Holloway

K Kingston

M Mortlake
MA *Amersham*
MH Muswell Hill

N Norwood
NB Norbiton
NF *Northfleet*
NS Romford (North Street)
NX New Cross

PB Potters Bar
PD Plumstead
PM Peckham
PR Poplar

Q Camberwell

R Hammersmith
RA Waterloo (Red Arrow)
RD Hornchurch
RE *Romford*
RG *Reigate*
RL Peckham (Rye Lane)

S Shepherds Bush
SE Stonebridge Park
SF Stamford Hill
SJ *Swanley*
SP Sidcup
ST *Staines*
SV *Stevenage*
SW Stockwell

T Leyton
TB Bromley
TC Croydon
TH Thornton Heath
TL Catford
TW *Tunbridge Wells*

U Upton Park
UX Uxbridge

V Turnham Green

W Cricklewood
WD Wandsworth
WG West Green
WH West Ham
WK Stanwell Buses
WL Walworth
WN Wood Green
WR *Windsor*
WW Walthamstow
WY *Addlestone*

X North Kensington

DEPOT CODE SUFFIX

s Staff Bus
t Driver Trainer
- Skid Bus at Chiwick Works
% Dedicated for use by BBC TV 'East Enders'